Word for Windo QuickStart

Elaine J. Marmel

Word for Windows QuickStart.

Copyright © 1992 by Que® Corporation.

Library of Congress Catalog Number: 92-70886

ISBN: 0-88022-920-9

94 93 92   6 5 4 3 2 1

Interpretation of the printing code: the rightmost double-digit number is the year of the book's printing; the rightmost single-digit number, the number of the book's printing. For example, a printing code of 92-1 shows that the first printing of the book occurred in 1992.

Screen reproductions in this book were created using Collage Plus from Inner Media, Inc., Hollis, NH.

Word for Windows QuickStart covers Word for Windows 2.0.

Publisher: Lloyd J. Short

Associate Publisher: Rick Ranucci

Product Development Manager: Thomas H. Bennett

Book Designer: Scott Cook

Production Team: Claudia Bell, Christine Cook, Jerry W. Ellis, Mark Enochs, Brook Farling, Dennis Clay Hager, Betty Kish, Bob LaRoche, Joy Dean Lee, Laurie Lee, Loren Malloy, Juli Pavey, Linda Quigley, Dennis Sheehan, Linda Seifert, John Sleeva, Kevin Spear, Suzanne Tully, Mary Beth Wakefield, Lisa Wilson, Phil Worthington, Christine Young

About the Author

Elaine Marmel is President of Marmel Enterprises, Inc., an organization which provides PC software training and support and specializes in assisting small- to medium-sized businesses computerize their accounting systems.

Elaine left her native Chicago for the warmer climes of Florida (by way of Cincinnati, OH; Jerusalem, Israel; Ithaca, NY; and Washington, D.C.) where she basks in the sun with her PC and her cat Tonto. Elaine also enjoys cross-stitching, and she sings in an internationally recognized barbershop chorus, the Toast of Tampa.

Product Director
Kathie-Jo Arnoff

Acquisitions Editor
Tim Ryan

Production Editor
Laura Wirthlin

Editor
Karen Grooms

Technical Editor
Ken German

*Composed in Garamond and MCPdigital
by Que Corporation*

Dedication

To my mother, Susan Marmel, and my brother and sister-in-law, Jim and Mariann Marmel, who always believe in me, and to the memory of my father, Harry Marmel (1914-1985), who would have been so very proud of me.

Acknowledgments

I would like to thank the following people:

Christopher Atkinson of CaptSure in Tampa for scanning images just to help out.

Richard Newrock of the Department of Physics at the University of Cincinnati for providing the Fourier Series equations.

Gloria Schuler for taking breaks with me when my brain quit working.

Kathie-Jo Arnoff for support and guidance.

Tim Ryan, even though he was a slave driver about everything, for encouraging me and making me laugh.

Laura Wirthlin for making this a better book.

Trademark Acknowledgments

Que Corporation has made every effort to supply trademark information about company names, products, and services mentioned in this book. Trademarks indicated below were derived from various sources. Que Corporation cannot attest to the accuracy of this information.

1-2-3 and Lotus are registered trademarks of Lotus Development Corporation.

dBASE is a registered trademark of Borland International, Inc.

IBM is a registered trademark of International Business Machines Corporation.

Intel is a registered trademark of Intel Corporation.

LaserJet is a registered trademark of Hewlett-Packard Co.

Microsoft, Microsoft Excel, Microsoft Windows, Microsoft Word, and Microsoft Word for Windows are registered trademarks and Toolbar is a trademark of Microsoft Corporation.

Rolodex is a registered trademark of Rolodex Corporation.

WordPerfect is a registered trademark of WordPerfect Corporation.

Contents at a Glance

Table of Contents

10 Working with Document Notation 219

Introduction

Word for Windows is one of the most popular word processing software packages available for the Windows environment. The program provides all the basic features you expect from a word processor as well as advanced features for more complicated operations. Word for Windows is well suited to your needs, whether you type short memos or create complex documents.

Word for Windows QuickStart takes you through Word for Windows step-by-step, covering all the fundamentals you need to know about the software package. The text supplies essential information, provides comments on what you see, and describes abstract ideas. Many illustrations guide you through procedures and help to clarify difficult concepts.

What Does This Book Contain?

Each chapter in *Word for Windows QuickStart* focuses on a particular Word for Windows operation or a related set of operations. The overall organization of the book reflects the typical steps you take as you create a document, from entering text to revising, proofreading, formatting, and printing.

Later chapters concentrate on more specialized topics: customizing Word for Windows; using the program's extensive document notation features; working with tables, frames, and pictures; automating your work with macros and glossaries; and merging. The last three chapters of *Word for Windows QuickStart* cover three additional software packages that Microsoft included when it shipped Word for Windows: Microsoft Graph, Microsoft Draw, and Microsoft Equation Editor.

Chapter 1, "Getting Started," begins with a brief overview of Word for Windows features, then covers the fundamentals of using the mouse and the keyboard. In the rest of the chapter, you learn how to start the Word for Windows program, understand the Word for Windows screen, and get help.

In Chapter 2, "Creating New Documents," you learn how to start a new document and use Word for Windows typing conventions. You also learn how to display documents in different "views" and how to save and print documents.

In Chapter 3, "Revising Documents," you learn the basics of editing a document. You learn how to open (retrieve) an existing document; how to move around in the document; and how to use basic editing techniques such as inserting blank lines and selecting, moving, copying, and deleting text. You also learn how to use the Undo feature and how to work in multiple windows.

In Chapter 4, "Proofreading," you learn how to find and replace information in a document and how to use the Thesaurus, Speller, and Grammar Checker. This chapter also includes information on formatting and proofing in foreign languages.

Chapters 5, 6, and 7 provide detailed information about formatting. Chapter 5, "Formatting Characters," describes how to apply different fonts and change font sizes, how to apply character styles such as boldface and italic type and underlining, and how to insert symbols and special characters. In Chapter 6, "Formatting Paragraphs," you learn how to work with tab stops and tab alignment, indentation, and paragraph alignment. You also learn how to set line spacing and apply borders and shading to paragraphs. Chapter 7, "Setting Up Documents," covers formatting pages to set margins; creating headers, footers, footnotes, and endnotes; and using paragraph numbering and bullets. You also learn how to create sections and how to work with newspaper columns.

In Chapter 8, "Managing and Printing Your Files," you learn how to create document summary information and how to use the program's file management features to find and print documents.

In Chapter 9, "Customizing Word for Windows," you learn how to work with styles, which were introduced in Chapter 6. You also learn how to work with document templates and how to change some of the many available options.

The rest of the chapters in this book deal with advanced topics. In Chapter 10, you learn how to work with the program's extensive document notation features. You learn to use bookmarks, cross-references, line numbers, and revision marks; to compare versions of a document; and to use annotations.

You also learn the advantages of Outline View and how to create a table of contents and an index.

In Chapter 11, "Working with Tables," you learn how to create a table; how to type, move, select, and edit in a table; and how to modify the table structure. You also learn how to add borders and shading to a table and how to sort table entries.

In Chapter 12, "Working with Frames and Pictures," you learn how to insert a frame and then type and edit in it, frame existing text, modify the size and placement of a frame, and remove a frame. You also learn how to work with clip art in Word for Windows by inserting a picture directly into a document or frame and then scaling or cropping the picture.

In Chapter 13, "Automating Your Work," you learn how to use glossaries and macros. You learn how to create and delete glossaries and macros and how to install the macros that Microsoft provided with Word. This chapter also includes a few sample macros.

Chapter 14, "Merging," covers all the basics of merging information for form letters. This chapter describes fields and records and explains how to plan a data file. You learn how to create a main merge document and how to create and edit a data file and attach it to the main merge document. You also learn how to merge to a document or to the printer.

Chapters 15, 16, and 17 cover the basics of the additional software packages that come with Word for Windows. Although you can use each of these software packages with other Windows products, the focus in this book is on using these packages with Word for Windows. In Chapter 15, "Using Microsoft Graph," you learn how to create and edit charts in a Word for Windows document. In Chapter 16, "Using Microsoft Draw," you learn how to draw pictures in a Word for Windows document. In Chapter 17, "Using Microsoft Equation Editor," you learn to use a specialized version of MathType to create and edit equations in a Word for Windows document.

Appendix A provides instructions for completely installing a single-user version of Word for Windows or for customizing the installation (if you have limited disk space).

The book concludes with a comprehensive index.

Who Should Use This Book?

Word for Windows QuickStart is an easy-to-use guide for anyone new to Word for Windows 2.0. This book presents enough basic information that a first-time Word for Windows user can quickly get started using the program. As that user's experience grows, later chapters of the book provide valuable information about tools that can enhance efficiency. An experienced Word for Windows user can easily find essential information and so can use this book as a reference tool.

Where To Find More Help

After you learn the Word for Windows basics covered in this QuickStart, you may want to explore some of the more advanced features of the program. Que Corporation has a complete line of Word for Windows books designed to meet the needs of all computer users. Other Word for Windows books include *Using Word for Windows 2*, Special Edition, and *Word for Windows 2 Quick Reference*. For more information about Que products, contact Que Corporation at 1-800-428-5331 (outside of Indiana). In Indiana, call 1-317-573-2500.

Word for Windows also has an extensive and effective on-line Help feature that can answer many specific questions. Chapter 1, "Getting Started," provides detailed information about using this feature.

If all else fails, you can call Microsoft for help. The phone number for Word for Windows support is (206)462-WORD. The telephone staff is courteous, helpful, and knowledgeable.

What Do You Need To Run Word for Windows 2.0?

To use Word for Windows 2.0, you must have the following computer hardware and software:

- A computer with an Intel 286 microprocessor or greater.
- At least 1 megabyte of RAM (to run the basic Word for Windows program) or 2 megabytes of RAM (to run all Word for Windows features), depending on the installation options you choose (see Appendix A for details on installation).

4

- A hard disk drive with at least 5.5 megabytes of free space (to install the basic program) or 15 megabytes of free space (to install all features), depending on the installation options you choose.
- A high-density floppy disk drive.
- An EGA monitor or better.
- DOS 3.1 or later.
- Windows 3.0 or later.

A mouse is recommended (it can make a number of tasks far more efficient), but is not required.

Conventions Used in This Book

Word for Windows QuickStart uses certain conventions to help you understand the information in this book:

- In this book, *selecting* means highlighting text (see Chapter 3 for details) and *choosing* means executing a command from a menu, the Toolbar, the Ribbon, the Ruler, or a dialog box.
- The keys you press and text you type appear in **boldface blue** type.

  To open a menu or choose a dialog box option by using the keyboard, you press Alt and then type the **boldface blue** letter. To open the **Help** menu, for example, you press Alt and then type **H**.

  To choose a command, you simply type the **boldface blue** letter. To choose the **Index** command from the **Help** menu, for example, you type **I**.

- Key combinations, such as Shift + F1, indicate that you hold down the first key as you press the second key. If the key combination consists of three keys, you hold down the first two keys as you press the third key.
- Important words or phrases appear in *italic* type when they are first discussed.
- Screen displays and messages appear in special type.

Getting Started

This chapter discusses the basics of Word for Windows: navigating in Windows by using a keyboard or the mouse, starting the program, understanding the Word for Windows screen, making choices, and getting help. The majority of this chapter is devoted to defining terms, identifying things you see when you use Word for Windows, and explaining how to open menus and how to make choices from the menus, the Toolbar, and dialog boxes.

Before you learn these basic skills, the chapter provides a brief overview of Word for Windows features. Because it is a *QuickStart*, this book does not cover some advanced features. You will learn, however, how to use Word for Windows to perform a variety of word processing tasks.

1

Key Terms in This Chapter

Mouse	A device you use to move the insertion point or pointer when working in a Windows program.
Pointer, mouse pointer	Various shapes on-screen that represent the position of the mouse.
Pointing	Positioning the mouse pointer directly on top of something on-screen. To click, double-click, or drag an item, you first point to that item.
Clicking	Pressing and releasing the mouse button one time. Unless otherwise specified, you click the left mouse button.
Double-clicking	Pressing and releasing the mouse button two times in rapid succession.
Dragging	Holding down the mouse button while moving the mouse. Unless otherwise specified, you hold down the left mouse button.
Insertion point	A flashing vertical bar on-screen that indicates where Word for Windows will place text when you start to type.
Selecting	Highlighting text (see Chapter 3 for details).
Choosing	Opening a menu or executing a command from a menu, the Toolbar, the Ribbon, the Ruler, or a dialog box by using the mouse or the keyboard.
Ctrl, X	Press and release the Ctrl key, and then press the X key.
Ctrl+X	Hold down the Ctrl key and press and release the X key (while holding down the Ctrl key).
Dialog box	A box that appears on-screen whenever Word for Windows needs additional information to complete an action.

An Overview of Word for Windows Features

Word for Windows 2 is a word processing program that can meet the needs of a variety of professionals in different industries. Word for Windows can easily support basic word processing features such as enhancing text with underlined, boldface or italic type and checking for spelling errors. Word for Windows also supports far more sophisticated features such as creating, editing, and publishing documents; automating work by using macros and glossaries; building tables and outlines; and merging text with graphics.

The following are just some of the features available in Word for Windows 2:

- Word for Windows 2 supports WYSIWYG (What You See Is What You Get) as well as several different views of a document.

- You can format characters in different fonts and sizes and add emphasis by using underlined, boldface, or italic type. You can define paragraph styles and apply them throughout a document. You can create document templates to store text and formatting you use regularly, such as a layout for a monthly report.

- You can move text by dragging it.

- You can automate repetitive work by using macros and glossaries.

- You can create tables of contents and indexes.

- You can use the document notation features of Word for Windows to indicate edited passages and to comment and ask questions within the document. You also can identify who made each comment or number the lines of a long document so that reviewers can refer to line numbers when commenting.

- You can easily create headers, footers, footnotes, and endnotes.

- You can break large documents into sections. You also can create newspaper-style columns that start anywhere on a page; for example, you can divide one part of a page into two columns and another part of that page into three columns.

- You can turn existing text into tables and existing tables into text. You also can add rows or columns anywhere in a table and change column sizes in a table by dragging.

- You can enhance pages with borders and shading.

- With the new Toolbar, you have immediate access to many Word for Windows menu commands. From the Toolbar, you can number lists or create bulleted entries, cut and paste text, open or save existing documents, and start new documents. You also can customize the Toolbar so that it provides the commands you use most often.

1

- In addition to the Spelling Checker and Thesaurus, Word for Windows has a new Grammar Checker (which also checks spelling).

- A screen preview feature enables you to check the contents of a document before you open it, making file management easier.

- With Microsoft Graph, you can create charts directly in Word for Windows. With Microsoft Draw, you can create logos, maps, and diagrams. Also, you can insert text and pictures into frames and then move them around a document.

- For WordPerfect users who want to learn Word for Windows quickly, Word for Windows provides an on-line Help feature that converts Word Help to WordPerfect Help. You also can use this feature to demonstrate WordPerfect commands in Word for Windows.

In the pages that follow, you will find step-by-step instructions for using these features and others. This upgrade of Word for Windows has made the software a most versatile document generator; its capabilities will enable you to achieve professional—and useful—results.

Reviewing Navigation in Windows

Although you can use Windows and Word for Windows with only a keyboard, both products are easier to use with a mouse *and* a keyboard. Before you start Windows, read this section to review navigation.

When you use DOS (non-Windows) programs, you generally navigate by using the arrow keys to move the *cursor* (usually a flashing underscore or a highlight). Moving the cursor is often called "pointing." To choose a command from a menu, for example, you "point" to that command and press ↵Enter.

In Windows programs, the cursor is usually called the *pointer* and has many different shapes. When you use Windows programs, you can use both the keyboard and the mouse to "point."

Also, most Windows programs have the same general appearance. When you start a Windows program, you see the name of the program in a bar at the top of the screen. When you start Windows, for example, the Program Manager appears.

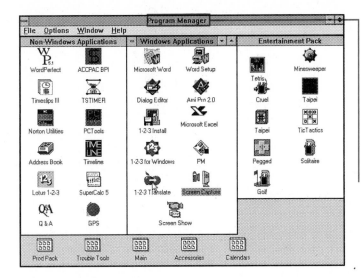

At the top of the screen, you see the name of the program currently running, the Program Manager.

Just below the program name, you see a *menu bar* that contains the names of the Windows menus: File, Options, Window, and Help. When you open a menu, you will see Windows commands.

Using the Keyboard

To activate the menu bar by using the keyboard, you press (Alt). Notice that a bar highlights the File menu's name.

After you activate the menu bar, you can open a menu in two ways:

- Move to the menu by pressing (←) or (→) until Windows highlights the name of the menu and then press (↵Enter).
- Type the underlined letter in the menu name. Note that you do not need to move to the menu before you type the letter.

Windows opens the menu and highlights the first command on that menu. To choose a menu command, you can press (↓) to "point to" the command and then press (↵Enter), or you can type the underlined letter in the command name. Throughout this book, the underlined letters appear in **boldface blue** type.

1

Using the Mouse

The mouse provides an alternative way to navigate in Windows. Using the mouse to navigate significantly reduces the number of keystrokes you need to work with Windows programs. Your mouse has two or three buttons. In Windows and in Word for Windows, you primarily use the left mouse button, but you occasionally use the right mouse button.

The words *pointer* and *mouse pointer* refer to the cursor shape that represents the position of the mouse on-screen. The mouse pointer's shape depends on its position. These shapes are discussed in detail later in this chapter. Usually, the mouse pointer is an arrow pointing up and slightly to the left.

To open a menu by using the mouse, point to the name of the menu (slide the mouse so that the mouse pointer is directly on top of the menu name) and then click the left mouse button. Windows opens the menu and highlights the first command on that menu. To choose a menu command, point to that menu command and then click the left mouse button.

Starting the Program

Word for Windows must operate in the Windows environment. You can, however, start the program in three ways:

- From the DOS command prompt.
- From the Windows Program Manager's File menu.
- From the Windows group icon for Word for Windows.

The last method is the easiest way to start Word for Windows, but this book provides instructions for all three methods. Starting Word for Windows by using one of the other methods is easier if you include the directory where you installed Word for Windows in your computer's PATH statement, which is generally stored in the AUTOEXEC.BAT file. If you installed Word for Windows with its defaults (see Appendix A, "Installing Word for Windows," for more information), you installed the program in the WINWORD directory. The following examples assume that you installed Word for Windows in the WINWORD directory on drive C.

Starting Word for Windows from the DOS Prompt

To start Word for Windows from the DOS prompt, follow these steps:

1

1. Type **WIN WINWORD** at the DOS command prompt.
2. Press ⏎Enter.

If the computer displays a message that this command failed, then the directory containing Word for Windows is not WINWORD or the directory containing Word for Windows is not included in the PATH statement. Change to the directory that contains Word for Windows and try the steps again.

Starting Word for Windows from the Program Manager's File Menu

To start Word for Windows from the File menu of the Windows Program Manager, follow these steps:

1. Type **WIN** at the command prompt and press ⏎Enter.

   The Windows Program Manager appears.
2. Open the File menu.
3. From the File menu, choose the Run command.

   The Run dialog box appears. Note that the insertion point—a slowly flashing vertical bar—appears in the Command Line text box.
4. Type **WINWORD** and press ⏎Enter. If the directory containing Word for Windows is not included in the PATH statement in your AUTOEXEC.BAT file, type the complete path (for example, type **C:\WINWORD\WINWORD.EXE** and press ⏎Enter).

Note: Using either of the preceding methods, you can start Word for Windows and open a document at the same time by adding the document name to the end of the command. For example, typing **WINWORD SAMPLE** starts Word for Windows and opens the document named SAMPLE.

Starting Word for Windows from the Windows Icon

To start Word for Windows from its Windows group icon, follow these steps:

1. Type **WIN** at the command prompt and press ⏎Enter.
2. Open the Windows group that contains the icon for Microsoft Word.
3. Double-click the Microsoft Word icon.

1 Understanding the Word for Windows Screen

Regardless of the method you use to start the program, you see the opening Word for Windows screen.

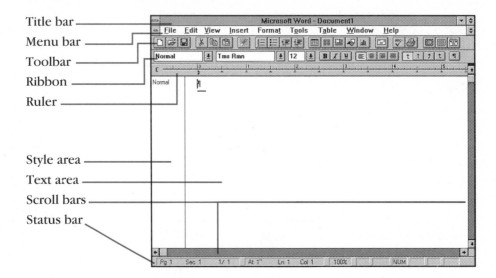

Title bar
Menu bar
Toolbar
Ribbon
Ruler

Style area
Text area
Scroll bars
Status bar

Note: The Style area appears only if you choose it as one of your options. You learn how to set options in Chapter 9.

When you start Word for Windows, the program opens Document1, a new document in which you can start typing.

You can open up to nine Word for Windows documents at one time, each in its own window (Chapter 3 discusses switching between documents). Word for Windows numbers additional new documents sequentially—Document2, Document3, and so on. When you exit and then restart Word for Windows, the program starts with Document1 again.

Identifying Screen Parts

In this section, you learn about the parts of the Word for Windows screen and how to use them.

1

Title Bar

The title bar appears at the top of the screen and, in Word for Windows, displays the program name and the name of the document in which you are working.

When you start Word for Windows, the program and Document1 are *maximized*, which means that they fill all the available work space on-screen. You can tell that Word for Windows and Document1 are maximized because they share the title bar. Working in a maximized window is not essential, but is usually easiest. You can change the size of the document window or the Word for Windows application window by using their Control menus or their Minimize or Maximize buttons.

Word Control Menu

The button that opens the Word Control menu is at the left end of the title bar, in the upper left corner of the screen.

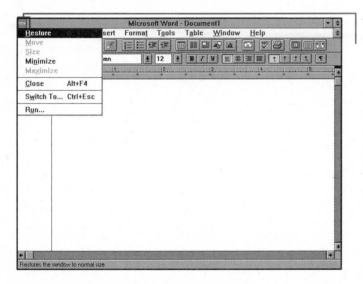

Word Control menu button

The Word Control menu includes commands for changing the size of the Word for Windows application screen.

Note that if you reduce the size of the Word for Windows application, you automatically reduce the size of the document in which you are working.

The Word Control menu also includes a command for switching to other programs.

1

Document Control Menu

Just below the Word Control menu is a similar button for the document Control menu.

Document
Control menu
button

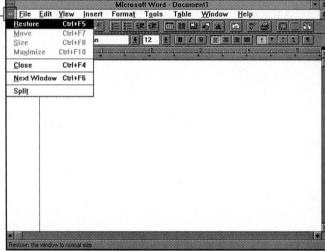

The commands
on the document
Control menu
enable you to
switch to the next
open document
and to split the
screen as well as
to change the size
of the document
window.

Minimize, Restore, and Maximize Buttons

Also at the top of the screen, but on the far right side, are the Minimize button and the Restore or Maximize button. These buttons provide a quick way to change the size of Word for Windows or the document:

- The Minimize button contains a small arrow that points down. If you click the Minimize button, Windows reduces the program to its Windows icon. The program is still running, but no longer fills the screen.

- The Restore button contains small arrows that point up and down. If you click the Restore button, Windows reduces the window to a size between the maximum (full screen) and minimum (icon) size, and the Restore button changes to the Maximize button.

- The Maximize button, which appears only if you previously chose the Restore button, contains a small arrow that points up. If you click the Maximize button, Windows maximizes the window, and the Maximize button changes to the Restore button.

Menu Bar

Next to the Document Control menu button is the menu bar, which contains the names of the Word for Windows menus. These menus contain Word for Windows commands grouped by function; for example, the File menu contains commands that open, close, save, and print documents and find information in document files. Word for Windows executes some commands, such as the Save command, as soon as you choose that command. For other commands, the program requires additional information to execute the command. Choosing Word for Windows menu commands and supplying additional information are discussed in detail later in this chapter.

Toolbar

Just below the menu bar is the Toolbar. The Toolbar contains a row of icons that provide shortcuts to Word for Windows menu commands. Choosing the command from the Toolbar saves keystrokes. To start the Spelling Checker, for example, you can open the Tools menu and then select the Spelling command, or you can click the Toolbar icon that represents the Spelling Checker. The Toolbar is also discussed in more detail later in this chapter.

Ribbon and Ruler

Just below the Toolbar are the Ribbon and the Ruler. The Ribbon and the Ruler also provide shortcuts to Word for Windows menu commands. You can use the Ribbon, which appears directly below the Toolbar, to make selected text boldface, underlined, or italic; to control paragraph alignment; and to customize tab settings. You can use the Ruler, which appears directly below the Ribbon, to change margins, adjust indents, and change the width of newspaper-style and table columns. The Ribbon and the Ruler are discussed in more detail in Chapters 5 and 6.

Text Area

Just below the Ruler is the text area. The text area is where you type text and insert tables and graphics. A horizontal bar marks the end of the document and a flashing vertical bar, the *insertion point*, appears in the upper left corner of the text area. The insertion point indicates where text will appear when you begin to type. The insertion point is discussed in more detail in Chapter 2.

1

Style Area

Word for Windows assigns a *style* to each paragraph you type. In the style area, you can see the name of the style for each paragraph. Chapter 9 provides information on styles and setting options.

In the screens in this book, the style area always appears. If you want to display the style area, see Chapter 9.

Scroll Bars

At the bottom and right side of the screen are the scroll bars. You use the horizontal scroll bar to move the text from side to side within the window. You use the vertical scroll bar to move forward and backward in the document. The *split box*, a small black box just above the arrow at the top of the vertical scroll bar, splits the current window into two panes. See Chapter 3 for further information on the scroll bars and the split box.

Status Bar

The last line of the screen is the status bar, which displays pertinent information about the page that contains the insertion point or about the highlighted command.

Insertion point ——

In this example, the first box on the status bar indicates that the insertion point is on page 2 in section 1 of the document, and that the page is page 2 of 3 (in section 1).

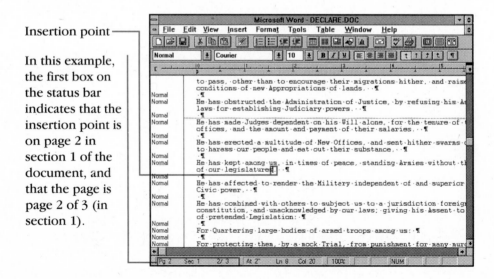

The second box on the status bar indicates the position of the insertion point, measured in inches from the top edge of the page (including any top margins); the number of the line containing the insertion point; and number of the column containing the insertion point, measured by counting the number of characters between the left margin and the insertion point. The next box on the status bar indicates the percentage of magnification. Other boxes on the status bar contain information if you press certain keys on the keyboard. If you press [Num Lock], for example, NUM appears in one of the boxes toward the right end of the status bar.

Recognizing Pointer Mouse Shapes

The mouse pointer can assume many different shapes, depending on where the pointer is on-screen.

Table 1.1
Mouse Pointer Shapes

Shape	Name	Appears when
	Menu pointer	The mouse pointer is pointing to a menu, a command, a scroll bar, the Toolbar, the Ribbon, or the Ruler.
	I-beam	The mouse pointer is in the text area. When the mouse pointer is within italic text, the I-beam slants (to make selecting text easier).
	Hourglass	The computer is working on a task. Please wait.
	Move text pointer	You are dragging text from one location to another. Position the vertical bar of the pointer where you want to place the text.
	Selection bar arrow	The mouse pointer is in the selection bar (or the style area) to the left side of the text area.
	Help pointer	You requested command help. When the mouse pointer has this shape and you choose a command, Word for Windows displays help information about the command rather than executing the command.

continues

19

1

Table 1.1 (continued)

Shape	Name	Appears when
Hand	Hand	The mouse pointer is pointing to a help topic for which more information is available.
Plus sign	Plus sign	In Print Preview mode, the mouse pointer is pointing to a margin, header, or footer. When the mouse pointer has this shape, you can move that margin, header, or footer.
Horizontal split box pointer	Horizontal split box pointer	The mouse pointer is pointing to the split box. When the mouse pointer has this shape, you can split the screen.
Vertical split box pointer	Vertical split box pointer	The mouse pointer is pointing to the line that separates the style area from the text area. When the mouse pointer has this shape, you can drag the line to increase or decrease the size of the style area.
Move/Size arrow	Move/Size arrow	You are changing the size of a window, but have not yet moved the mouse pointer to one of the boundaries of the window.
Move/Size vertical or horizontal arrows	Move/Size vertical or horizontal arrows	You are moving a window or changing its size and have moved the mouse pointer to one of the boundaries of the window.
Outline arrow	Outline arrow	In Outline View, the mouse pointer is pointing to the icon of a heading. When the mouse pointer has this shape, you can drag the heading.
Outline vertical or horizontal arrows	Outline vertical or horizontal arrows	In Outline View, you are dragging a heading vertically or horizontally.
Down arrow for tables	Down arrow for tables	The mouse pointer is above a table column.

20

See Chapter 10 for more information on working in Outline View.

Making Choices

When you are working in Word for Windows, you choose items from the menu, the Toolbar, and dialog boxes. This section describes how to choose items and how to undo your action if you change your mind.

Choosing from a Menu by Using the Mouse

To open a menu by using the mouse, follow these steps:

1. Move the mouse pointer into the menu bar.
2. Point to the name of the menu you want to open.
3. Click the menu name.

Word for Windows opens the menu and displays the commands. To choose a command from the menu, follow these steps:

1. Move the mouse pointer into the menu.
2. Point to the command you want to choose.
3. Click the command.

If the command is followed by an ellipsis (...), Word for Windows displays a dialog box to request more information. Otherwise, Word for Windows executes the command immediately. If a command is gray, that command is not currently available.

1

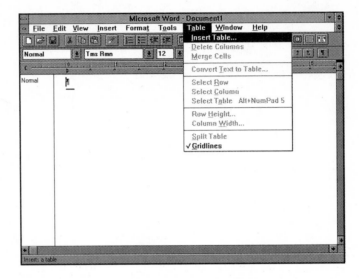

When the insertion point is not in a table, most of the commands on the Table menu are gray. These commands would be available if the insertion point were in a table.

If you open a menu and then change your mind, you can close the menu by clicking the mouse button anywhere in the text area, or you can open a different menu by clicking that menu's name.

Choosing from a Menu by Using the Keyboard

To open a menu and choose a command by using the keyboard, follow these steps:

1. Press Alt. The document Control menu button becomes darker.

2. Type the underlined letter in the name of the menu you want to open. In this book, the underlined letter appears in **boldface blue** type. To open the Table menu, for example, press A.

Word for Windows displays the menu. To choose a command from the menu, type the underlined letter in the command or press ↓ to point to (highlight) the command and then press ⏎Enter.

If you open a menu and then change your mind, you can do any of the following:

• Close the menu by pressing Esc two times.

• Open a different menu by pressing Esc one time and then pressing the underlined letter in the menu name.

• Open a different menu by pressing ← or → to point to (highlight) the menu name.

Choosing a Command by Using the Toolbar

To take advantage of the shortcuts provided by the Toolbar, you must use the mouse. To choose a command from the Toolbar, click the button for that command. Word for Windows executes most Toolbar commands immediately. Table 1.2 describes the buttons on the Toolbar.

Table 1.2
Toolbar Buttons

Button	Name	Effect
	New	Opens a new document.
	Open	Opens an existing document.
	Save	Saves the current document.
	Cut	Cuts the highlighted text to the Windows Clipboard.
	Copy	Copies the highlighted text to the Windows Clipboard.
	Paste	Inserts the contents of the Windows Clipboard into the current document at the insertion point.
	Undo	Reverses the last action. (You cannot reverse some actions.)
	Numbered List	Formats the selected text with Arabic numbers and indents each line 1/4 inch to the right of the number position.
	Bullets	Formats the selected text with bullets and indents each line 1/4 inch to the right of the bullet position.
	Unindent	Moves the selected text left to the preceding tab position.
	Indent	Moves the selected text right to the next tab position.

continues

1

Table 1.2 (continued)

Button	Name	Effect
	Table	Inserts a table at the insertion point.
	Columns	Formats the current section of the document in newspaper-style columns.
	Frame	Inserts a frame at the insertion point.
	Draw	Enables you to draw images that you can insert into Word for Windows documents.
	Chart	Enables you to create a chart without leaving Word for Windows.
	Envelope	Creates an envelope and then prints the envelope or adds it to the current document for later printing.
	Spelling Checker	Checks the spelling in the document.
	Print	Prints the active document.
	Zoom Whole Page	Reduces the page so that an entire page appears in the window.
	Zoom 100%	Displays the document in Normal View at full size. For typing and editing, you usually use this view.
	Zoom Page Width	Temporarily reduces the character size so that complete lines appear in the window.

You can change the Toolbar icons or modify Toolbar commands by choosing the Options command from the Tools menu (described in more detail in Chapter 9).

Choosing Options from Dialog Boxes

Whenever you choose a menu command that is followed by an ellipsis (...), Word for Windows displays a dialog box where you supply additional information. Each dialog box is different and may contain any or all of the following types of options:

- A *list box* contains a list of options. Word for Windows has two kinds of list boxes. The Print list box in the Print dialog box is an example of a "pull-down" list box and is closed when the dialog box appears. To open a pull-down list box, click the down arrow at the right end of the box or hold down Alt and type the underlined letter in the list box name. The other type of list box is already open when the dialog box appears. To choose an option from either type of list box, click the option or press ↓ to point to the option and then press ↵Enter. If the list box is not long enough to display all the available options, hold down ↓ to move beyond the options that appear in the box.

- An *option button* is a small round button you use to choose one option from a group of related options. A black dot appears in the button of the current option. To choose an option button, click the option button or hold down Alt and type the underlined letter in the option name.

- A *check box* is a small square box you use to choose an option. You can choose more than one check box from a group of related options. An X appears in the check boxes of the activated options. To choose a check box, click the check box or hold down Alt and type the underlined letter in the option name. To deactivate the option and remove the X from the box, choose the check box again.

- A *text box* is a rectangular box where you enter text. When a dialog box opens, the current text is usually selected. To replace the selected text, just type the new information.

- A *command button* is an oblong button that performs an action. The OK button accepts the settings in the dialog box. The Cancel and Close buttons cancel your changes to the settings in the dialog box. To choose a command button, click the button or highlight the button and press ↵Enter.

- A *tunnel-through command button* is a command button that opens another dialog box. To choose a tunnel-through command button, click the button, highlight the button and press ↵Enter, or hold down Alt and type the highlighted letter in the option name. In the Print dialog box, the Setup button and the Options button are tunnel-through command buttons.

Most dialog boxes provide only *some* of these types of options.

1

The Print dialog box contains examples of each type of option.

Command buttons ——————

List box ——————

Option buttons ——————

Text boxes ——————

Check boxes ——————

Tunnel-through command buttons ——————

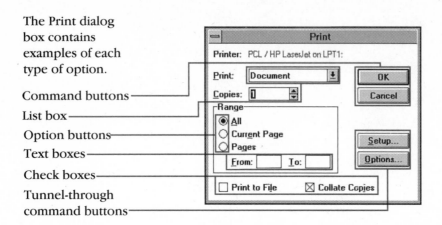

In the Print dialog box, the Print box is a list box, but the Copies box is a text box. The Range box contains option buttons (All, Current Page, and Pages) and two text boxes (From and To). At the bottom of the box are the Print to File and Collate Copies check boxes. At the right side of the dialog box, the OK and Cancel buttons are command buttons and the Setup and Options buttons are tunnel-through command buttons.

You also may notice a dotted line surrounding an option. This line indicates the current mouse pointer position. To choose dialog box options by using the mouse, you click the button or box. To choose dialog box options by using the keyboard, you hold down [Alt] and type the underlined letter in the option name. To choose the OK button or the Cancel button, you press [Tab↨] to highlight the button and then press [↵Enter].

Getting Help

You can use Word for Windows' extensive Help feature in three ways:

- Activate general Help.
- Use context-sensitive Help.
- Get Help before selecting a command.

Activating General Help

To activate general Help, follow these steps:

1

1. Open the **H**elp menu.

2. Choose the Help **I**ndex command.

Or, press F1 without pointing to any command.

Note: If you installed WordPerfect Help when you installed Word for Windows, you disabled the Word for Windows Help key (F1). See "A Note to WordPerfect Users" later in this chapter to learn how to use the **O**ptions command (on the **T**ools menu) to disable and enable WordPerfect Help as you need it.

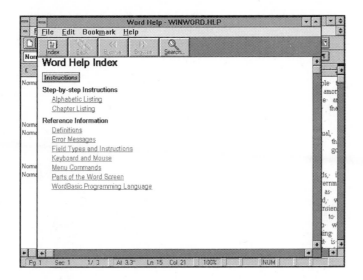

When you activate general Help, Word for Windows displays the Word Help Index in the Word Help window.

From left to right at the top of the Word Help window are the Control menu button, the Word Help window's title bar, and the Minimize and Maximize buttons. Just below the title bar is the Help menu bar. The boxes below the Help menu bar are Help buttons. Help information appears below the Help buttons.

To print a topic you view in Help, choose the **P**rint Topic command from the **F**ile menu. Word for Windows prints the topic that appears in the Help window. You cannot, however, print part of a topic.

Note: Word for Windows also provides two on-line tutorials: Getting Started, a quick overview, and Learning Word, a longer, more extensive set of lessons. You can choose either tutorial from the **H**elp menu.

When you view topics, you will see topics that have solid underlines and topics that have dashed underlines. If you choose a topic that has a solid

1

underline, Word Help jumps to the help information on that topic. If you point to a topic that has a dashed underline and hold down the left mouse button, Word Help displays a box that contains a brief definition of the word(s) you chose.

Looking through Help Topics

The Browse Forward and Browse Backward buttons are available whenever Word Help has topics before or after the current topic. If the Browse Forward and Browse Backward buttons are available, you can use these buttons to view topics in the order that they appear in Word Help. The Browse Forward button displays the next screen. The Browse Backward button displays the preceding screen.

Searching for Topics

You can use the Search button to search for Word Help topics by using *keywords*.

When you choose the Search Help button, Word for Windows displays the Search dialog box.

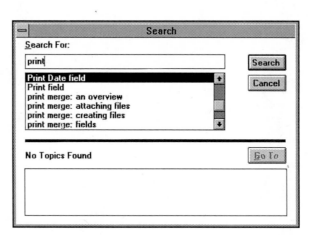

You can type the keyword you want Word for Windows to find in the Search For text box or choose a keyword from the list box. After you type or choose a keyword, choose the Search button. In the lower portion of the Search dialog box, Word for Windows identifies any related topics it finds. To view a topic directly, click that topic and then choose the Go To button.

Marking Topics To Return to Them Later

If you find topics to which you might want to return later, you can define bookmarks for them.

To define a bookmark, follow these steps:

1. When you are looking at a help topic for which you want to define a bookmark, open the Bookmark menu.

2. Choose the Define command.

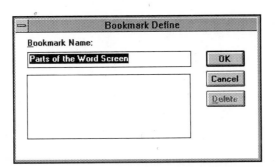

Word for Windows displays the Bookmark Define dialog box. The topic name appears in the Bookmark Name text box.

3. To accept the name, choose OK or press ⏎Enter. To enter a different name, type the name.

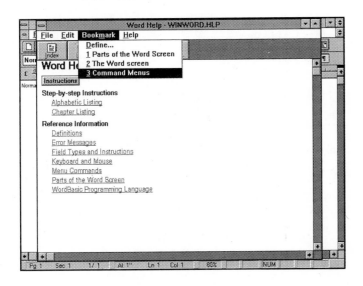

The bookmarks you define appear on the Bookmark menu.

1

To use one of the bookmarks you defined, choose the Bookmark menu and then choose the bookmark for the topic you want to view.

To delete a bookmark, follow these steps:

1. Open the Bookmark menu.
2. Choose the Define command.
3. Choose the bookmark you want to delete.
4. Choose the Delete button.
5. Choose OK or press ⏎Enter.

Adding Comments to Help

You also can add your own comments to Word Help topics. To annotate a topic, follow these steps:

1. Display the help topic on which you want to comment.
2. Open the Edit menu.
3. Choose the Annotate command.

The Help Annotation dialog box appears.

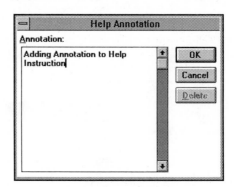

4. Type your comment in the Annotation text box.
5. Choose OK or press ⏎Enter.

Word for Windows adds the comment to the current topic. Note that a small green paper clip appears to the left of the topic to indicate that an annotation exists for this help topic. If you click the green paper clip, Word for Windows displays the annotation.

1

Copying Help to the Clipboard

You can copy the contents of the Help window to the Clipboard by choosing the Copy command from the Help window's Edit menu. Chapter 3 discusses copying in more detail.

Getting Help about Using Help

To get information about how Word Help works, choose the Using Help command from the Help window's Help menu.

Using Context-Sensitive Help

You can get help about any Word for Windows command by pointing to that command and pressing F1. You also can get this kind of help about the Ribbon by positioning the insertion point in the Style, Font, or Point Size text boxes and pressing F1.

Note: If you installed WordPerfect Help when you installed Word for Windows, you disabled the Word for Windows Help key (F1). See "A Note to WordPerfect Users" later in this chapter to learn how to use the Options command (on the Tools menu) to disable and enable WordPerfect Help as you need it.

Getting Help before Choosing a Command

You can turn the mouse pointer into a "help requester." When operating in this mode, you do not actually choose commands, but rather choose to see the help topic related to the command or the area of the screen to which you pointed.

To get help about the area or command to which you are pointing, you press ⇧Shift + F1. The mouse pointer changes shape (to include a question mark) until you make a help request. When you exit Help, the mouse pointer returns to normal operation.

A Note to WordPerfect Users

Microsoft has incorporated help for WordPerfect users into Word for Windows. This feature not only provides help text, but also demonstrates the Word for Windows equivalent of the WordPerfect command you choose. (You

1

can set up this option when you install Word for Windows and turn it off later by using the Help for WordPerfect Users dialog box.) You can use the WordPerfect Help feature in two ways:

- You can make WordPerfect Help available anytime you press a key combination that has meaning in WordPerfect ("automatically").

- You can make WordPerfect Help available only when you specifically request it.

To access WordPerfect Help, choose WordPerfect Help from the Help menu.

Word for Windows displays the Help for WordPerfect Users dialog box.

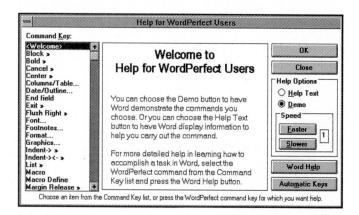

The center of the Help for WordPerfect Users dialog box contains a brief explanation of how to use the equivalent Word for Windows feature. The area on the right contains Word for Windows command buttons. In the Help Options box, you can set the WordPerfect Help feature so that Word for Windows provides help text when you choose a WordPerfect command (Automatic Keys) or so that Word for Windows actually demonstrates the equivalent of that command (Demo). You also can speed up or slow down the demonstration.

To get Word Help about the Word for Windows version of a WordPerfect command, choose the WordPerfect command in the list box on the left side of the dialog box and then choose the Word Help command button on the right side of the dialog box. If the WordPerfect command you choose is followed by an ellipsis (...), Word for Windows displays a Word Help Index of topics related to the WordPerfect command. If the WordPerfect command is followed by a greater-than symbol (>), Word for Windows displays help text for the command or demonstrates the command.

32

The last button on the right side of the dialog box toggles between automatic and manual access to help with WordPerfect commands. When this button is Automatic keys, you are using Word for Windows keys for help. If you choose the Automatic keys button, the button changes its name and function to Disable Automatic. When this button is Disable Automatic, you are using WordPerfect keys for help. Note that when you access WordPerfect Help automatically, you disable some Word for Windows functions. You cannot get Help by pressing F1, for example, because in WordPerfect F1 is the Cancel key.

If you want to see Word for Windows demonstrate a WordPerfect command by pressing the keys that represent that WordPerfect command, choose the Automatic keys button and the Demo option button. Then, close the Help for WordPerfect Users dialog box and press the WordPerfect key combination. Word for Windows demonstrates the equivalent WordPerfect command by using Word for Windows commands.

Instead of a demonstration, you can ask Word for Windows to display text that tells you what Word for Windows commands you choose to perform a WordPerfect command. If you want information on how to execute a WordPerfect command using Word for Windows commands, choose the Automatic keys button and the Help Text option button. Then, close the Help for WordPerfect Users dialog box and press the WordPerfect key combination. Word for Windows displays text that describes the equivalent Word for Windows commands.

Chapter Summary

In this chapter, you learned the basics of starting Word for Windows and using the mouse or the keyboard. This chapter also described the parts of the Word for Windows screen and the mouse pointer shapes. Specifically, you learned the following information about Word for Windows:

- You can start Word for Windows from the DOS prompt, from the Windows Program Manager, or from the Windows icon.

- The Word for Windows screen contains a title bar, Word Control menu, document Control menu, Minimize and Restore or Maximize buttons, menu bar, Toolbar, Ribbon, Ruler, style area, scroll bars, and status bar.

- The mouse pointer assumes different shapes depending on the pointer's position on-screen.

1

- You can open or cancel menus and choose commands from menus by using the keyboard or the mouse. You can choose commands from the Toolbar only by using the mouse.

- You supply additional information to Word for Windows by choosing options in dialog boxes. Dialog boxes can contain list boxes, option buttons, check boxes, text boxes, and command buttons.

- You can browse or search through Word for Windows' extensive Help feature. You can insert bookmarks in Word Help so that you can return to specific topics easily, and you can add your own notes to the help information.

- You can have Word for Windows demonstrate or provide text instructions for the equivalent Word for Windows commands when you press a WordPerfect key combination.

In Chapter 2, you will learn how to create new documents in Word for Windows.

Creating New Documents

2

In this chapter you will learn how to start a new document, how to type text and correct simple mistakes in a document, and how to display different views of a document. You also will learn how to save and print a document.

Starting new documents

Typing text

Displaying documents in different views

Saving documents

Printing the active document

2

Key Terms in This Chapter

Document template An empty document in which Word for Windows stores standard settings such as margins, typeface and type size, tab stops, and line spacing. If you use document templates as a basis for your documents, you do not have to create standard settings each time you start a new document.

Word wrap A concept that describes how Word for Windows automatically moves the insertion point to the beginning of a new line when you fill the current line with text.

Insert mode The opposite of Overtype mode. In Insert mode, existing text moves to the right as you type new text. Insert mode is the default mode for Word for Windows.

Overtype mode The opposite of Insert mode. In Overtype mode, new text replaces existing text as you type.

Starting a New Document

You can begin typing text as soon as you start Word for Windows. The document which appears on-screen, Document1, is based on a document template called NORMAL.DOT. This template provides basic settings established by Word for Windows. The NORMAL.DOT template includes the following settings:

- A typeface with an average size.
- Left and right margins of 1.25 inches.
- Top and bottom margins of 1 inch.
- Single-spaced paragraphs aligned flush with the left margin.
- Tab stops set every .5 inch.

2

Word for Windows provides a number of document templates; each template includes some different settings. If you base your documents on Word for Windows templates, you do not have to create basic settings each time you start a new document; rather, Word for Windows uses the settings in the template as a guideline for formatting the document. You can change the settings before you start typing or at any time while you are typing. Chapter 9 discusses document templates in greater detail.

You can start a new document of your own (Document2) by choosing a command from a menu or a button from the Toolbar. If you start a new document by choosing a menu command, you must make more decisions.

To start a new document by choosing a menu command, follow these steps:

1. Open the File menu.

2. Choose the New command.

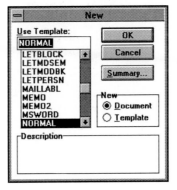

The New dialog box appears. NORMAL is the default document template.

Because NORMAL is a very basic template, you probably will use it more than you use other templates.

3. Choose NORMAL (by choosing the OK button or pressing ⏎Enter).

Document2 appears on-screen.

To start a new document from the Toolbar, you choose the New button. (To choose a button from the Toolbar, you must use the mouse.)

2

The New button
is the first button
on the Toolbar.

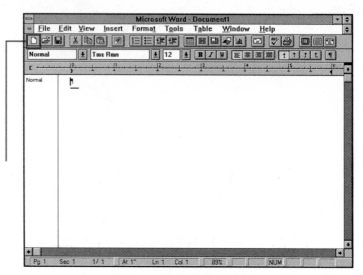

A new, blank document appears on-screen. When you start a new document from the Toolbar, Word for Windows automatically uses NORMAL.DOT as the document template.

Note: In the figures in this book, the style area appears at the left side of the window. Chapter 9 discusses how to set this option.

Typing

Typing words in a word processor can be much faster and easier than writing them on paper. With a word processor, you can make revisions quickly. If you change your mind about the structure of a sentence or the organization of a paragraph, you can insert words and sentences, delete phrases you don't want, and move information from one location to another. The Spelling Checker can find typographical errors better than most people, so you don't need to worry about your typing accuracy.

Understanding the Insertion Point

The insertion point is the flashing vertical bar in the text area of the document. In a new document, the insertion point appears in the upper left corner of the text area. When you type, text appears to the left of the insertion point, and the insertion point moves to the right. The insertion point is the place marker for where Word for Windows inserts text into the document. You can move the insertion point by using the keyboard or the mouse, but you cannot move the insertion point beyond the last character in the document.

Understanding Word Wrap

As you reach the end of a line, the insertion point automatically moves to the next line. This phenomenon, known as *word wrap*, occurs because Word for Windows calculates when you reach the right margin and "returns the carriage" for you. Don't press ⏎Enter until you want to start a new paragraph.

Using the Backspace and Delete Keys

When you type, you may make mistakes that you notice immediately and want to correct. You can use ←Backspace or Del to remove one character at a time. When you press ←Backspace, you delete the character immediately to the left of the insertion point.

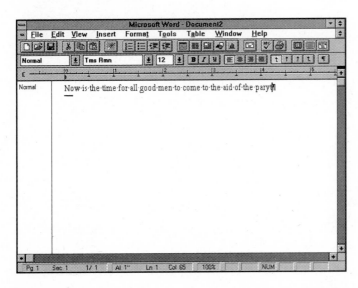

If you typed this line, you could correct the mistake by pressing ←Backspace two times to remove the letters *t* and *y* (in that order).

After you remove incorrect letters by pressing ←Backspace, you can retype the correct letters (in the correct order) without moving the insertion point.

Whereas ⌫Backspace deletes the character to the left of the insertion point, Del deletes the character immediately to the right of the insertion point.

2

If you pressed ← two times (to position the insertion point between the *r* and the *y*), you press Del two times to remove the letters *y* and *t* (in that order).

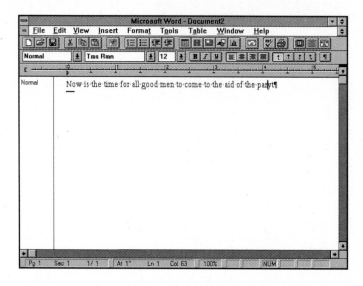

Understanding Insert and Overtype Modes

When you first open a Word for Windows document and start typing, you are in Insert mode. As you type, Word for Windows inserts the characters to the left of the insertion point. Any text already on-screen moves to the right. If you want to replace text that appears on-screen, you can change to Overtype mode by pressing Ins.

Note: If NUM appears on the status bar, you have pressed Num Lock so that the keys on the numerical keypad type numbers rather than work as directional keys. You must press the gray Ins key to change to Overtype mode or press Num Lock again to make the numerical keypad work as directional keys (and then press Ins on the numeric keypad to change to Overtype mode).

Two things happen when you change to Overtype mode:

- The indicator OVR appears at the right end of the status bar.
- Any characters you type replace existing text rather than moving existing text to the right.

The Ins key is a "toggle" switch. Press Ins one time to change to Overtype mode. Press Ins again to change back to Insert mode. OVR appears on the status bar only when Word for Windows is operating in Overtype mode. This indicator disappears from the status bar when you toggle back to Insert mode.

Displaying Documents in Different Views

Word for Windows can display several different *views* of the same document. You can use these views to focus on various aspects of a document and to make editing easier. You can display a document in the following four views:

- Normal
- Outline
- Page Layout
- Print Preview

The remaining screens in this chapter use the document CRUISE.DOC as an example. Later in this book, you will learn how to create documents with all the features you see in CRUISE.DOC—and more.

Changing to Normal View

Normal View is the default, and generally the most useful, view. You probably will do the majority of your work in Normal View.

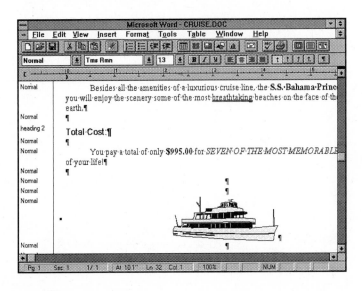

In Normal View, you can see character and paragraph formatting; alignment; tab stops; and line, section, and page breaks.

2

To change to Normal View, follow these steps:

1. Open the View menu.

2. Choose the Normal command. (If a dot appears to the left of the Normal command when you open the View menu, you are already in the Normal View—you don't need to choose the command.)

If you open the View menu again, you see a dot to the left of the Normal command, indicating that Word for Windows is displaying the document in the Normal View.

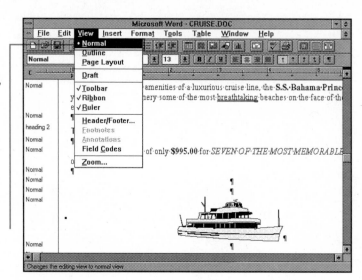

You can add Draft mode to the Normal View to speed up redrawing the screen or printing the document. When you add Draft mode to the Normal View, character formatting appears as underlining and graphics appear as frames.

Follow these steps to add Draft mode to the Normal View:

1. Open the View menu.

2. Choose the Draft command.

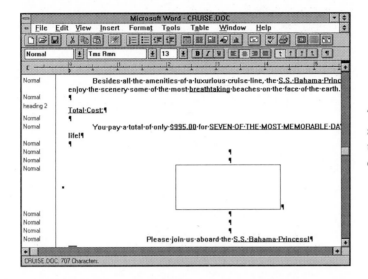

The on-screen appearance of text and graphics changes.

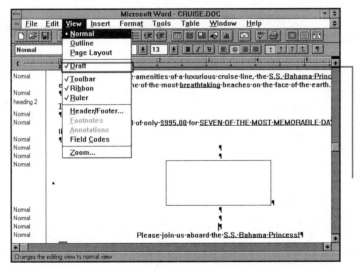

If you open the **V**iew menu again, you see a check mark to the left of the **D**raft command.

Note: Draft mode is available only when you choose Normal View.

Changing to Outline View

You can create an outline from the headings in a Word for Windows document by changing to Outline View. Outline View can be very useful when you are working with long documents—particularly when you want to check or change their organization. (Chapter 10 provides more information on using Outline View.)

In Outline View, the headings in a document appear as an outline.

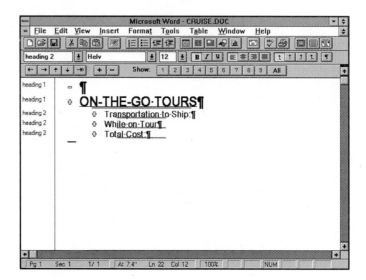

To change to Outline View, follow these steps:

1. Open the View menu.

2. Choose the Outline command. (If a dot appears to the left of the Outline command when you open the View menu, you are already in Outline View—you don't need to choose the command.)

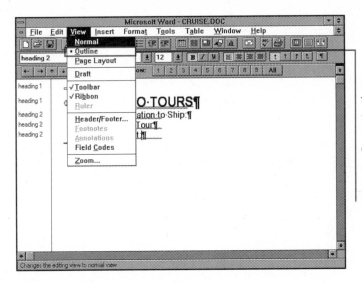

2

If you open the View menu again, you see a dot to the left of the Outline command, indicating that you chose Outline View.

Changing to Page Layout View

When you choose Page Layout View, you can see all the document's formatting—including headers, footers, footnotes, columns, and frames—in their correct positions. You can edit and format text in Page Layout View. The zero point on the Ruler aligns with the left margin. Page Layout View is the best view for positioning frames (see Chapter 12 for more information on frames).

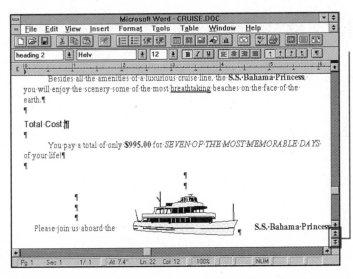

In Page Layout View, two additional buttons appear on the vertical scroll bar. When you choose the up or down button, the document scrolls up or down one page at a time.

2

To change to Page Layout View, follow these steps:

1. Open the View menu.

2. Choose the Page Layout command. (If a dot appears to the left of the Page Layout command when you open the View menu, you are already in Page Layout View—you don't need to choose the command.)

If you open the View menu again, you see a dot to the left of the Page Layout command, indicating that you chose Page Layout View.

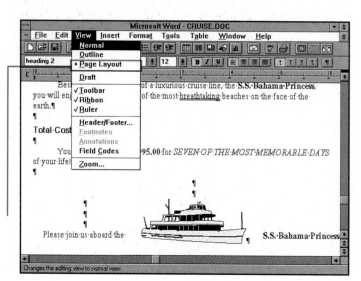

Changing to Print Preview

When you choose the Print Preview command, you see a version of the document that appears exactly as it will print, but reduced to fit on-screen. You cannot (and are not intended to) read the text.

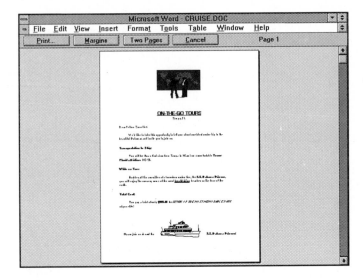

2

Using Print Preview enables you to check the alignment and placement of information on the page.

You cannot edit the text in Print Preview, but you can adjust margins and page breaks and move headers and footers. You also can print the document (see Chapter 8 for more information).

Follow these steps to choose the Print Preview command:

1. Open the File menu.
2. Choose the Print Preview command.

To view facing pages (for example, pages 2 and 3 in a book), choose the Two Pages button from the bar at the top of the Print Preview screen. When you choose the Two Pages button, this button changes from Two Pages to One Page, and the Cancel button changes to Close.

To return to editing, choose the Cancel (or Close) button.

Tip: To go directly from Print Preview to Page Layout View, you can double-click the left mouse button anywhere on the Print Preview screen.

Enlarging or Reducing the View

You can enlarge the view of a document if you want to examine the text or graphics more closely. You also can reduce the view of the document if you want to see more text or graphics on-screen at one time. You use the Zoom feature to enlarge or reduce the view.

To enlarge or reduce a document on-screen by choosing a menu command, follow these steps:

1. Open the View menu.

2. Choose the Zoom command.

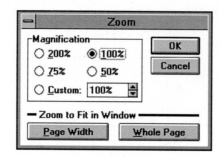

The Zoom dialog box appears.

3. To enlarge or reduce the view by a percentage, choose a Magnification option button: 200%, 100%, 75%, or 50% (of Normal View size) or Custom (a custom size from 25 to 200 percent).

   Or, to change the view so that the widest line on the page fits in the window, choose the Page Width button.

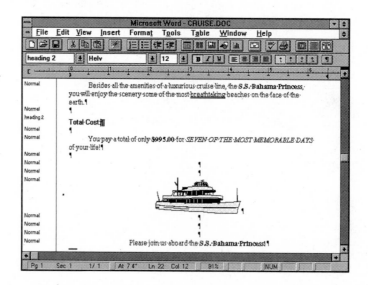

Compare the view you see here to the view of the same page in Normal View (in the "Changing to Normal View" section of this chapter).

Or, to reduce the text so that the entire page appears on-screen (similar to the view you see when you choose the Print Preview command), choose the Whole Page button.

4. If you selected a Magnification option button, choose OK.

On the Toolbar, you can choose from three Zoom options: Zoom Whole Page, Zoom 100%, and Zoom Page Width.

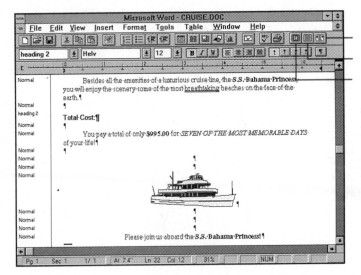

Zoom Page Width button
Zoom 100% button
Zoom Whole Page button

The Zoom Whole Page, Zoom 100%, and Zoom Page Width buttons are the last three buttons on the Toolbar.

The Zoom Whole Page button on the Toolbar performs the same function as choosing the Whole Page Button in the Zoom dialog box. The Zoom 100% button on the Toolbar performs the same function as choosing the 100% option button from the Zoom dialog box and then choosing OK. The Zoom Page Width button on the Toolbar performs the same function as choosing the Page Width button in the Zoom dialog box.

You can customize the Zoom 100% button so that you can zoom to any magnification from 25 to 200 percent. Follow these steps:

1. Open a new document based on the Normal template.

2. Open the Tools menu and choose the Options command.

3. In the Category box on the left side of the dialog box, choose Toolbar.

4. In the Tool To Change box, choose ViewZoom100.

5. In the Show box, choose Commands.

2

6. In the Commands box, choose ViewZoom.

7. Choose the Change button.

8. Choose the Close button to return to the document.

9. Choose the Zoom 100% button from the Toolbar.

   Word for Windows displays a graphical arrow.

10. Drag the mouse pointer down the arrow.

    As you drag, Word for Windows displays percentages (from 25 to 200 percent) in the box below the graphical arrow.

11. When you see the magnification percentage you want Word for Windows to use whenever you choose the Zoom 100% button from the Toolbar, release the mouse button.

When you save the document, the customized Zoom 100% button becomes available to all documents based on the Normal template.

Saving Documents

You can save documents by choosing a command from a menu or a button from the Toolbar. The File menu provides three commands for saving documents:

- The Save Command
- The Save As Command
- The Save All Command

On the Toolbar, the Save button is the third button from the left.

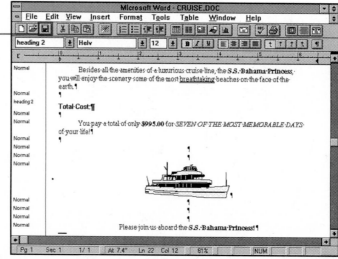

Saving a New Document

To save a new document (accepting as many default options as possible) choose the Save button from the Toolbar or follow these steps:

1. Open the File menu.

2. Choose the Save or Save As command.

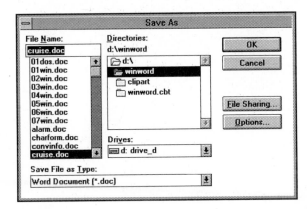

The Save As dialog box appears.

3. In the File Name text box, type a name (of up to eight characters) for the document.

4. To save the document to the current drive and directory, choose OK. (Other options are discussed at the end of these steps.)

5. If the Summary Info dialog box appears, you can type a title, subject, key words, and comments for the document. (Summary information is optional; the Summary Info dialog box is discussed later in this section.)

6. To save the document (whether or not you typed any summary information), choose OK.

The Save As dialog box always appears when you save a new document, whether you choose the Save button from the Toolbar or the Save or Save As command from the File menu. The Save As dialog box also appears when you save an existing document by choosing the Save As command from the File menu. (Deciding whether to choose the Save or Save As command is discussed later in this chapter.)

2

The Save As dialog box provides the following options:

- In the File Name text box, you must provide a name (of up to eight characters) for the document. You can add a three-character extension (separated from the name by a period), but if you do not type an extension, Word for Windows automatically adds the DOC extension to the file name you type. Using the DOC extension for all Word for Windows documents makes file management easier (for more information on file management, see Chapter 8).

  Note: Word for Windows automatically assigns an extension that corresponds to the type of document you are saving. If you are saving a template, Word for Windows assigns the DOT extension (see Chapter 9 for more information on document templates).

- You can change the drive and directory where Word for Windows will save the document. Because Word for Windows can convert documents to other file formats, you also can save the document in another format.

- If you choose the File Sharing command button, Word for Windows displays the File Sharing dialog box where you can lock the file or protect the file with a password. If you lock the file, other users cannot change the document, but they can insert annotations (see Chapter 10 for more information on annotations). If you protect the file with a password, no one (including you) can open the file without entering the password.

- If you choose the Options command button, Word for Windows displays the Save Options dialog box, which contains the default options for saving documents. You also can set these options by choosing the Options command from the Tools menu (see Chapter 9 for more details on setting options).

The Save Options dialog box.

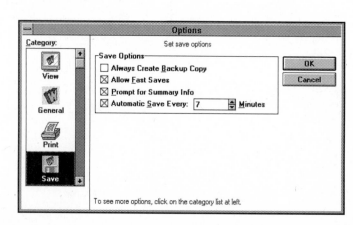

52

2

The Save Options dialog box provides the following options:

- If you choose the Always Create Backup Copy check box, Word for Windows saves the current version of the document and keeps the preceding version in a file with the same name but the extension BAK. (This option uses additional disk space.)

- If you choose the Allow Fast Save check box, Word for Windows saves only the changes you made since the last time you saved. To speed up the saving process, choose the Allow Fast Save check box rather than the Always Create Backup Copy check box.

- If you choose the Automatic Save Every check box, Word for Windows automatically saves the document according to the schedule you specify in the Minutes text box. This option is particularly valuable to guard against data loss from power failures. If a power failure occurs, the only work you lose is the work you did since the last automatic save.

- If you choose the Prompt for Summary Info check box, Word for Windows prompts you for summary information each time you save a new document. If you enter summary information when you save each document, you make searching for documents easier (see Chapter 8).

Summary Info	
File Name:	CRUISE.DOC
Directory:	D:\WINWORD
Title:	Cruise Promotion
Subject:	Sample with Graphics in it
Author:	Elaine J. Marmel
Keywords:	View
Comments:	

OK Cancel Statistics...

The Summary Info dialog box.

You can display the Summary Info dialog box in two ways: by setting the Word for Windows options so that this dialog box appears whenever you save a new document or by choosing the Summary Info command from the File menu.

In the Summary Info dialog box, you can type up to 255 characters in the Title and Subject text boxes. Your name should already appear in the Author text box because you supplied your name when you installed Word for Windows. You also can enter key words that appear in the document (in the Keywords

2

text box) and comments about the document (in the Comments text box). Later, you can search for documents by using the information you enter in the Title, Subject, Author, and Keywords text boxes (see Chapter 8 for more information).

If you choose the Statistics button, Word for Windows displays the Document Statistics dialog box, which contains such information as when you created and last saved the document.

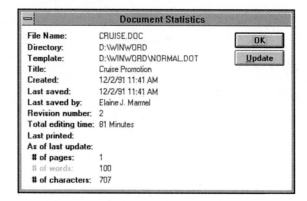

Word for Windows updates this information, but you can edit it.

Saving an Existing Document

After you save a document the first time, you can save the document again (to the same name, drive, and directory) by choosing the Save button from the Toolbar or the Save (or Save As) command from the File menu. If you watch the status bar, you see the percentage saved increase to 100 percent as Word for Windows saves the document.

Deciding Whether To Choose the Save or Save As Command

The Save As command provides choices that the Save command does not; you can specify the drive and directory where you want to store the document, the document type, and the access rights of other users. When you need to change these options, choose the Save As command from the File menu.

If you don't need to change the file name, drive, directory, file format, or access rights, choose the Save command from the File menu or the Save button on the Toolbar.

Using the Save All Command

Choose the Save All command (also on the File menu) when you are working with more than one document at a time and you want to save all the documents (see Chapter 3 for more information on working with more than one document). When you choose the Save All command, Word for Windows asks whether you want to save the changes to each document you have open.

Tip: If you choose the Exit command from the File menu when you have multiple documents open, Word for Windows prompts you to save any unsaved changes to each document before you exit the program.

Printing the Active Document

You can print the active document by choosing the Print button from the Toolbar or the Print command from the File menu. (Chapter 8 provides a more detailed discussion of other printing choices.)

Before you print, you may want to choose the Print Preview command from the File menu to see a reduced version of the document layout. Or, you may want to change to the Normal View to see the character and formatting information.

After you check the layout and formatting, follow these steps to print the active document by choosing a menu command:

1. Open the File menu.
2. Choose the Print command.

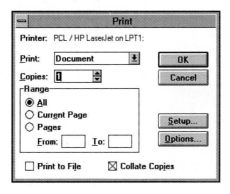

The Print dialog box appears.

2

3. From the Print list box, choose Document, Summary Information, Annotations, Styles, Glossaries, or Key Assignment. (To print the entire document, choose Document, the default.)

   In the Print dialog box, you also can specify the number of copies to print, the range of pages to print, whether to collate multiple copies, and whether to print to a file (rather than on paper). The Setup and Options command buttons open dialog boxes that contain printer setup and default printing options. Word for Windows established the printer setup during installation; you usually do not need to change this setup. You also usually do not need to change the default printing options. (You can access the default printing options by choosing the Options command from the Tools menu as well as by using the Print dialog box.)

4. To print the document using the default options, choose OK.

If you print the active document by choosing the Print button from the Toolbar, the document prints immediately (according to the default printing options).

The Print button on the Toolbar.

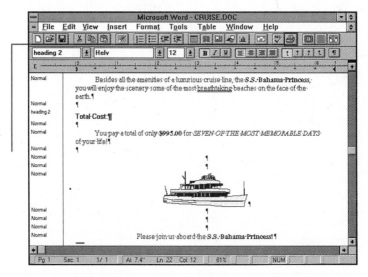

Word for Windows displays messages on-screen to indicate which page is currently printing.

Chapter Summary

In this chapter, you learned how to work with new documents in Word for Windows. Specifically, you learned how to do the following:

- Start a new document by choosing the New button from the Toolbar or the New command from the File menu.

- Type text in a document, correct basic mistakes by using ⎡⬅Backspace⎤ and ⎡Del⎤, and switch between Insert and Overtype modes.

- Change the view of a document by choosing commands from the View menu or the Print Preview command from the File menu.

- Enlarge or reduce the view of a document by choosing a button from the Toolbar or the Zoom command from the View menu.

- Save a new or existing document by choosing the Save button from the Toolbar or the Save or Save As command from the File menu.

- Print a document by choosing the Print button from the Toolbar or the Print command from the File menu.

In the next chapter, you will learn how to make revisions to the documents you create.

Revising Documents

3

In this chapter, you will learn how to make changes to existing documents. You will learn how to open an existing document and how to move the insertion point to the locations where you want to edit. You will learn how to move, copy, and delete text in the document. Because Word for Windows enables you to open more than one document at a time, you also will learn how to move and copy text between documents.

Opening an existing document

Moving around in a document

Basic editing

3

Key Terms in This Chapter

Select   The action you take to identify the text with which you want to work. When you select text, Word for Windows highlights it.

Clipboard   A "holding area" provided by Windows and used by all Windows applications to store information temporarily. The Clipboard holds only one entry at a time; whenever you cut or copy information to the Clipboard, Windows replaces the preceding entry.

Cut   Eliminating selected text. When you choose the Cut command from the Edit menu or the Cut button from the Toolbar, Word for Windows removes the selected text, but stores it on the Clipboard. When you combine cutting with pasting, you can move text from one location to another.

Copy   Making a duplicate of selected text. When you choose the Copy command from the Edit menu or the Copy button from the Toolbar, Word for Windows places a copy of the selected text on the Clipboard. When you combine copying with pasting, you can copy text from one location to another.

Paste   Placing the contents of the Clipboard into a document. When you combine pasting with cutting or copying, you can move or copy text from one location to another.

Spike   Word for Windows' specialized version of the Clipboard. You can store multiple entries in the Spike.

Window   A rectangular area on-screen in which you work when using a Windows program. You can open up to nine documents at one time; Word for Windows places each document in its own window. When you *maximize* a window, that window fills the screen, blocking other windows from view.

Pane   A portion of a window. When you divide a window into more than one part, each part is called a pane.

Scroll bars   Gray bars that appear at the bottom and right side of a document window. You use the mouse and scroll bars to move, or "scroll," through the document.

Opening an Existing Document

As you learned in Chapter 2, a new document (Document1) appears when you start Word for Windows. If you want to start a new document, you can simply start typing. If you want to work on an existing document, however, you must open that document.

You can open an existing document by choosing a command from a menu or a button from the Toolbar.

To open an existing document by choosing a menu command, follow these steps:

1. Open the File menu.
2. Choose the Open command.

To choose a command from the Toolbar, you must use the mouse. To open an existing document from the Toolbar, you choose the Open button.

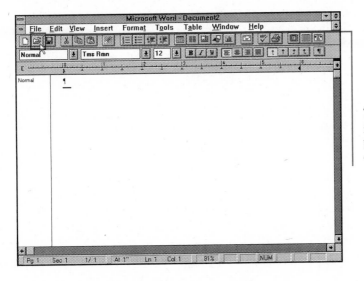

The Open button is the second button on the Toolbar.

Whether you choose the Open command from the File menu or the Open button from the Toolbar, the Open dialog box appears.

61

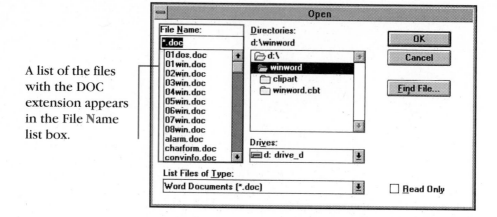

A list of the files with the DOC extension appears in the File Name list box.

3. If the name of the document you want to open appears in the File Name list box, choose its name and then choose OK.

Tip: Instead of choosing the name of the document and then choosing OK, you can simply double-click the name of the document in the File Name list box.

The other options in the Open dialog box help you to handle special situations:

- If the name of the document you want to open does not appear in the File Name list box, the file may be stored on a different drive or in a different directory. Choose the correct drive from the Drives list box and the correct directory from the Directories list box.

- The options in the List Files of Type list box are somewhat misleading. The option names imply that you can choose to see, for example, all Word documents. Instead, you see all documents whose extension is DOC. If you saved some documents from another program with the DOC extension, these files also appear in the File Name list box when you choose the Word Documents (*.doc) option.

    If, however, you follow Word for Windows' naming conventions when you save documents, only Word documents will appear when you choose the Word Documents (*.doc) option. See the Word for Windows manual for more information about each file type.

- If you choose the Find File button, Word for Windows displays the Find File dialog box, in which you can search for the document you want to open. See Chapter 8 for more information on using the File Find feature.

- If you choose the **R**ead Only check box, you can open the document, but you cannot save any changes. This option can be valuable if you want to create two versions of the same document. Choose the **R**ead Only check box when you open the original file. Make the changes and then save the new version by choosing the Save **A**s command from the **F**ile menu, typing a different file name, and then choosing OK. The original file remains unchanged.

3

Word for Windows "remembers" the last four documents you opened and lists their names at the bottom of the **F**ile menu. You can open any of these documents by choosing the document name from the **F**ile menu.

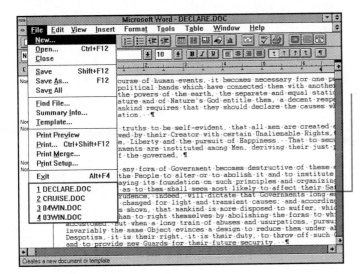

The names of the last four documents you opened appear at the bottom of the **F**ile menu.

Word for Windows also "remembers" the position of the insertion point when you last saved the document. You can return to that location by pressing ⇧Shift + F5.

Moving around in a Document

As you create longer documents, you will need to move the insertion point around the document efficiently. You can move the insertion point by using the mouse or the keyboard.

3

Moving the Insertion Point by Using the Mouse

To move the insertion point by using the mouse, you position the mouse pointer where you want the insertion point to be and then click the left mouse button. If you want to move the insertion point to a part of the document that does not appear in the window, you first use the vertical scroll bar (at the right side of the window) to display that part of the document.

The position of the scroll box (the gray box that appears on the scroll bar somewhere between the up and down arrows) on the vertical scroll bar indicates the position of the text in the window relative to the beginning and the end of the document. If the scroll box is approximately in the middle of the scroll bar, for example, the text that appears in the window is approximately in the middle of the document.

To use the mouse and the scroll box to move to a different area of the document, follow these steps:

1. Position the mouse pointer on the scroll box on the vertical scroll bar.

2. Hold down the left mouse button.

3. Drag the scroll box up to move toward the beginning of the document or down to move toward the end of the document.

4. Release the mouse button when the scroll box indicates the approximate position in the document of the text you want to view.

   The text in the corresponding position in the document appears in the window.

5. Move the mouse pointer into the text area.

   When the mouse pointer is over the text area, it has an I-beam shape.

6. Position the mouse pointer where you want the insertion point to be and then click the left mouse button.

The last step is very important—the insertion point does not move until you click the new location. If you start typing before you click the new location, Word for Windows inserts the text at the original insertion point location.

You also can move to a different area of the document by using the arrows at the ends of the scroll bar to scroll through the document. Follow these steps:

1. To scroll toward the beginning of the document, position the mouse pointer on the up arrow at the top of the vertical scroll bar. To scroll toward the end of the document, position the mouse pointer on the down arrow at the bottom of the vertical scroll bar.

2. Hold down the left mouse button.

   The text of the document scrolls toward the beginning or end of the document.

3. Release the mouse button when the text you want to view appears in the window.

4. Move the mouse pointer into the text area.

   When the mouse pointer is over the text area, it has an I-beam shape.

5. Position the mouse pointer where you want the insertion point to be and then click the left mouse button.

Again, the last step is very important—the insertion point does not move until you click the new location. If you start typing before you click the new location, Word for Windows inserts the text at the original insertion point location.

Moving the Insertion Point by Using the Keyboard

Moving the insertion point by using the keyboard can be very efficient at times. To move the insertion point, you use the directional keys individually or in combination with Ctrl.

Table 3.1 lists key combinations for moving the insertion point.

Table 3.1
Moving the Insertion Point by Using the Keyboard

Key combination	Effect
←	Moves the insertion point one character to the left.
→	Moves the insertion point one character to the right.
↑	Moves the insertion point one line up.
↓	Moves the insertion point one line down.
Ctrl + ←	Moves the insertion point one word to the left.
Ctrl + →	Moves the insertion point one word to the right.
Home	Moves the insertion point to the beginning of the line.
End	Moves the insertion point to the end of the line.
Ctrl + ↑	Moves the insertion point one paragraph up.

continues

3

Table 3.1 (continued)

Key combination	Effect
Ctrl + ↓	Moves the insertion point one paragraph down.
PgUp	Moves the insertion point up one window length.
PgDn	Moves the insertion point down one window length.
Ctrl + PgUp	Moves the insertion point to the top of the window.
Ctrl + PgDn	Moves the insertion point to the bottom of the window.
Ctrl + Home	Moves the insertion point to the beginning of the document.
Ctrl + End	Moves the insertion point to the end of the document.

Word for Windows also enables you to return to previous editing locations. The program stores the last three locations where you typed or edited text; to return to these locations, you press ⇧Shift + F5 one, two, or three times. Each time you press this key combination, the insertion point returns to the preceding editing location. The fourth time you press ⇧Shift + F5, the insertion point returns to its original location.

Tip: When you save a document, Word for Windows stores the last three locations where you typed or edited text. When you reopen the document, you can press ⇧Shift + F5 to find the location where you stopped working.

You can go directly to a specific location in a document in two ways:

- Press F5 (the Go To key).
- Open the Edit menu and choose the Go To command.

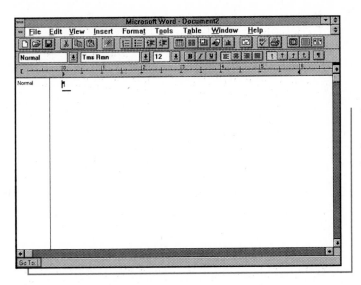

When you press
F5, the prompt
Go To: appears
on the status bar.

3

Type the location you want to "go to" (such as a page number) and press
↵Enter. The insertion point moves to that location.

If you change your mind and don't want to "go to" another location, press
Esc or click anywhere outside the status bar.

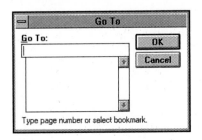

If you choose the
Go To command
from the Edit
menu, the Go To
dialog box
appears.

Type the location you want to "go to" (such as a page number) and choose
OK. The insertion point moves to that location.

If you change your mind and don't want to "go to" another location, choose
the Cancel button.

You can "go to" a variety of locations in a document. Table 3.2 lists the codes
you use to move to specific locations.

3

Table 3.2
Moving to a Specific Location

To "go to"	Type
A specific line	An **l** followed by a line number.
A section	An **s** for the next section or an **s** followed by a number for a specific section.
A page	A **p** for the next page or the page number (or a **p** followed by the page number).
A specified distance into the document	A number followed by %; for example, type **25%** to move one quarter of the way into the document.
A specific location	A combination of the instructions in this table. For example, to "go to" page 4, line 17, type **p4l17**.
A footnote	An **f** for the next footnote or an **f** followed by the footnote number.
An annotation	An **a** for the next annotation or an **a** followed by an annotation number.
A bookmark	The bookmark name (or choose the bookmark name from the list).

See Chapter 10 for more information on bookmarks and annotations.

Basic Editing

In this section, you will learn how to insert blank lines; how to select, copy, move, and delete text; and how to use the Undo feature.

Inserting Blank Lines

To insert blank lines into your document, Word for Windows must be in Insert mode. If OVR appears on the status bar, Word for Windows is in Overtype mode. Press Ins to switch to Insert mode. The OVR indicator disappears from the status bar.

After making certain that Word for Windows is in Insert mode, position the insertion point where you want to insert a blank line and press ⏎Enter two times.

Selecting Text

3

Word for Windows operates on the principal that you must identify the text you want to change *before* you can change it. To identify the text you want to change, you *select* it. You can select text by using the mouse or the keyboard.

Selecting Text by Using the Mouse

When you select text by using the mouse, you often use the *selection bar*, an area at the left side of the text area. The selection bar is not marked in any way, but when you position the mouse pointer in the selection bar, the pointer appears as an arrow pointing up and slightly to the right.

Table 3.3 lists techniques for selecting text by using the mouse.

Table 3.3
Selecting Text by Using the Mouse

To select	*Use the mouse to*
Any block of text	Click the beginning or the end of the text and then drag the mouse pointer to the other end of the text you want to select. Word for Windows highlights the text as you select it.
	Or
	Click the beginning or the end of the text and then hold down ⬆Shift as you click the other end of the text you want to select. Word for Windows highlights the text when you click the second time.
A word	Double-click the word.
A line	Click in the selection bar to the left of the line.
Multiple lines	Click in the selection bar to the left of the first or last line and then drag the mouse pointer down or up the selection bar to the left of the other lines you want to select. Word for Windows highlights the lines as you select them.

continues

Table 3.3 (continued)

To select	Use the mouse to
A sentence	Hold down Ctrl and click anywhere in the sentence.
A paragraph	Double-click in the selection bar to the left of the paragraph. Or Click in the style area to the left of the paragraph.
Multiple paragraphs	Double-click in the selection bar to the left of the first or last paragraph and then drag the mouse pointer down or up the selection bar to the left of the other paragraphs you want to select. Word for Windows highlights the paragraphs as you select them.
A document	Hold down Ctrl and click in the selection bar.

Selecting Text by Using the Keyboard

Table 3.1 (in the "Moving Around a Document" section of this chapter) provides information on moving the insertion point by using the keyboard. To *select* text by using the keyboard, you use very similar techniques. In many cases, you simply add ⇧Shift to the key combination you use to move the insertion point.

Table 3.4 lists key combinations for selecting text.

Table 3.4
Selecting Text by Using the Keyboard

Key combination	Effect
⇧Shift + ←	Selects one character to the left.
⇧Shift + →	Selects one character to the right.
Ctrl + ⇧Shift + ←	Selects to the beginning of the word.
Ctrl + ⇧Shift + →	Selects to the end of the word.
⇧Shift + Home	Selects to the beginning of the line.
⇧Shift + End	Selects to the end of the line.
⇧Shift + ↑	Selects one line up.

Key combination	Effect
⌖Shift + ↓	Selects one line down.
Ctrl + ⌖Shift + ↑	Selects to the beginning of the paragraph.
Ctrl + ⌖Shift + ↓	Selects to the end of the paragraph.
⌖Shift + PgUp	Selects one window length up.
⌖Shift + PgDn	Selects one window length down.
Ctrl + ⌖Shift + Home	Selects to the beginning of the document.
Ctrl + ⌖Shift + End	Selects to the end of the document.
Ctrl + 5 (on the numeric keypad)	Selects the entire document.

3

To deselect the selected text, press any arrow key.

Word for Windows also has an Extend key, F8, that you can use to select text.

To select text by using the Extend key, follow these steps:

1. Position the insertion point anywhere in the text you want to select.
2. Press F8.

   The EXT indicator appears in the status bar.

3. Press F8 repeatedly to select the text. The selected text increases in the following increments: word, sentence, paragraph, section, entire document. To reduce the selected text to the next smaller increment, press ⌖Shift + F8.

   Or

   Press the key for a letter or other character (including ., Tab↹, or ↵Enter) to extend the selection to the next occurrence of that letter or character. For example, press ↵Enter to select text from the insertion point to the end of the paragraph.

   Or

   Press ↑, ↓, ←, →, PgUp, PgDn, Home, or End to select the text.

To cancel Extend mode, press Esc.

3

Moving Text

Moving text involves removing the text from its current location (called "cutting") and placing it in a new location (called "pasting"). You can move text in several ways:

- Choose the Cut and Paste buttons from the Toolbar.
- Choose the Cut and Paste commands from the Edit menu.
- Use the Move key.
- Use the mouse.
- Use the Spike.

The first two methods of moving text use the Clipboard. The Clipboard is a holding area supplied by Windows where Word for Windows temporarily places the information you cut. The Clipboard can hold only one entry at a time; each time you place information on the Clipboard, you wipe out any information previously stored there. You can place information on the Clipboard from many Windows programs and then move or copy it to other Windows programs.

To see the contents of the Clipboard, follow these steps:

1. Open the Word Control menu (at the upper left corner of the window).

2. Choose the Run command.

The Run dialog box appears.

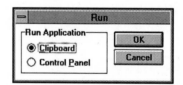

3. Because the Clipboard option button is the default, choose OK.

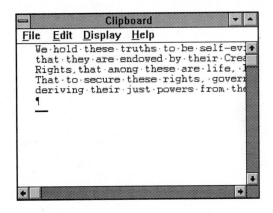

When you choose
OK, the Clipboard
appears.

3

To close the Clipboard, open the Clipboard Control menu and choose the
Close command.

Using the Toolbar To Move Text

You also can use the Toolbar to move text.

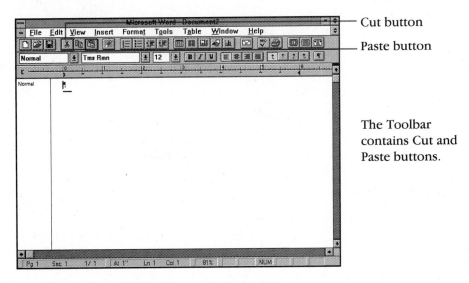

Cut button

Paste button

The Toolbar
contains Cut and
Paste buttons.

To move text by using the Cut and Paste buttons, follow these steps:

1. Select the text you want to move.

2. Choose the Cut button from the Toolbar.

3

Word for Windows removes the text from the document and stores it on the Clipboard.

3. Position the insertion point where you want the text to appear. Don't forget to click the left mouse button to move the insertion point from its previous location.

4. Choose the Paste button from the Toolbar.

The text appears in the new location.

Using the Edit Menu To Move Text

You also can move text by choosing menu commands. Follow these steps to move text by using the Edit menu:

1. Open the Edit menu.

2. Choose the Cut command.

Word for Windows removes the text from the document and stores it on the Clipboard.

3. Position the insertion point where you want the text to appear. Don't forget to click the left mouse button to move the insertion point from its previous location.

4. Open the Edit menu again.

5. Choose the Paste command.

The text appears in the new location.

Using the Move Key To Move Text

Using the Move key, F2, to move text differs from all the other methods: you do *not* select the text before you start the Move process, and the text is *not* stored on the Clipboard.

To move text by using the Move key, follow these steps:

1. Position the insertion point where you want the text to appear.

2. Press F2 (the Move key).

The prompt Move from where? appears on the status bar.

3. Move the insertion point to the beginning of the text you want to move. You can scroll or press ↑, ↓, ←, or →.

4. Select the text you want to move. You cannot use the Extend key (F8) to select the text.

As you select the text, Word for Windows does not highlight the text with a reverse video bar; instead, a dotted underline indicates the selected text.

5. Press [↵Enter].

The insertion point returns to the new location for the text, and the text appears there.

Using the Mouse To Move Text

You can use the mouse to move text in two ways: by dragging the text or by using the right mouse button.

To move text by dragging, follow these steps:

1. Select the text you want to move.

2. Position the mouse pointer anywhere within the selected text.

   When you move the mouse pointer over the selected text, the pointer becomes an arrow.

3. Hold down the left mouse button.

   The mouse pointer changes shape again, becoming a dotted insertion point in a dotted box (⌐).

4. Drag the mouse pointer to the new location for the text.

   Hint: Use the dotted insertion point, not the box to align the text.

5. Release the left mouse button.

   The text disappears from its original location and reappears in the new location.

To move text by using the right mouse button, follow these steps:

1. Select the text you want to move.

2. Position the mouse pointer at the new location for the text.

3. Hold down [Ctrl] and click the *right* mouse button.

Using the Spike To Move Text

The Spike is Word for Windows' specialized version of the Clipboard. The major difference between the Spike and the Clipboard is that the Spike can hold more than one entry at a time. You can repeatedly select information and place it in the Spike without losing previously selected text.

Use the Spike when you need to move information from several different locations to one new location. When you retrieve the text from the Spike, the text blocks appear in the same order that you cut them to the Spike and are separated by paragraph marks. Also, when you retrieve text from the Spike, you can leave the text in the Spike or clear the Spike.

Follow these steps to move text to the Spike:

1. Select the text you want to move to the Spike.
2. Press `Ctrl` + `F3`.

    The selected text disappears from the document, and Word for Windows adds it to the Spike.
3. Repeat Steps 1 and 2 for each block of text you want to move.

To insert the text and empty the Spike:

1. Position the insertion point where you want to insert the contents of the Spike. Make sure that the insertion point is at the beginning of a line or is preceded by a space.
2. Press `Ctrl` + `⇧Shift` + `F3`.

    The text stored in the Spike appears in the new location, and Word for Windows deletes the text from the Spike.

To insert the text without emptying the Spike:

1. Place the insertion point where you want to insert the text.
2. Type **spike**.
3. Press `F3`.

    The text stored in the Spike appears in the document, but also remains in the Spike. If you repeat steps 1 through 3, the same text appears in the document again. If you move more text to the Spike, Word for Windows adds that text to the text already stored in the Spike.

Copying Text

Copying text involves making a duplicate of the text ("copying") and placing the duplicate in a new location ("pasting"). The original text remains in its current location. You can copy text in several ways:

*   Choose the Copy and Paste buttons from the Toolbar.
*   Choose the **C**opy and **P**aste commands from the **E**dit menu.

- Use the Copy key.
- Use the mouse.

The first two methods use the Clipboard as a temporary storage area for the text you are copying. See the "Moving Text" section of this chapter for information on the Clipboard and how to view its contents.

Using the Toolbar To Copy Text

You can use the Toolbar to copy text.

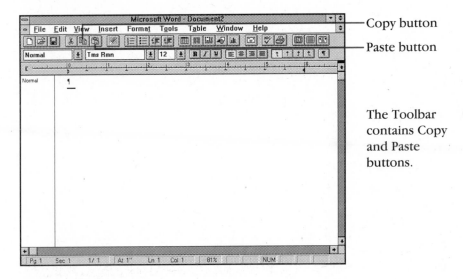

Copy button

Paste button

The Toolbar contains Copy and Paste buttons.

To copy text by using the Copy and Paste buttons, follow these steps:

1. Select the text you want to copy.
2. Choose the Copy button from the Toolbar.
3. Position the insertion point where you want a duplicate of the text to appear. Don't forget to click the left mouse button to move the insertion point from its previous location.
4. Choose the Paste button from the Toolbar.

   A duplicate of the text appears in the new location.

Using the Edit Menu To Copy Text

You also can copy text by choosing menu commands. Follow these steps to copy text by using the Edit menu:

3

1. Open the Edit menu.

2. Choose the Copy command.

3. Position the insertion point where you want a duplicate of the text to appear. Don't forget to click the left mouse button to move the insertion point from its previous location.

4. Open the Edit menu again.

5. Choose the Paste command.

   A duplicate of the text appears in the new location.

Using the Copy Key To Copy Text

Using the Copy key combination, Shift+F2, to copy text differs from all the other methods: you do *not* select the text before you start the Copy process, and the text is *not* stored on the Clipboard.

To copy text by using the Copy key, follow these steps:

1. Position the insertion point where you want the new, duplicated text to appear.

2. Press Shift+F2 (the Copy key combination).

   The prompt Copy from where? appears on the status bar.

3. Move the insertion point to the beginning of the text you want to copy. You can scroll or press ↑, ↓, ←, or →.

4. Select the text you want to copy. You cannot use Extend mode (F8) to select the text.

   As you select the text, Word for Windows does not highlight the text with a reverse video bar; instead, a dotted underline indicates the selected text.

5. Press Enter.

   The insertion point returns to the new location for the text and the copied text appears there.

Using the Mouse To Copy Text

You also can copy text by using the right mouse button. Follow these steps:

1. Select the text you want to copy.

2. Position the mouse pointer at the new location for the text.

3. Hold down Ctrl+Shift and click the *right* mouse button.

Deleting Text

In Chapter 2, you learned how to delete a few characters by pressing
⟨◆Backspace⟩ or ⟨Del⟩. When you need to delete more than a few characters at
a time, you can select the text you want to delete and then press ⟨◄Enter⟩,
⟨◆Backspace⟩, or ⟨Del⟩. Word for Windows also provides keyboard shortcuts for
deleting blocks of text without selecting the text.

Table 3.5 lists key combinations for deleting text.

Table 3.5
Deleting Text

Key combination	Effect
⟨◆Backspace⟩	Deletes the selected text or deletes one character to the left of the insertion point.
⟨Ctrl⟩+⟨◆Backspace⟩	Deletes one word to the left of the insertion point.
⟨Del⟩	Deletes the selected text or deletes one character to the right of the insertion point.
⟨Ctrl⟩+⟨Del⟩	Deletes one word to the right of the insertion point.
⟨Ctrl⟩+⟨X⟩ or ⟨◆Shift⟩+⟨Del⟩	Deletes the selected text and stores the deleted text on the Clipboard.
⟨Ctrl⟩+⟨Z⟩	Reverses the last action (also known as "undo").

Using the Undo Feature

You can "undo" the preceding action and restore deleted text by using Word
for Windows' Undo feature. You can "undo" an action by choosing the Undo
button from the Toolbar or by choosing a menu command.

3

The Undo button
on the Toolbar.

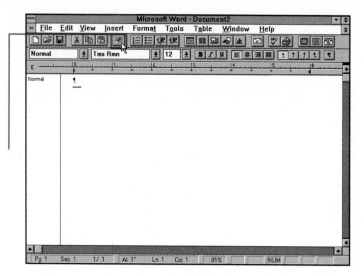

To "undo" the preceding action by choosing a menu command, follow these
steps:

1. Open the Edit menu.

2. Choose the Undo command.

   Because Word for Windows keeps track of your actions, the words
   next to Undo change, depending on what you are trying to undo. If
   you cut some text and then open the Edit menu, for example, the
   Undo command is Undo Cut.

Working in Multiple Windows

In Word for Windows, you view and work on documents in windows. You can
open up to nine documents at the same time, each in its own window. By
default, Word for Windows maximizes the document window, so only one of
the open windows is visible at a time. The *active window* is the window that
contains the document on which you are currently working and, thus, the
insertion point. You can type and edit text in the active document only.

Windows capabilities enable you to do the following:

• Work with different documents in different full-sized windows.

• Split the window into smaller parts (called "panes") and work with
  different documents in different panes.

- Work with one document in two panes.
- Work with one document in more than one full-sized window (by making multiple copies of the document).

Working with Different Documents in Full-Sized Windows

To open more than one Word for Windows document, you open each document just as you open a single document. To make an open document active, you switch to its window by using the Window menu.

To make an open document active, follow these steps:

1. Open the Window menu.

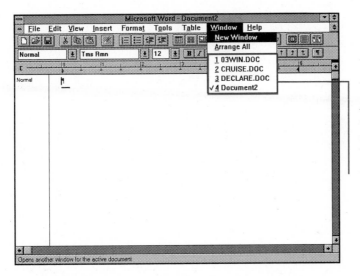

A list of open documents appears at the bottom of the menu.

2. Choose the document you want to make active.

Each Word for Windows document is independent; you can work in any document without affecting the other open documents. You also can move and copy text between documents by using the Window menu and the Clipboard.

To move or copy text between documents, follow these steps:

1. Use the Window menu to switch to the document that contains the text you want to move or copy.

2. Select the text.

3. Cut or copy the text by choosing the Cut or Copy button from the Toolbar or by choosing the Cut or Copy command from the Edit menu.

4. Use the Window menu to switch to the document where you want to place the cut or copied text.

5. Position the insertion point where you want the cut or copied text to appear.

6. Paste the text into the document by choosing the Paste button from the Toolbar button or by choosing the Paste command from the Edit menu.

Working with Different Documents on the Same Screen

You cannot use the Move key, the Copy key, or the mouse to move or copy text between two documents unless both documents appear on-screen at the same time.

To make more than one document appear on-screen at the same time, choose the Arrange All command from the Window menu.

The open documents appear in separate panes.

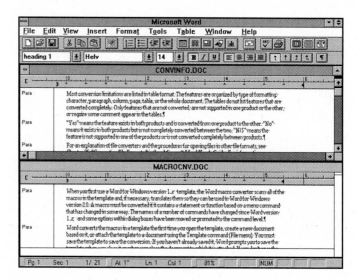

To make a document active, click anywhere inside that document's pane.

Note: Word for Windows divides the screen into as many panes as needed to display all the open documents. If four documents are open, for example, Word for Windows divides the screen into four panes, and each open document occupies one pane. Working in very small panes is difficult, so do not choose the Arrange All command when many documents are open unless you need to see all the open documents on one screen.

To return to working in a full-sized window, you can do either of the following:

- Close all the other open documents.

- Maximize an open document. To maximize a document, you can use the document Control menu (at the left end of the document's title bar) or the Maximize button (at the right end of the document's title bar). To save steps, first activate the document in which you want to work. Word for Windows maximizes all open documents. (You then can switch between the open documents by using the Window menu.)

3

Working with One Document in Two Panes

To view and work in two parts of the active document at the same time, you can divide the document into two panes. You can scroll through—and work in—each pane independently. This feature is particularly useful when you need to move or copy text between distant parts of a long document. You can split the screen into two panes and then view the source text in one pane and the destination area in the other pane.

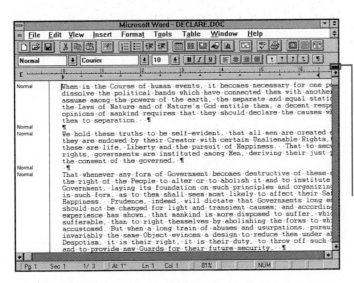

To split the screen into panes by using the mouse, you use the *split box* at the top of the vertical scroll bar.

When you position the mouse pointer over the split box, the mouse pointer shape changes to ⬍.

3

To divide the text area into two equal panes, double-click the split box. To create panes of different sizes, drag the split box down the vertical scroll bar to indicate where you want the screen to split.

The pane that contains the insertion point is the active pane. To switch between the panes, press ⟨F6⟩. To return to working in a full-sized window, double-click the split box again.

Working with One Document in More than One Full-sized Window

Working with one document in more than one full-sized window is similar to working with the document in two panes, but you can see more of the document at one time. Movement within each document window is independent, but any changes you make in one window also occur in the other. This feature is particularly useful when you need to see different parts of the same document, but those parts are too large to fit into a pane.

To create multiple full-sized windows for the same document, follow these steps:

1. Activate the document with which you want to work in more than one window.

2. Open the Window menu.

3. Choose the New Window command.

The document title now has a colon (:) and a number at the end of the file name.

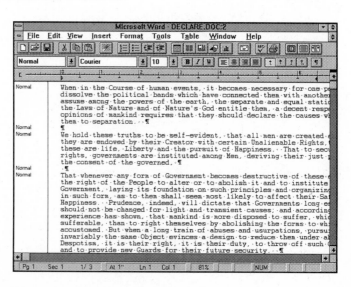

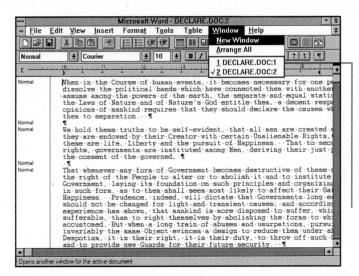

When you open the Window menu again, you see multiple versions of the same document with numbers appended to the file name.

To return to working in only one window, choose the Close command from the document Control menu to close each additional window.

Chapter Summary

In this chapter, you learned how to open an existing document, how to move around in a document, and how to use basic editing techniques to make changes to a document.

Specifically, you learned the following key information:

- You can open an existing document by choosing the Open command from the File menu or the Open button on the Toolbar. You can retrieve any of the last four documents you opened by choosing the document name from the File menu.

- You can move the insertion point by using the mouse or the keyboard. When you use the mouse, moving the I-beam mouse pointer does not move the insertion point; before you begin typing, you must click the location where you want to position the insertion point.

- You can insert a blank line in a document by pressing ⏎Enter two times.

- You can select text by using the mouse or the keyboard. You must select text before you can change it.

3

- You can move selected text by using the Cut and Paste buttons on the Toolbar, the Cut and Paste commands on the Edit menu, the Move key (F2), the mouse, or the Spike.

- You can copy text by using the Copy and Paste buttons on the Toolbar, the Copy and Paste commands on the Edit menu, the Copy key (⇧Shift + F2), or the mouse.

- You can delete a word by pressing Ctrl + ⇧Backspace or Ctrl + Del .

- You can "undo" most actions by choosing the Undo button from the Toolbar or the Undo command from the Edit menu.

- You can work in multiple windows by using the Window menu. You can split a window into two panes by using the split box on the vertical scroll bar.

In Chapter 4, you will learn about the proofreading tools that Word for Windows provides.

Proofreading

4

In this chapter, you will learn about the basic Word for Windows proofing tools. You will learn how to search a document for text, special characters, or formatting and how to replace the text, special characters, or formatting with other information. You will learn how to use the Word for Windows Thesaurus, Spelling Checker, and Grammar Checker. For information on Word for Windows' more advanced tools for document notation (such as revision marks and annotations), see Chapter 10.

Finding and replacing information in a document

Using the Thesaurus

Using the Spelling Checker

Using the Grammar Checker

Formatting and proofing text in foreign languages

> ## Key Terms in This Chapter
>
> *Synonym*   A word that means the same (or nearly the same) as the
> original word. The Thesaurus finds synonyms.
>
> *Antonym*   A word that means the opposite (or nearly opposite) of the
> original word. In some cases, the Thesaurus also finds
> antonyms.

4

Finding and Replacing Information in a Document

Often, when you review a document, you discover that you need to find—and possibly change—certain information. The Find command enables you to search for text, special characters (such as paragraph or tab marks), or formatting (such as bold or italic). The Replace command enables you not only to find this information, but also to replace it with other information. This chapter describes how to search for and replace text, commonly used special characters, and formatting.

Note: Making changes with the Replace command uses a lot of memory. To free memory after using the Replace command, save the document.

Finding Text, Special Characters, or Formatting

Follow these steps to search a Word for Windows document for text, special characters, or formatting:

1. Open the Edit menu.
2. Choose the Find command.

The Find dialog box appears.

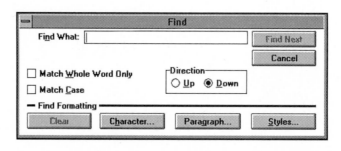

3. In the Find What text box, type the text or special characters for which you want to search.

4. If you want to find the information only when it appears as an entire word, choose the Match Whole Word Only check box.

5. If you want to find the information only when it has exactly the specified combination of upper-and lowercase letters, choose the Match Case check box.

6. If you want to search from the insertion point toward the beginning of the document, choose the Up option button. The default search direction is toward the end of the document (the Down option button).

7. If you want to search for formatting, choose the Character, Paragraph, or Styles button. (For more information on the dialog boxes associated with these formatting options, see Chapters 5, 6, and 9, respectively.) To remove any previous formatting search requests, choose the Clear button.

8. Choose the Find Next button.

   Word for Windows finds and displays the first occurrence (after or before the insertion point) of the information you specified.

9. To find the next occurrence of the information, choose the Find Next button again. To stop the search, choose the Cancel button or press Esc

   If Word for Windows reaches the end (or beginning) of the document without searching the entire document, a dialog box asks whether you want to continue the search.

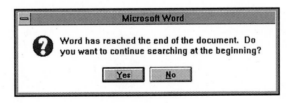

Choose Yes to continue the search or No to stop the search.

You also can use keyboard shortcuts to specify special character or formatting information. Table 4.1 provides a list of frequently used special characters and formats; for a complete list, see the *Word for Windows User's Guide.*

Table 4.1
Searching for Special Characters and Formatting

Key combination	Searches for
^t	A tab mark.
^p	A paragraph mark.
^n	A line break.
^?	A question mark.
Ctrl+U	Any underlined text.
Ctrl+B	Any boldface text.
Ctrl+I	Any italic text.
Ctrl+D	Any double-underlined text.

Replacing Text, Special Characters, or Formatting

You can find and replace text, special characters, or formatting in part or all of a Word for Windows document. To limit the area of the document in which Word for Windows finds and replaces the specified information, select the part of the document you want to search before you start the process. Otherwise, Word for Windows searches forward from the insertion point, and you can replace any or all occurrences of the information throughout the document.

To search for and replace text, special characters, or formatting, follow these steps:

1. Open the Edit menu.
2. Choose the Replace command.

The Replace dialog box appears.

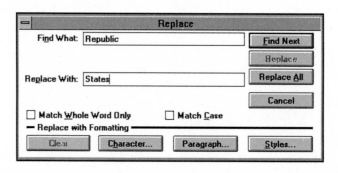

90

3. In the Find What text box, type the text or special characters for which you want to search.

4. In the Replace With text box, type the text or special characters you want to substitute.

5. If you want to find the information only when it appears as an entire word, choose the Match Whole Word Only check box.

6. If you want to find the information only when it has exactly the specified combination of upper-and lowercase letters, choose the Match Case check box.

7. If you want to replace the formatting, choose the Character, Paragraph, or Styles button. (For more information on the dialog boxes associated with these formatting options, see Chapters 5, 6, and 9, respectively.) To remove any previous formatting search requests, choose the Clear button.

8. Choose the Find Next button.

   Word for Windows finds and displays the first occurrence (after the insertion point) of the information you specified.

9. If you want Word for Windows to replace the information and find the next occurrence, choose the Replace button.

   If you want Word for Windows to replace all occurrences of the information in your document, choose the Replace All button.

   If you want Word for Windows to skip the current occurrence of the information and find the next occurrence, choose the Find Next button again.

   If Word for Windows reaches the end of your document without searching the entire document, a dialog box asks whether you want to continue the search. Choose Yes to continue the search or No to stop the search.

To stop the search and replace procedure, choose the Cancel button or press Esc.

You can undo the preceding search and replace operation by choosing the Undo command from the Edit menu or the Undo button on the Toolbar immediately after you close the Replace dialog box.

Tips: To replace the search text or special characters with nothing, delete all information from the Replace With text box and choose the Clear button to remove any formatting.

To add text to the text you typed in the Find What text box, type ^m in the Replace With text box and then type the text you want to add. For example, to

replace *Robert Smith* with *Robert Smith, Jr.*, type **Robert Smith** in the Find
What text box and ^**m, Jr.** in the Replace With text box.

Using the Thesaurus

You can use the Thesaurus to find synonyms, antonyms, and related words as
you are creating or editing a Word for Windows document. To use the Thesaurus, follow these steps:

1. Position the insertion point on or immediately before or after the
   word for which you want to find synonyms, antonyms, or related
   words.

2. Open the Tools menu.

3. Choose the Thesaurus command.

Word for Windows selects the word and opens the Thesaurus dialog box.

In the Thesaurus dialog box, the word for which you want to find a synonym
appears in the Synonyms For box. Possible meanings of the word appear in
the Meanings list box. The synonyms for the highlighted meaning appear in
the Synonyms list box, and the first synonym in the list appears in the Replace
With text box.

In the Thesaurus dialog box, you can do any of the following:

- Choose a word from the Synonyms list box and then choose the Replace button. Word for Windows replaces the selected word in the document with the word you chose.

- Choose a word from the Synonyms list box and then choose the Look Up button. Word for Windows moves the word you chose into the Synonyms For box and displays new lists of meanings and synonyms.

- Choose a word from the Meanings list box. Word for Windows displays a new list of synonyms in the Synonyms list box. If you choose a word from the Synonyms list box and then choose the Look Up button, Word for Windows moves the word you chose into the Synonyms For box and displays lists of meanings and synonyms for that word.

  Hint: Double-clicking the word produces the same result as choosing the word and then choosing the Look Up button.

- The Meanings list box also may include an entry for Antonyms or Related Words. If you choose the Antonyms entry or the Related Words entry, the Synonyms list box changes to an Antonyms list box or a Related Words list box. The Antonyms list box contains words that mean the opposite of the original word. The Related Words list box contains words related to the original word. To return to the Synonyms list box, click any other word in the Meanings list box.

- Type a word in the Replace With text box. If you choose the Look Up button, Word for Windows looks up the word you typed. If you choose the Replace button, Word for Windows replaces the selected word in the document with the word you typed.

If you change your mind and want to cancel the operation, choose the Cancel button or press Esc.

Note: If Word for Windows cannot find a synonym for the word you selected, the program displays words with similar spellings in the Meanings box.

Using the Spelling Checker

You can use the Spelling Checker to check a single word, a selected block of text, or an entire document. Word for Windows uses a standard dictionary to check spelling. When the Spelling Checker encounters a word that is not in this dictionary, you can correct the word or add it to a custom dictionary.

In Word for Windows, you can create more than one custom dictionary. Then, when you add a word to a custom dictionary, you can specify the custom

4

dictionary. For more information on creating and using custom dictionaries, see the *Word for Windows User's Guide*.

If you installed the appropriate language proofing files, you also can check the spelling in foreign-language text. For more information, see the *Word for Windows User's Guide*.

Note: The Grammar Checker checks grammar *and* spelling; if you plan to check both, using the Grammar Checker is more efficient.

You can start the Spelling Checker in three ways:

- Choose the Spelling Checker button 🗹 on the Toolbar.
- Choose the Spelling command from the Tools menu.
- Press F7 to check the spelling of a selected word.

To check the spelling in a document, follow these steps:

1. Position the insertion point where you want to begin checking. To check the spelling in a block of text, select the block of text.
2. Choose the Spelling Checker button from the Toolbar.

   Or

   Open the Tools menu and choose the Spelling command.

When Word for Windows finds a word that is not in the standard dictionary (or the available custom dictionaries), the program highlights the word and opens the Spelling dialog box.

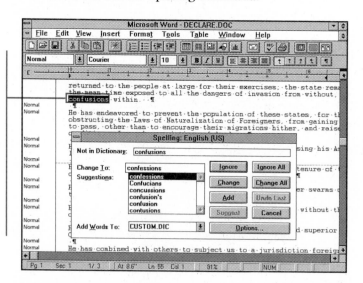

The Not in Dictionary text box contains the highlighted word. The Change To text box contains the first word from the Suggestions list box.

In the Spelling dialog box, you can do any of the following:

- Choose the Ignore button. Word for Windows continues checking spelling without taking any action on the highlighted word.

- Choose the Ignore All button. Word for Windows continues checking spelling without taking any action on the highlighted word *or any other occurrence of the same word* in the document.

- Choose a word from the Suggestions list box and then choose the Change button. Word for Windows replaces the highlighted word in the document with the word from the Suggestions list box.

- Choose a word from the Suggestions list box and then choose the Change All button. Word for Windows replaces the highlighted word *and all other occurrences of the same word* in your document with the word from the Suggestions list box.

- Choose a custom dictionary from the Add Words To list box and then choose the Add button to add the word to a custom dictionary. Use this option if the word is one you use regularly (such as a street name). When you add a word to a custom dictionary, Word for Windows adds the word exactly as it appears in the document (including upper- and lowercase letters) and no longer identifies it as misspelled.

- Click somewhere in the document window (or press Ctrl+Tab⇥) and then edit the word in the document. Word for Windows changes the Ignore button to the Start button. When you are ready to resume checking spelling, choose the Start button.

- Choose the Undo Last button to reverse up to five preceding spelling changes. Each time you choose the Undo Last button, Word for Windows returns the last word you changed to its original condition.

- Choose the Delete button (usually the Change button) to delete one occurrence of a duplicated word (for example, "to to").

- Type what you think is the correct spelling for the word in the Change To text box and choose the Suggest button. Word for Windows displays similar words in the Suggestions list box.

You can choose the Cancel button or press Esc to stop checking spelling at any time.

You also can choose the Options button to control some of the ways Word for Windows checks spelling:

- You can control which custom dictionaries Word for Windows uses to check spelling.

- You can control whether Word for Windows always makes suggestions when it encounters an unknown word.

- You can control whether Word for Windows ignores words in upper-case letters.

- You can control whether Word for Windows ignores words that include numbers.

By default, Word for Windows uses only one custom dictionary (CUSTOM.DIC), always suggests alternative ways of spelling the highlighted word, and *does not* ignore words in uppercase letters or words that include numbers.

To check the spelling of a single word, you also can position the insertion point on or immediately before or after the word you want to check and press F7. If the word is spelled incorrectly, Word for Windows selects the word in the document and displays the Spelling dialog box.

If the word is spelled correctly, Word for Windows asks whether you want to check the rest of the document.

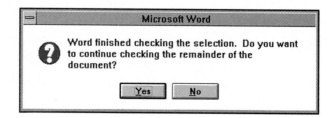

Choose Yes to continue checking the document or No to stop checking and return to editing. If you choose Yes, Word for Windows begins to check the spelling from the insertion point to the end of the document.

When Word for Windows reaches the end of the document, another dialog box asks whether you want to continue checking spelling from the beginning of the document. Choose Yes to continue checking spelling or No to stop checking spelling and return to editing.

Using the Grammar Checker

The Grammar Checker helps you to identify sentences that have questionable style or grammatical structure. For many grammatical errors, the Grammar Checker suggests corrections. By default, the Grammar Checker uses grammar and style rules for business writing, checks spelling, and provides readability statistics after checking the grammar. To change these and other options for the Grammar Checker, you can choose the **O**ptions button in the Grammar Checker dialog box or the **O**ptions command from the **T**ools menu. See Chapter 9 for more information on changing options.

Like the Spelling Checker, the Grammar Checker can check all or part of a document. To check only part of a document, select the text you want to check before you start the Grammar Checker.

To run the Grammar Checker, follow these steps:

1. Position the insertion point where you want to begin checking. To check the grammar for a block of text, select the block of text.

2. Open the **T**ools menu.

3. Choose the **G**rammar command.

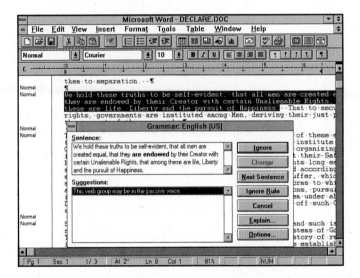

When Word for Windows finds a sentence with questionable grammatical structure or style, the program highlights the sentence and displays the Grammar dialog box.

The **S**entence box contains the questionable sentence. The part of the sentence that the Grammar Checker questions appears in boldface type. The S**u**ggestions list box displays information about the suspected problem.

In the Grammar dialog box, you can do any of the following:

- Make a suggested change by choosing a suggestion from the S**u**ggestions list box and then choosing the **C**hange button.

    Note: You also can choose a suggestion by double-clicking it.

- Click somewhere in the document window (or press $\boxed{\text{Ctrl}}$+$\boxed{\text{Tab⇥}}$) and then edit the sentence in the document. Word for Windows changes the Ignore button to the Start button. When you are ready to resume checking grammar, choose the Start button.

- Choose the Ignore button to make Word for Windows skip the questionable item. If the Grammar Checker found other problems within the same sentence, Word for Windows displays the next problem in the Sentence box.
- Choose the Next Sentence button to make Word for Windows skip all problems associated with the current sentence and continue checking from the next sentence.
- Choose the Ignore Rule button to make Word for Windows skip the current problem and all occurrences of the same problem in this document.
- Choose the Explain button to display the grammar rule.

You can stop checking grammar at any time by choosing the Cancel button or pressing [Esc].

If Word for Windows is checking spelling as well as grammar and finds a misspelled word, the Spelling dialog box appears over the Grammar dialog box. You can choose the same options that you can choose from the Spelling Checker.

When the Grammar Checker reaches the end of the document, a dialog box asks whether you want to continue checking grammar from the beginning of the document.

If you did not change the defaults, the Readability Statistics dialog box appears when you finish checking the grammar.

Readability Statistics	
Counts:	
Words	70
Characters	328
Paragraphs	1
Sentences	1
Averages:	
Sentences per Paragraph	1.0
Words per Sentence	70.0
Characters per Word	4.7
Readability:	
Passive Sentences	0%
Flesch Reading Ease	5.3
Flesch Grade Level	17.0
Flesch-Kincaid	29.9
Gunning Fog Index	32.6
OK	

For an explanation of the document's readability statistics, see the *Word for Windows User's Guide*.

Formatting and Proofing Text in Foreign Languages

You can work in languages other than English and still use Word for Windows' proofreading tools to check your documents; however, you first must purchase and install proofreading files for that foreign language. Contact Microsoft's Customer Service Department at the phone number listed on your Word for Windows registration card.

To format text in a foreign language, follow these steps:

1. Type the text in the foreign language.
2. Select the text.
3. Open the Format menu.
4. Choose the Language command.

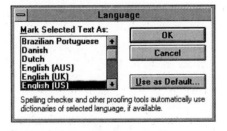

The Language dialog box appears.

5. Choose the language from the Mark selected text as list box and then choose OK.

   When you use the Thesaurus, Spelling Checker, or Grammar Checker for that text, Word for Windows works in the foreign language.

Chapter Summary

In this chapter, you learned how to use proofing tools to check a Word for Windows document. Specifically, you learned the following key information:

■ You can search for or replace text, special characters, and formatting in a Word for Windows document by choosing the Find or Replace commands from the Edit menu.

■ You can find synonyms, antonyms, and related words by choosing the Thesaurus command from the Tools menu.

■ You can check spelling by choosing the Spelling Checker button on the Toolbar or the Spelling command from the Tools menu.

■ You can check grammar and spelling by choosing the Grammar command from the Tools menu.

■ You can format text in foreign languages and use Word for Windows' proofing tools in those languages.

4

Formatting Characters

5

Often, you want to change the appearance of certain text in a document—for example, you may want to enhance the appearance of a word or phrase by using underlining or boldface type. *Formatting* is the process of specifying the appearance of text. Word for Windows divides formatting into three categories: character formatting, paragraph formatting, and page formatting. Within each category, you can format text in many ways. In this chapter, you will learn about the available character formats and how to use them.

> ## Key Terms in This Chapter
>
> *Character formatting* The process of specifying the appearance of letters, numbers, punctuation, and symbols. You can specify the font, point size, style, color, and placement of characters.
>
> *Ribbon* A Word for Windows feature that provides shortcuts for character and paragraph formatting.

5

An Overview of Character Formatting

Characters are letters, numbers, punctuation marks, and symbols. When you format characters, you specify their appearance. In Word for Windows, you can change the font, point size, style, color, and placement of characters. You also can use hidden characters to insert nonprinting text into a document. In addition, Word for Windows makes it easy to insert symbols and fractions (such as ©, ¢, £, §, ¼, and ¾) into a document.

Note: You can apply character formatting before you type the characters, or you can type the characters, select them, and then apply the formatting.

Word for Windows enables you to apply character formatting by using the Ribbon, the keyboard, or the Character dialog box. Table 5.1 lists the character attributes you can apply by using each of these methods.

Table 5.1
Character Formatting Methods

Method	*Character attributes*
Ribbon	Enables you to specify the font; the point size; and the bold, italic, and single underline styles.
Keyboard	Enables you to specify the continuous underline, word underline, double underline, bold, italic, all caps, small caps, and hidden character styles and the character case.

Method	Character attributes
Character dialog box	Enables you to specify the font; the point size; the bold, italic, strikethrough, hidden, small caps, all caps, single underline, word underline, and double underline styles; the color; superscript or subscript position; and expanded, condensed, or normal spacing.

Although the Character dialog box provides the most options, applying character formatting by using the Ribbon or the keyboard is often faster than using the dialog box.

To use the Ribbon, you must display the Ribbon on-screen and then use the mouse to choose character formatting options.

To display the Ribbon, follow these steps:

1. Open the View menu.

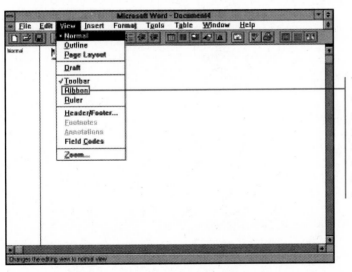

When the Ribbon does not appear at the top of the text area, no check mark appears to the left of the Ribbon command.

2. Choose the Ribbon command. (If a check mark appears to the left of the Ribbon command when you open the View menu, the Ribbon already appears at the top of the text area—you don't need to choose the command.)

103

Font list box ——————

Point size list box ——————

Bold button ——————

Italic button ——————

Underline button ——————

The Ribbon
appears at the top
of the text area.

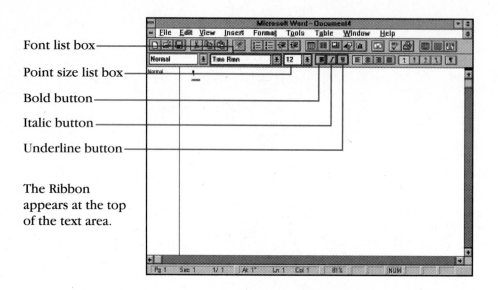

5

If you open the View menu again, a check mark appears to the left of the
Ribbon command.

Fonts and Point Size

Fonts are collections of typefaces, such as Courier and Dom Casual. Each font
has a distinctive look. Because Word for Windows supports WYSIWYG (What
You See Is What You Get), you must consider two types of fonts: screen fonts
and printer fonts. Screen fonts display text on-screen; printer fonts actually
print the text. For Word for Windows to display *and* print a font correctly,
both the screen font and the printer font must be available.

Most fonts are available in a range of sizes. You measure the size of a font in
points (one point is equal to 1/72 inch); smaller point sizes produce smaller
text. In Word for Windows, you can use point sizes from 4 to 127 points in
.5 point increments, but Word for Windows can display *and* print a point size
correctly only if that point size is available for *both* the screen and printer font.

Note: If the fonts and point sizes you choose do not appear as expected, consult Chapter 6 of the *Word for Windows User's Guide*, which contains an excellent section on troubleshooting.

To print Word for Windows documents, you can use the "hardware" fonts and point sizes available on your printer (the fonts supplied with your printer or fonts you added to your printer by using font cartridges), or you can use "software" fonts (if your printer supports them).

Note: If you install software fonts (such as Adobe Type Manager fonts), you may find some apparent inaccuracies in translation and, therefore, certain inconsistencies when you use these fonts in Word for Windows. If, for example, you use a software font manager, the I-beam mouse pointer does not slant when positioned over italic text. Also, when a software font manager is active, you cannot use the Toolbar or the Tools menu to print envelopes in Word for Windows (see Chapter 8 for more information on printing envelopes).

Sometimes, you may want to create a document on one computer, but print it from another computer. The two computers may have different screen and printer fonts available. When you create the document, you can use fonts that are not available on that computer—just be aware that the characters will not appear correctly on-screen nor print correctly until you move to the computer that has the necessary screen and printer fonts available.

You can choose a font and point size before you type the characters, or you can type the characters, select them, and then choose a font and point size. You can choose the font and point size by using the Ribbon or the Character dialog box.

Using the Ribbon To Change the Font or Point Size

To change the font by using the Ribbon, follow these steps:

1. Position the insertion point where you want to change the font or select the characters for which you want to change the font.

2. Open the Ribbon's Font list box by clicking the down arrow button to the right of the box.

5

Printer fonts

Screen fonts

If an icon appears
to the left of a
font name, you
can print that
font. And, al-
though the
Modern, Roman,
and Script fonts
do not have
icons, you also
can print these
three fonts.

5

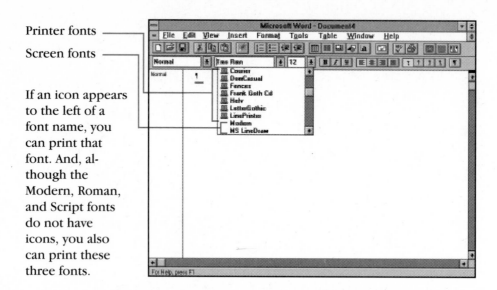

If no icon appears to the left of a font name, only the screen font is
available. When you try to print that font (except in the case of the
Modern, Roman, and Script fonts), Word for Windows uses an available printer font, such as Courier.

3. Choose a font from the list of available printer and screen fonts.

   If you plan to print the document on another printer and want to use
   a font that is not available on the current printer, you can type the
   name of the font in the Font list box. (When you open the document
   on a computer system where the printer font is available, Word for
   Windows will use the correct font.)

To change the point size by using the Ribbon, follow these steps:

1. Position the insertion point where you want to change the point size
   or select the characters for which you want to change the point size.

2. Open the Ribbon's Point Size list box by clicking the down arrow
   button to the right of the box.

3. Choose a point size from the list of available sizes.

Using the Character Dialog Box To Change the Font or Point Size

To change the font or point size by using the Character dialog box, follow these steps:

1. Position the insertion point where you want to change the font or point size or select the characters for which you want to change the font or point size.

2. Open the Format menu.

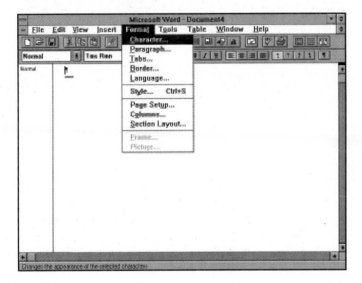

The Format menu contains the Word for Windows formatting commands.

3. Choose the Character command.

5

Font list box ————

Points list box ————

The Character dialog box appears.

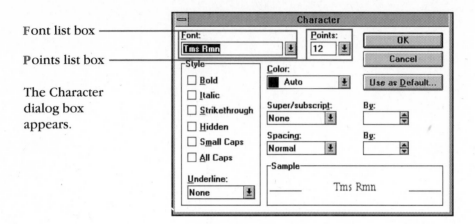

4. From the Font list box, choose one of the available screen or printer fonts.

5. From the Points list box, choose one of the available point sizes.

   The Sample box displays the character formatting changes as you choose them. Watch the text in the Sample box to see how the text in the document will look.

6. Choose OK to accept the font or point size and return to the document.

Tip: You also can open the Character dialog box by double-clicking any of the spaces between buttons on the Ribbon.

Character Styles

You can use character styles to enhance the appearance of text in many ways. In Word for Windows, you can create text in the following styles:

Table 5.2
Character Styles

Character Style	Effect
bold	Characters appear in boldface type.
italic	Characters appear in italic type.
~~strikethrough~~	Characters appear as though they should be removed from the text.

108

Character Style	Effect
Hidden	Characters do not appear on-screen unless you choose to display them or print unless you choose to print them. See Chapter 9 for information on setting the hidden text default options.
SMALL CAPS	Characters are all uppercase, but the first character of each word is the assigned point size and the rest of the characters have a slightly smaller point size.
ALL CAPS	Characters are all uppercase.
single underline	Both words and spaces are underlined.
word underline	Words are underlined, but spaces are not.
double underline	Both words and spaces have a double underline.
Character Case	The first character of each word is uppercase.

You can choose a character style before you type the characters, or you can type the characters, select them, and then choose a character style. You can choose a character style by using the Ribbon, the keyboard, or the Character dialog box.

Using the Ribbon To Change Character Styles

By using the Ribbon, you can apply or remove the bold, italic, and single underline styles in two ways:

1. Before you type the text, click the Bold, Italic, or Underline button on the Ribbon.
2. Type the text.
3. When you finish typing the text you want to be boldface, italic, or underlined, click the Bold, Italic, or Underline button again.

   Or

1. Type the text.
2. Select the text you want to be boldface, italic, or underlined.
3. Click the Bold, Italic, or Underline button on the Ribbon.

5

Using the Keyboard To Change Character Styles

You can use the key combinations in Table 5.3 to apply the bold, italic, underline, case, and hidden text character styles in two ways:

- Before you type the text you want to format, press the appropriate key combination to turn on the character style. If the Ribbon is visible, you can see the corresponding button change shade. After you finish typing the text you want to format, press the key combination again to turn off the character style.

- Type the text you want to format, select the text, then press the appropriate key combination to apply the character style. If the Ribbon is visible, you can see the corresponding button change shade.

Table 5.3
Character Style Keyboard Shortcuts

Key combination	Style
Ctrl + U	Single Underline
Ctrl + W	Word Underline
Ctrl + D	Double Underline
Ctrl + B	Bold
Ctrl + I	Italic
Ctrl + A or Caps Lock	All Caps
Ctrl + K	Small Caps
Ctrl + H	Hidden

You also can press ⇧Shift + F3 to change the character case. Follow these steps:

1. Select the characters whose case you want to change.
2. Press ⇧Shift + F3.

The case of the characters change as follows:

Selected characters	Effect
all lowercase	ALL CHARACTERS CHANGE TO UPPERCASE.
ALL UPPERCASE	The First Character Of Each Word Changes To Uppercase, But All Other Characters Are Lowercase.
First Character Uppercase	all characters change to lowercase.
first character lowercase	ALL CHARACTERS CHANGE TO UPPERCASE.

Using the Character Dialog Box To Change Character Styles

You can change more aspects of character style by using the Character dialog box than you can by using the Ribbon or the keyboard. In the Character dialog box, you can specify the bold, italic, strikethrough, hidden, small caps, all caps, and underline styles. You also can apply a color to the characters.

To change character styles by using the Character dialog box , follow these steps:

1. Position the insertion point where you want to change the character styles or select the characters for which you want to change the character styles.

2. Open the Format menu.

3. Choose the Character command.

    The Character dialog box appears.

4. In the Style box, you can choose from the Bold, Italic, Strikethrough, Hidden, Small Caps, and All Caps styles. Because these styles have check boxes, you can choose more than one style at a time.

    When you choose a style, an X appears in its check box.

5. To underline the characters, choose Single, Words Only, or Double from the Underline list box.

6. To apply a color to the characters, choose a color from the Color list box. On-screen, you see only those colors that your monitor can display.

In this example, *breathtaking beaches* will have bold, italic, and word underline styles and will appear in blue.

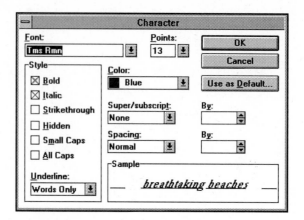

5

7. Choose OK to accept your formatting changes and return to the document. (Choose Cancel to ignore your formatting changes.)

Note: See Chapter 9 for information on the Use as Default button.

Character Placement

You also can affect the placement of text in a Word for Windows document by using character formatting options:

- You can use superscript or subscript characters for such characters as copyright and trademark symbols and scientific and mathematical expressions. (Superscript characters are placed above the baseline of normal type; subscript characters are placed below the baseline of normal type.)
- You can expand or condense the spacing between characters.

You can change character placement only by using the Character dialog box. Follow these steps:

1. Position the insertion point where you want to change the character placement or select the characters for which you want to change the character placement.

2. Open the Format menu.

3. Choose the Character command.

   The Character dialog box appears.

4. From the Super/subscript list box, choose Superscript, Subscript, or None. If you choose Superscript or Subscript, enter the amount by

112

which you want to raise or lower the text in the By text box to the right of the Super/subscript list box.

5. From the Spacing list box, choose Normal, Expanded, or Condensed. If you choose Expanded or Condensed, enter the amount by which you want to to expand or condense the space between characters in the By text box to the right of the Spacing list box.

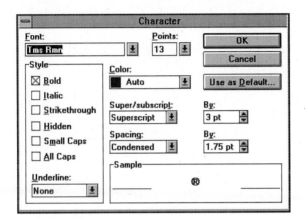

In this example, the ® symbol will become ®.

Removing, Repeating, and Copying Character Formatting

If you change your mind about the character formatting you applied, you can remove any of the character style formatting (for example, bold or italic) and change any of the other character format options (for example, font, point size, and superscript). You also can repeat or copy character formatting.

Removing or Changing Character Formatting

To remove character styles, simply select the text from which you want to remove a character style and then choose the character style again. You can remove a character style in the same ways that you can apply a character style: by using the Ribbon, the keyboard, or the Character dialog box.

If you use the Character dialog box, you can see all the currently applied styles. To remove a character style, simply choose its check box again.

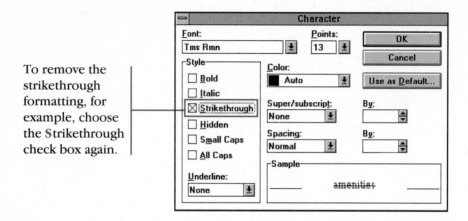

To remove the strikethrough formatting, for example, choose the Strikethrough check box again.

To remove any other format options in the Character dialog box, you must choose another format from the same list. When you finish removing character formats, choose the OK button to return to the document.

Repeating Character Formatting

To repeat character formatting, follow these steps:

1. Select the first block of text you want to format.

2. Apply the character formats.

3. Select the next block of text you want to format (don't perform any other actions between steps 2 and 3).

4. Open the **E**dit menu and choose the **R**epeat Formatting command.

    Or

    Press F4.

If, in step 1, you applied multiple formats by using the Character dialog box, Word for Windows repeats all the formats. If you applied formats by using the Ribbon or the keyboard, however, Word for Windows repeats only the most recently applied format.

Copying Character Formatting

You also can copy the formatting of characters without copying the characters. To copy only the character formatting, follow these steps:

1. Select the text you want to format.

2. Position the insertion point anywhere in the text that has the formatting you want to apply.

3. Hold down `Ctrl` + `⇧Shift` and click the left mouse button.

   Word for Windows formats the selected text with the same character formats as the text that contains the insertion point.

Inserting Symbols and Special Characters

Word for Windows also makes it easy for you to insert symbols and special characters. Follow these steps:

1. Position the insertion point where you want the symbol or special character to appear.

2. Open the Insert menu.

3. Choose the Symbol command.

   The Symbol dialog box appears.

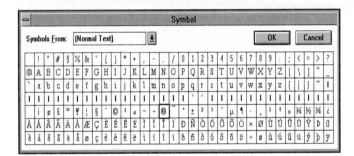

In the Symbol dialog box, you see characters available for the character set shown in the Symbols From list box.

You can change the available symbols and special characters by choosing a different character set from the Symbols From list box.

4. Choose the symbol or special character you want to insert (by pressing `↑`, `↓`, `←`, or `→` or by clicking) and then choose OK. You also can double-click the symbol instead of choosing the character and then choosing OK.

Chapter Summary

In this chapter, you learned about the many ways you can format characters in Word for Windows. You learned how to apply character formatting by using the Ribbon, the keyboard, and the Character dialog box and how to remove, repeat, and copy character formatting. You also learned how to insert symbols and special characters. Specifically, you learned the following information:

- You can change the font, point size, style (including bold, italic, strikethrough, hidden, small caps, all caps, and underlining), color, position (superscript and subscript), and spacing of characters.

- You can change character formatting by using the Ribbon, the keyboard, or the Character dialog box (which you open by choosing the Character command from the Format menu).

- You can change more character formatting options by using the Character dialog box, but the Ribbon and the keyboard provide some excellent shortcuts.

- You can insert special characters by using the Symbol command on the Insert menu.

In Chapter 6, you will learn about paragraph formatting.

5

Formatting Paragraphs

6

In Chapter 5, you learned how to enhance the appearance of text by using character formatting. In this chapter, you will learn about the available paragraph formatting options and how to use them. You will learn how to set and align tabs, indent and align paragraphs, set line spacing, and use other options in the Paragraph dialog box. You also will learn how to apply borders and shading to paragraphs. The last section of this chapter provides a brief introduction to styles.

An overview of paragraph formatting

Tab stops and tab alignment

Indentation

Paragraph alignment

Line spacing

Removing, repeating, and copying paragraph formatting

Applying borders and shading to paragraphs

Introducing styles

Key Terms in This Chapter

Paragraph formatting	The process of specifying the appearance of paragraphs. You can specify the position and alignment of tabs, the indentation and alignment of paragraphs, and line spacing.
Ribbon	A Word for Windows feature that provides shortcuts for character and paragraph formatting.
Ruler	A Word for Windows feature that provides shortcuts for paragraph formatting.
Border	A line that appears around text. You can use a border to surround the text, or you can place individual lines above, below, or to the left or right of the text.
Shadow	A box that appears behind a border to create the effect of a shadow. A shadow adds a three-dimensional look to the border.
Shading	A dotted pattern that appears over text to create the effect of a highlight.

An Overview of Paragraph Formatting

In Word for Windows, the word *paragraph* has a special meaning: a paragraph is not necessarily a series of related sentences, but rather is any amount of text or graphics followed by a *paragraph mark* (which appears on-screen as ¶ if you are displaying paragraph marks).

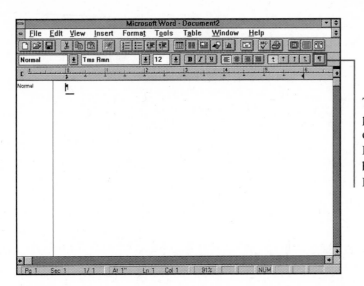

To display paragraph marks, choose the Paragraph Mark button from the Ribbon.

6

Word for Windows stores all paragraph formatting in the paragraph mark at the end of the paragraph. If you move, copy, or delete a paragraph mark, you also move, copy, or delete the paragraph formatting of that paragraph.

You can control the following attributes of paragraph formatting:

- Tab stops and tab alignment
- Indentation
- Paragraph alignment
- Line spacing

Note: In most cases (just as with character formatting), you can apply paragraph formatting before or after you type the text. To apply paragraph formatting after you type the text, select the paragraphs you want to format and then apply the format.

Word for Windows enables you to apply paragraph formatting in many ways:

- You can use the Ruler and the mouse.
- You can use the Ruler and the keyboard.
- You can use the Tabs dialog box.
- You can use the Paragraph dialog box.
- You can use the keyboard.
- You can use the Ribbon.
- You can use the Toolbar.

Table 6.1 lists the paragraph attributes you can apply by using each of these methods.

Table 6.1
Paragraph Formatting Methods

Method	Paragraph attributes
Ruler and mouse	Enables you to specify tab stops and indentation.
Ruler and keyboard	Enables you to specify tab stops, tab alignment, and indentation.
Tabs dialog box	Enables you to specify default tab stop spacing, custom tab stops, tab alignment, and leaders.
Paragraph dialog box	Enables you to specify all the Tabs dialog box options (default tab stop spacing, custom tab stops, tab alignment, and leaders) plus indentation, paragraph alignment, line spacing (before, after, and within the paragraph), page breaks within the paragraph, and line number suppression.
Keyboard	Enables you to specify hanging indents and paragraph alignment.
Ribbon	Enables you to specify tab alignment and paragraph alignment.
Toolbar	Enables you to specify indentation.

The Paragraph dialog box provides the most complete way to format paragraphs because it includes all the paragraph formatting options. Although using the Ribbon or the Ruler is faster than using the Paragraph dialog box, fewer paragraph formatting options are available on the Ribbon and the Ruler.

Remember that to apply formatting by using the Ribbon, you must display the Ribbon (by choosing the Ribbon command from the View menu) and then use the mouse to choose formatting options.

Similarly, to apply formatting by using the Ruler, you must display the Ruler (by choosing the Ruler command from the View menu) and then use the mouse or the keyboard to choose formatting options. The Ruler appears at the top of the text area and displays measurements (in inches, by default), margins, and custom tab stops.

Tab Stops and Tab Alignment

Often, you don't want all the text in a document to begin at the left margin—for example, you may want to indent the first line of each paragraph. In Word for Windows, you use tab stops to position text at locations other than the left margin. When you press [Tab↹], the insertion point moves to the next tab stop, and a tab character (→) appears in the space (if you are displaying tabs).

Word for Windows provides default tab stops at .5-inch intervals from the left margin. You can delete a default tab stop or change the distance between default tabs, but to make other changes, you must create a *custom* tab stop. (To delete a default tab stop, set a custom tab to its right. When you set a custom tab, Word for Windows deletes all default tabs to the left of the custom tab.)

Default tabs are left-aligned, which means that when you press [Tab↹] and then type, the text you type flows toward the right margin. For custom tabs, you can specify the alignment of text (left, center, right, or decimal) relative to the tab stop. Text you type from a center tab is centered around that tab. Text you type from a right tab flows back toward the left margin. A decimal tab, which you use to align columns of numbers, combines a right tab and a left tab. Text flows toward the left margin until you type a period (.), which represents the decimal point in a number. Then, text flows toward the right margin.

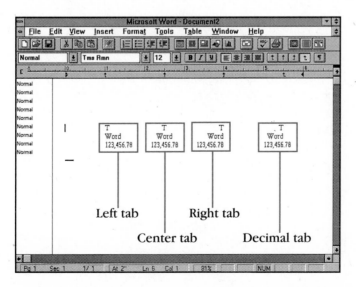

Here, you can see the effect on text and numbers of choosing left, center, right, or decimal tab alignment. Each T indicates the position of a custom tab stop.

6

121

You also can fill the space before a custom tab stop with dots, dashes, or underscore characters (known as *leader characters*).

Throughout this section, the term *tab stops* refers to custom tabs unless otherwise stated. You can set (and delete) custom tab stops and change tab alignment in the following ways:

- You can use the Ruler and the mouse.
- You can use the Ribbon.
- You can use the Ruler and the keyboard.
- You can use the Tabs dialog box.

The Ruler has three *scales* (sets of markings), each for a different kind of work. For paragraph formatting, you use the Indent scale.

Indent scale symbol ——

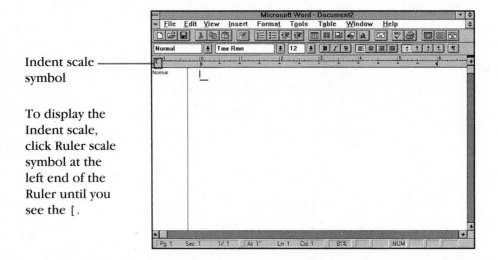

To display the Indent scale, click Ruler scale symbol at the left end of the Ruler until you see the [.

On the Indent scale, the upside-down T's at .5-inch intervals represent the default tab stops. The Indent scale also contains three triangles: one larger triangle toward the right end of the Ruler and two smaller triangles toward the left end of the Ruler. You use these three triangles to control indentation (discussed later in this chapter).

Using the Ruler and the Mouse To Set Tab Stops

You can use the Ruler and the mouse to set and delete custom tab stops.

To set custom tab stops by using the Ruler and the mouse, follow these steps:

1. Position the insertion point where you want to begin using the tab stops or select the paragraphs to which you want to add the tab stops.

2. Position the mouse pointer in the Ruler where you want to add a tab stop (below the Ruler's scale—where the upside-down T's are).

3. Click the Ruler.

   Word for Windows creates a custom tab stop at that location and deletes all the default tab stops to the left of the custom tab.

4. Repeat steps 2 and 3 to set additional custom tab stops.

To move a custom tab stop, drag it right or left on the Ruler. To remove a custom tab stop, drag it down off the Ruler.

Using the Ribbon and the Mouse To Set Tab Alignment

You can use the Ribbon and the mouse to set the alignment of custom tab stops.

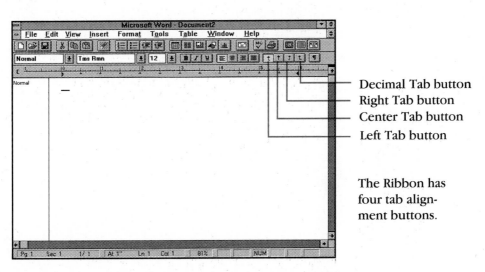

Decimal Tab button
Right Tab button
Center Tab button
Left Tab button

The Ribbon has four tab alignment buttons.

The default alignment for custom and default tabs is left. To set a tab with a different alignment, choose a tab alignment button from the Ribbon before you set the tab on the Ruler.

Using the Ruler and the Keyboard To Set Tab Stops and Tab Alignment

To set custom tab stops and alignment by using the Ruler and the keyboard, follow these steps:

1. Position the insertion point where you want to begin using the tab stops or select the paragraphs to which you want to add the tab stops.

2. Press [Ctrl]+[⇧Shift]+[F10] to activate the Ruler.

   A black box, the Ruler cursor, appears beneath the Ruler scale symbol at the left end of the Ruler.

3. Press [←] or [→] to position the Ruler cursor at the location where you want to add a tab stop and set the tab alignment.

4. Type **1** for a left tab, **2** for a center tab, **3** for a right tab, or **4** for a decimal tab. If you skip this step, the tab will have the same alignment as the last tab you set.

5. Press [Ins] to set a new left, center, right, or decimal tab.

6. Repeat steps 3 through 5 to set additional custom tabs.

7. Press [↵Enter] to return to the document.

Using the Tabs Dialog Box To Set Tab Stops and Tab Alignment

To set custom tab stops and alignment by using the Tabs dialog box, follow these steps:

1. Position the insertion point where you want to begin using the tab stops or select the paragraphs to which you want to add the tab stops.

2. Open the Format menu.

3. Choose the Tabs command.

The Tabs dialog box appears.

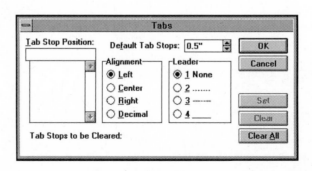

4. In the Default Tab Stops list box, you can change the interval between default tabs. Normally, the default tab stops are set at .5-inch intervals.

5. To set a custom tab, type its position relative to the left margin (in inches, by default) in the Tab Stop Position text box.

6. To align text or numbers at the custom tab stop, choose Left, Center, Right, or Decimal from the Alignment box. The default option button is Left.

7. To fill the space preceding the custom tab with dots, dashes, or a line, choose an option from the Leader box.

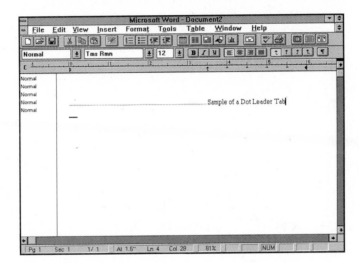

When you press Tab : Word for Windows will fill the space before the leader tab stop with the leader character.

8. After you set the position, alignment, and leader (if any) for the custom tab, choose the Set button to store the custom tab setting.

   When you set a custom tab, Word for Windows deletes all default tabs to the left of the custom tab.

9. Repeat steps 4 through 7 to set additional custom tabs.

10. Choose OK to accept the tab stop settings or Cancel to ignore them.

To clear a custom tab, choose it from the Tab Stop Position list box and then choose the Clear command button. To clear all custom tabs, choose the Clear All command button. (The Set and Clear command buttons are available only when a custom tab position appears in the Tab Stop Position text box.)

Tip: You also can open the Tabs dialog box from the Paragraph dialog box or by double-clicking any tab stop on the Ruler. If you double-click a tab stop, Word for Windows sets a custom tab stop at that location and deletes all default tab stops to the left, but you can clear the tab from the Paragraph dialog box.

Indentation

Rather than indenting just the current line of text, you can position an entire paragraph at a particular tab stop. Word for Windows enables you to create a variety of indents, including hanging indents. (You often use hanging indents, which align the first line of the paragraph at the left margin and indent subsequent lines of the paragraph to the next tab stop, in bibliographies.) You can change indentation in the following ways:

- You can use the Toolbar.
- You can use the keyboard.
- You can use the Ruler and the mouse.
- You can use the Ruler and the keyboard.
- You can use the Paragraph dialog box.

Using the Toolbar To Set Indentation

The Indentation buttons enable you to indent paragraphs to the next or preceding tab stop.

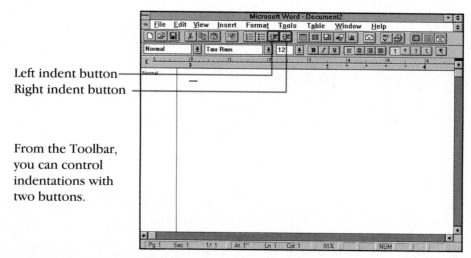

Left indent button
Right indent button

From the Toolbar, you can control indentations with two buttons.

Follow these steps to use the Toolbar for indenting paragraphs:

1. Position the insertion point where you want to begin indenting or select the paragraphs you want to indent.

2. Choose the Right Indent button to indent the text to the next tab stop. Choose the Left Indent button to move the text to the preceding tab stop.

Using the Keyboard To Set Indentation

To create a hanging indent at the first tab stop, you can use the following shortcut:

1. Position the insertion point where you want to begin indenting or select the paragraphs you want to indent.

2. Press Ctrl + T. Word for Windows indents all lines except the first line to the first tab stop.

   If you want to align the body of the paragraph at the next tab stop, press Ctrl + T again. Word for Windows leaves the first line at the left margin and indents the rest of the paragraph to the next tab stop.

To move the body of the text to the preceding tab stop, press Ctrl + G.

Using the Ruler and the Mouse To Set Indentation

You can indent a paragraph from the right margin by dragging the triangle at the right end of the Ruler to the position where you want to align the text. You can indent a paragraph from the left margin by dragging both triangles at the left end of the Ruler to the position where you want to align the text.

You can create a hanging indent in two ways. Follow these steps:

1. Drag both triangles to the desired location.

2. Drag the top triangle back to its original position.

Or, hold down Shift as you drag the bottom triangle to the desired location. (When you hold down Shift, only the bottom triangle moves.)

Using the Ruler and the Keyboard To Set Indentation

You can create left, right, and first line indentations by following these steps:

1. Position the insertion point where you want to begin indenting or select the paragraphs you want to indent.

127

2. Press ⌐Ctrl⌐+⌐Shift⌐+⌐F10⌐ to activate the Ruler.

3. Press ⌐←⌐ or ⌐→⌐ to position the Ruler cursor at the location for the indentation.

4. Type **L** to set a left indentation, **R** to set a right indentation, or **F** to indent the first line of the paragraph(s).

5. Press ⌐Enter⌐ to return to the document.

Follow these steps to create hanging indents:

1. Position the insertion point where you want to begin indenting or select the paragraphs you want to indent.

2. Press ⌐Ctrl⌐+⌐Shift⌐+⌐F10⌐ to activate the Ruler.

3. Press ⌐←⌐ or ⌐→⌐ to position the Ruler cursor at the location for the left indentation.

4. Type **L** to set a left indentation.

5. Press ⌐←⌐ or ⌐→⌐ to position the Ruler cursor at the location for the first line indentation.

6. Type **F** to indent the first line of the paragraph.

7. Press ⌐Enter⌐ to return to the document.

Using the Paragraph Dialog Box To Set Indentation

To open the Paragraph dialog box, open the Format menu and choose the Paragraph command.

From the Indentation box, you can indent from the left or right margin or indent the first line.

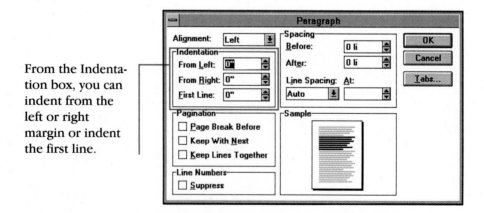

Note: You also can open the Paragraph dialog box by double-clicking the Ruler above the scale.

You can choose indentation measurements from the From Left, From Right, or First Line list boxes, or you can type measurements in the boxes. Word for Windows sets the indentations relative to the left margin. If you choose indentation measurements from the list boxes, watch the Sample box as you scroll through the list. The picture in the Sample box changes to simulate the current choice. If you type measurements in the boxes, click one of the other boxes in the Paragraph dialog box to change the Sample box picture.

Use the From Left list box to specify the distance you want to move *all* text from the left margin. Use the From Right list box to specify the distance you want to move text from the right margin. You also can indent a paragraph's first line differently than its other lines. Use the First Line list box to specify the distance you want to move the first line of a paragraph from the *left indent setting* (not the left margin). You can create hanging indents by changing the First Line setting to the negative equivalent of the From Left setting.

6

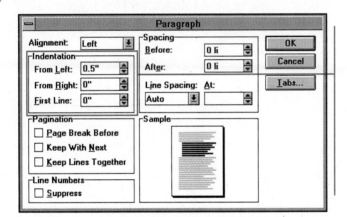

If you change the From Left list box to .5 inch and leave the From Right and First Line settings at 0, all lines in the paragraph will be indented .5 inch from the left margin.

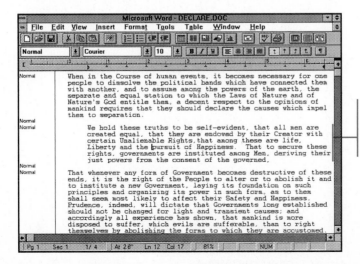

This paragraph is indented .5 inch from the left margin.

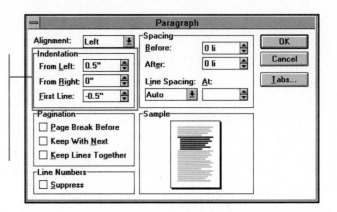

You can create a hanging indent by setting the From Left list box to .5 inch and the First Line list box to –.5 inch.

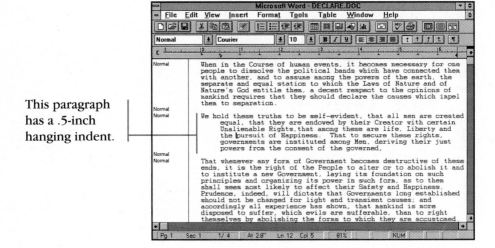

This paragraph has a .5-inch hanging indent.

Paragraph Alignment

In Word for Windows, you can align text to the left margin, center text, align text to the right margin, or justify text.

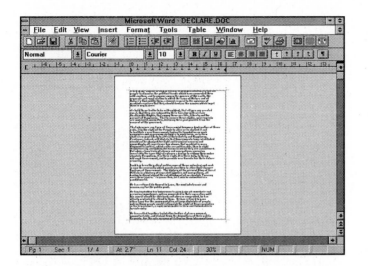

Aligning text to
the left margin,
produces a
ragged right
margin.

6

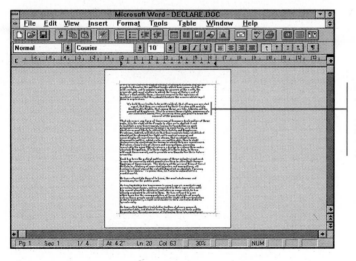

Centering text
between the
margins makes
both margins
ragged.

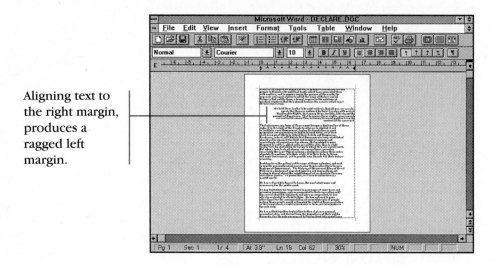

Aligning text to the right margin, produces a ragged left margin.

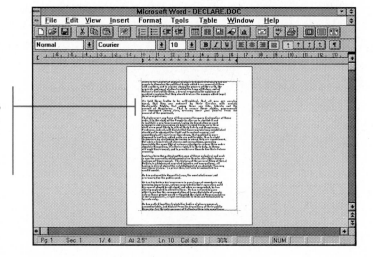

Justifying text aligns the text to both margins by expanding the spaces between words.

You can change paragraph alignment in three ways:

- You can use the Ribbon.
- You can use the keyboard.
- You can use the Paragraph dialog box.

Using the Ribbon To Set Paragraph Alignment

When changing paragraph alignment, you can choose an alignment button and then type the text, or you can type the text, select it, and then choose the alignment button.

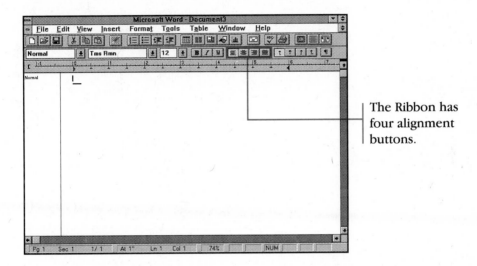

The Ribbon has four alignment buttons.

Using the Keyboard To Set Paragraph Alignment

You also can control paragraph alignment by using just the keyboard:

- To align text to the left, press Ctrl + L.
- To center text, press Ctrl + E.
- To align text to the right, press Ctrl + R.
- To justify text, press Ctrl + J.

Using the Paragraph Dialog Box To Set Paragraph Alignment

To open the Paragraph dialog box, open the Format menu and choose the Paragraph command or double-click the Ruler above the scale.

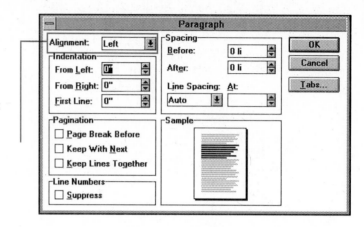

You use the
Alignment list box
to set paragraph
alignment.

6

From the Alignment list box, you can choose to align text to the left margin or to the right margin, to center the text between the left and the right margins, or to justify the text between the left and right margins.

Line Spacing

Through paragraph formatting, you can control line spacing, both within and between paragraphs. You can, for example, single space lines within a paragraph, but double space between paragraphs. You can control line spacing only by using the Paragraph dialog box.

To set line spacing, position the insertion point where you want to change the line spacing and open the Paragraph dialog box. (To open the Paragraph dialog box, open the Format menu and choose the Paragraph command or double-click the Ruler above the scale.)

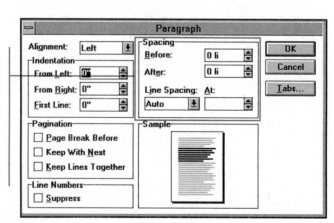

In the Spacing
box, you can
control the
amount of space
before a para-
graph, after a
paragraph,
and within a
paragraph.

134

From the **Before** and **After** list boxes, you can choose (or type) the number of lines you want before or after a paragraph. From the **Line Spacing** list box, you can choose the amount of vertical space Word for Windows uses for each line. If you choose Auto, each line is as tall as the tallest character in the line. Single, 1.5 Lines, and Double set line spacing at one line, one and one-half lines, and two lines respectively. The At Least option enables you to set a minimum spacing between lines. The Exactly option enables you to set a specific line spacing in the **At** list box (such as 1.25 lines or .75 line—you can choose a number from the list or type a number).

Using Other Paragraph Dialog Box Options

By using other Paragraph dialog box options, you can control line number suppression and some elements of pagination. You also can open the Tabs dialog box by choosing the **Tabs** button in the Paragraph dialog box.

6

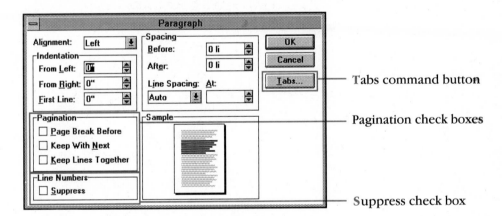

Tabs command button

Pagination check boxes

Suppress check box

Line Numbers

The Line Numbering feature (discussed in Chapter 7) enables you to number each line of a page. You usually use this feature to make reviewing a document easier (because reviewers can refer to a place in the document by its line number). If you don't want to number every line of the document, however, you can choose the **S**uppress check box to conceal line numbers for selected paragraphs or text.

Pagination

Because Word for Windows includes page sizes, font sizes, line spacing, and top and bottom margin settings, the program calculates when you fill a page with text. Whenever you fill a page, Word for Windows inserts a "soft" page break. Sometimes these soft page breaks occur in places where you don't want them (for example, in the middle of a list). You use the options in the Pagination box to prevent unwanted soft page breaks within paragraphs. You can move the page break before a selected paragraph (Page Break Before), or you can force two paragraphs to appear on the same page by preventing a page break between them (Keep With Next). You also can prevent a page break within a paragraph (Keep Lines Together). For more information on pagination and page breaks, see Chapter 7.

6

Command Buttons

The Tabs command button opens the Tabs dialog box. You also can choose the OK button to accept your paragraph formatting settings or the Cancel button to ignore your changes.

Removing, Repeating, and Copying Paragraph Formatting

To save your work, Word for Windows has some features that enable you to remove, repeat, and copy formatting quickly. You also can use styles (discussed at the end of this chapter and in Chapter 9) to perform these functions.

Removing Paragraph Formatting

To remove all paragraph (and character) formatting you applied to selected text, follow these steps:

1. Select the text from which you want to remove formatting.
2. Press Ctrl+Q.

These steps remove the paragraph formatting *and* character formatting you applied to the selected text.

Repeating Paragraph Formatting

To repeat paragraph formatting from one paragraph to another, follow these steps:

1. Apply paragraph formatting to the first paragraph.
2. Select the paragraph(s) to which you want to apply the same formatting.
3. Open the Edit menu and choose the Repeat Paragraph command.

   Or

   Press `F4`.

If you applied multiple formats by using the Toolbar, the Ruler, the Ribbon, or the keyboard, Word for Windows repeats the most recently applied format only. If you used the Paragraph dialog box to apply multiple formats, Word for Windows repeats all the paragraph formatting.

Copying Paragraph Formatting

You also can copy paragraph formatting without copying the text. Follow these steps:

1. Select the text you want to format.
2. Hold down `Ctrl`+`⇧Shift` and click in the selection bar (on the left side of the text area) next to the text that has the formatting you want to copy.

Applying Borders and Shading to Paragraphs

Word for Windows enables you to place borders around, above, below, or beside a block of text or to shade a block of text. These techniques, which you can use separately or together, are excellent ways to emphasize text.

Borders

The term *borders*, as used in Word for Windows, can be somewhat confusing. Borders can surround a block of text or appear above, below, or to the left or right of the text.

6

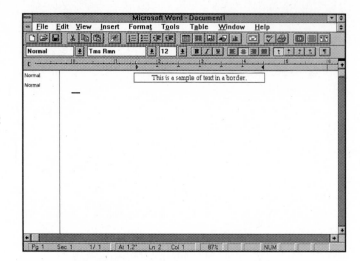

You can place text
inside a boxed
border.

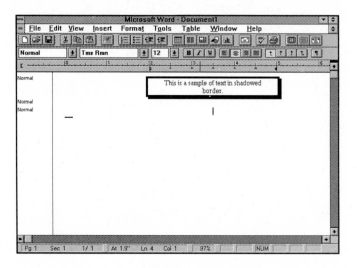

You can use
a shadow to
create a three-
dimensional
effect.

6

138

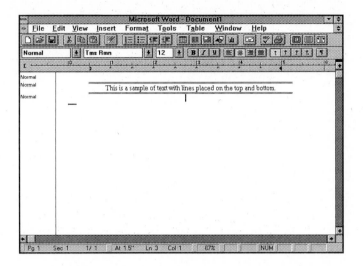

You can place border lines on any side or sides of the text.

6

To apply a border to one or more paragraphs, follow these steps:

1. Select the text to which you want to apply a border. If you don't select any text, Word for Windows applies the border to the paragraph that contains the insertion point.

2. Open the Format menu.

3. Choose the Borders command.

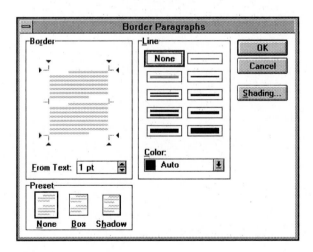

The Border Paragraphs dialog box appears.

139

If you simply want to place a thin box around the selected text, you can choose **B**ox from the Preset box. If you choose Sh**a**dow from the Preset box, the top and left side lines are thin, but the bottom and right side lines are thicker, producing a shadowed effect.

Alternatively, you can use the Border sample box to identify the parts of the selected text to which you want to apply a border. When the Border Paragraphs dialog box first appears, border markers appear on all sides of the Border sample box. To place a border on the bottom of a paragraph, for example, first click the bottom of the text in the Border sample box.

When you click the bottom of the text, Word for Windows removes all border markers except the ones in the lower left and right corners.

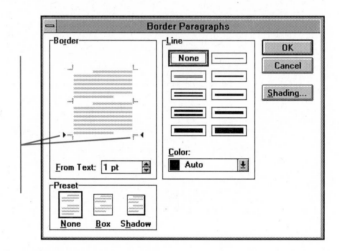

Next, choose a border style from the **L**ine choice box. If you intend to use a color printer, you can choose a color from the **C**olor list box. (You can always choose a color, but the color prints only if you use a color printer.) If you don't want the line to appear directly below the selected text, you can specify the border's distance from the text by using the **F**rom Text list box. The distance is measured in points.

Tip: You can place a line approximately halfway between two paragraphs by using the same point size in the **F**rom Text box as the point size of the font you are using in the two paragraphs.

By default, lines you place at the top or the bottom of selected text extend from the left margin to the right margin. Boxes that surround text extend into the left and right margins. You can change the length of the line (and keep the line inside the left and right margins) by changing the indentation of the paragraph to which you apply the line: move the left indent to the right and move the right indent to the left.

You can remove borders completely by choosing None from the Preset box. You can remove borders partially by clicking the line you want to remove in the Border box and then choosing the None option from the Line box.

Shading

To shade text, choose the Shading button from the Border Paragraphs dialog box.

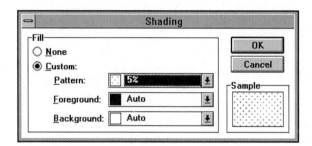

The Shading dialog box appears.

If you choose the Pattern, Foreground, or Background list box, Word for Windows automatically chooses the Custom option button.

From the Pattern list box, you can choose the percentage of gray in the shading. From the Foreground and Background list boxes, you can choose shading colors. By default, the Foreground color is black (the color in which you type text) and the Background color is white (the background color of the window). If you don't have a color printer, you may get unusual results by changing these colors.

Be aware that shading affects readability—darker shading makes text more difficult to read, particularly with smaller fonts.

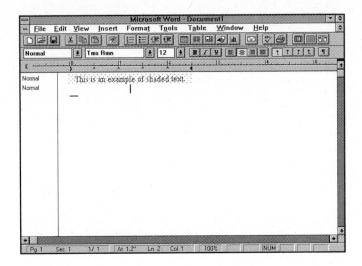

If you use the settings in the preceding illustration, the shaded text looks like this.

Introducing Styles

Often, you apply many character and paragraph attributes to a block of text. Then, you find that you need to apply the same attributes to many other blocks of text in the document. You can copy the formatting to the other blocks of text, but that technique involves a considerable amount of work.

Word for Windows enables you to store formatting information as a *style* so that you can easily apply a set of formats to more than one block of text. In addition, Word for Windows enables you to use *document templates*, which are like empty documents that contain a set of styles for a certain type of work. Word for Windows comes with several different document templates, each containing different styles. Using styles and document templates makes formatting Word for Windows documents easy.

In Chapter 2, you learned that when you open a new document, you generally work with the Normal document template (the default template). The Normal document template contains margin and tab defaults and a minimum number of styles, including the Normal style. The Normal style contains information about the default font, point size, and text alignment.

You can change both the Normal style and the Normal document template if Word for Windows' definition of "normal" does not meet your everyday work needs. In Chapter 9, you will learn about the document templates and styles that come with Word for Windows and how to create your own styles and document templates to save your character, paragraph, and document formatting.

Chapter Summary

In this chapter you learned about the many ways you can format paragraphs in Word for Windows. You learned about the paragraph attributes available for formatting and how to apply paragraph formatting by using the dialog boxes, the keyboard, the Ribbon, the Ruler, and the Toolbar. You learned how to remove, repeat, and copy formatting. Specifically, you learned the following information:

- You can use paragraph formatting techniques to control tab stops, tab alignments, indentations, paragraph alignment, and line spacing.
- You can change paragraph formatting by using the Tabs dialog box, the Paragraph dialog box, the keyboard, the Ruler and the mouse, the Ruler and the keyboard, the Ribbon, and the Toolbar.
- You can control the most paragraph formatting options by using the Paragraph dialog box (which includes access to the Tabs dialog box), but the Ruler, Ribbon, and Toolbar offer excellent shortcuts.
- You can apply borders and shading to text by choosing the Borders command from the Format menu.

This chapter also introduced the concepts of styles and document templates as ways to store often-used formatting information.

In the next chapter, you will learn how to set up documents and use page-related functions in Word for Windows.

6

Setting Up Documents

7

In Chapter 5 you learned how to format characters in Word for Windows, and in Chapter 6 you learned how to format paragraphs. To format characters and paragraphs, you used dialog boxes, the Ribbon, the Ruler, and the Toolbar. In this chapter you will learn how to format pages and sections. Specifically, you will learn how to set margins, paper size, and orientation; use page numbering and insert page breaks; create headers and footers, footnotes, and endnotes; use paragraph numbering and bullets; format sections; and work with newspaper columns.

Formatting pages

Formatting sections

Working with newspaper columns

Key Terms in This Chapter

Portrait	A paper orientation for which text flows across the 8 1/2-inch side of the paper from the left margin to the right margin.
Landscape	A paper orientation for which text flows across the 11-inch side of the paper from the left margin to the right margin.
Soft page break	A page break that Word for Windows inserts after calculating that the text has filled the page from the top margin to the bottom margin.
Hard page break	A page break you insert to force Word for Windows to begin a new page.
Header	Text that appears at the top of each page.
Footer	Text that appears at the bottom of each page.
Reference mark	A mark, usually a superscript number, that indicates the existence of explanatory or reference text.
Footnote	Reference text that appears at the bottom of the page containing the corresponding reference mark.
Endnote	Reference text that appears at the end of the section or document containing the corresponding reference mark. You use endnotes when you want to collect all references in one place.
Bullet	A character, such as •, that appears at the beginning of a paragraph. You usually use bullets for emphasis.
Newspaper columns	Text that appears in columns and flows from the bottom of one column to the top of the next column.

Formatting Pages

When you first open a document, Word for Windows provides basic default settings. These default settings include the following:

- Left and right margins of 1.25 inches.
- Top and bottom margins of 1 inch.
- A typeface of average size.
- Single-spaced paragraphs aligned to the left margin.
- Tab stops set every .5 inch.

In Chapter 5 you learned how to change the font (typeface) and point size; in Chapter 6 you learned how to change the paragraph alignment and spacing and the tab stops. Now, you will learn how to change the page formatting.

Setting Margins

By changing margin settings, you can affect the document's length, improve the clarity of the document, or leave room for binding the document. As you will learn later in this chapter, you also can divide a document into different sections, and each section can have its own set of margins. You can change the left and right margins of a document in three ways:

- Use the Ruler.
- Use the Print Preview command.
- Use the Page Setup command.

Setting Margins by Using the Ruler

You can use the Ruler to set the left and right margins for the section of the document that contains the insertion point or for all selected sections. You can set different margins in different sections of a document.

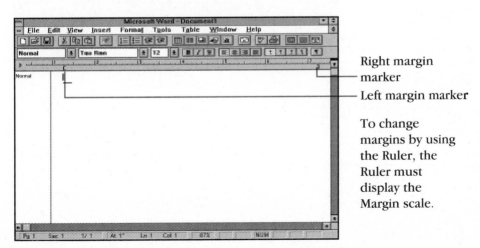

Right margin marker

Left margin marker

To change margins by using the Ruler, the Ruler must display the Margin scale.

To change margins by using the Ruler, follow these steps.

1. Click the Ruler scale symbol until the Ruler displays the Margin scale.
2. Drag the margin markers to the new margin positions.

   When you release the mouse button, the text adjusts to the new margins.

Setting Margins by Using the Print Preview Command

You can set all four margins (top, bottom, left, and right) from Print Preview mode. When you change margins by using the Print Preview command, you affect the margins of the section that contains the page you are previewing.

To change margins by using the Print Preview command, follow these steps:

1. Position the insertion point on any page in the section for which you want to set the margins.
2. Open the File menu.
3. Choose the Print Preview command.
4. Choose the Margins button.

Margin indicators —
Handles ——

The current
margin bound-
aries appear
with handles.

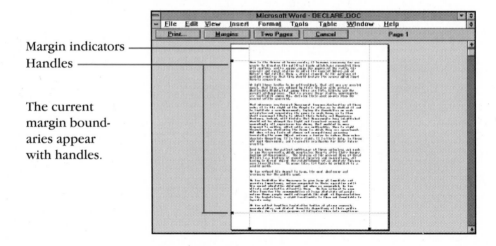

5. Drag the handles to change the margins.

   Note: The Undo feature cannot change the margins back to their original values.
6. To see the effect of your changes, click anywhere outside the page.

7. When you finish setting the margins, choose the Close button or press
   Esc.

Setting Margins by Using the Page Setup Command

You also can change all four margins by using the Page Setup command on
the Format menu. You have the most flexibility when you change margins by
using the Page Setup command. You can choose the portions of the document
you want to affect: selected text, the current section, all text from the insertion
point forward, or the entire document. (If you choose to affect the selected
text or the text from the insertion point forward, Word for Windows inserts
section breaks. New sections always begin on a new page.) You also can set up
a "gutter" margin to provide extra space for binding the document or set up
margins for "facing pages" so that you can assemble the document as a book.

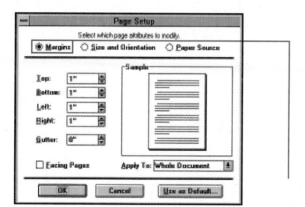

When you select
the Page Setup
command from
the Format menu,
the Page Setup
dialog box
appears. **Margins**
is the default page
attribute option.

Set the margins, including any gutter margin, by typing margin measurements
in the Top, Bottom, Left, Right, or Gutter text boxes or by clicking the arrows
at the end of the text boxes to increase or decrease the current measurement.
Watch the picture in the Sample box to see the effect of your choices. If you
plan to assemble the document as a book, choose the Facing Pages check box.
The choices in the Apply To list box vary depending on whether you created
sections in the document and whether you selected text before opening the
Page Setup dialog box.

To save the new margin settings in the current document template, choose
the Use as Default button. If you choose this option, all future documents
based on the current template use the margins you establish here. When you
finish setting the margins, choose OK to accept your choices or Cancel to
ignore them.

149

Setting Paper Size and Orientation

From the Page Setup dialog box, you also can change the paper size and orientation. To set the paper size or orientation, follow these steps:

1. Open the Format menu.
2. Choose the Page Setup command.

   The Page Setup dialog box appears.
3. Choose the Size and Orientation option button at the top of the Page Setup dialog box.

The dialog box changes to display size and orientation options. In the Paper Size list box, you can see the paper sizes that your printer supports.

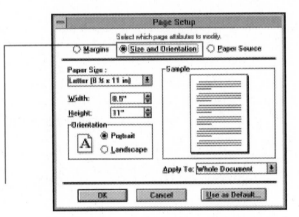

4. Choose a paper size from the Paper Size list box or enter a custom paper size in the Width and Height text boxes (by typing the paper measurements or by clicking the arrows to increase or decrease the current measurements). Watch the picture in the Sample box to see the effects of your changes.

5. In the Orientation box, choose Portrait or Landscape.

6. From the Apply To list box, choose the portions of the document you want to affect. The options in this list box vary depending on whether you selected text before you opened the Page Setup dialog box. If you selected text, Word for Windows inserts section breaks before and after the selected text.

7 To save these size and orientation settings in the current document template, choose the Use as Default button. If you choose this option, all future documents based on the current template have the size and orientation you establish here.

8. Choose OK to accept your choices or Cancel to ignore them.

To see the overall effect of your changes, choose the Print Preview command from the File menu.

Choosing a Paper Source

In Word for Windows, you can print the first page of each section on different paper than the rest of the pages. Most printers that Word for Windows supports offer at least two ways to feed paper into the printer: by using the paper tray and by feeding the paper manually through the printer. Some printers have two paper trays, enabling you to use different paper in each tray.

To choose the paper source, follow these steps:

1. Open the Format menu.
2. Choose the Page Setup command.

   The Page Setup dialog box appears.
3. Choose the Paper Source option button.
4. From the First Page list box, choose the paper source for the first page of each section.
5. From the Other Pages list box, choose the paper source for the remaining pages of each section.
6. From the Apply To list box, choose the portions of the document you want to affect. The options in this box vary depending on whether you selected text before you opened the Page Setup dialog box. If you selected text, Word for Windows inserts section breaks before and after the selected text.
7. To save these paper source settings in the current document template, choose the Use as Default button. If you choose this option, all future documents based on the current template use the paper source you establish here.
8. Choose OK to accept your choices or Cancel to ignore them.

Setting Pagination

When formatting documents, you often need to control pagination. In this section you will learn about page breaks, repagination, and page numbering.

7

Setting Page Breaks

Because Word for Windows calculates page sizes, font sizes, line spacing, and margins, the program can determine when you have filled a page with text. Whenever this occurs, Word for Windows inserts a "soft" page break in the document. As you edit or move text, Word for Windows continually recalculates the amount of text on each page and moves the soft page breaks accordingly.

Occasionally, you may want to begin a new page in a specific location. To do this, you insert a "hard" page break. Hard and soft page breaks differ in two ways:

- Word for Windows inserts soft page breaks automatically, but you insert hard page breaks manually.
- You cannot delete a soft page break, but you can delete a hard page break.

You can insert and delete hard page breaks by using menu commands or by using the keyboard.

To insert a hard page break, follow these steps:

1. Position the insertion point just before the text you want to begin the new page.
2. Open the **Insert** menu.
3. Choose the **Break** command.
4. Choose the **Page** Break option button (the default).
5. Choose OK.

Or, follow these steps:

1. Position the insertion point just before the text you want to begin the new page.
2. Press Ctrl + ⏎Enter.

To delete a hard page break, follow these steps:

1. Select the hard page break you want to delete.
2. Open the **Edit** menu.
3. Choose the Cut command.

Or, follow these steps:

1. Select the hard page break you want to delete or position the insertion point on or immediately after the hard page break.

2. If you selected the page break or positioned the insertion point on the page break, press ⌈Del⌉. If you positioned the insertion point immediately after the page break, press ⌈◆Backspace⌉.

You also can make some adjustments to the placement of page breaks by using Print Preview mode. Follow these steps:

1. Open the File menu.

2. Choose the Print Preview command.

3. Choose the Margins button.

4. Drag the page break to the new position:

   You can drag a soft page break (thin dotted line) up to make the page shorter. If you move a soft page break up, it becomes a hard page break.

   You can drag a hard page break (a darker dotted line) up or down to make the page shorter or longer or you can drag a hard page break off the page to delete it.

5. Choose the Close Button.

For information on controlling pagination by keeping text together and inserting page breaks before certain paragraphs, see Chapter 6.

Repaginating

By default, Word for Windows calculates pagination in *background mode—* that is, whenever you pause while typing or editing. Background repagination uses some memory, so if you experience memory problems, you may want to turn off this option. To turn off background repagination, follow these steps:

1. Open the Tools menu.

2. Choose the Options command.

3. From the Category options, choose General.

4. Choose the Background Repagination check box to turn off this option.

   Word for Windows removes the X from the check box.

5. Choose OK.

If background repagination is off, Word for Windows stills repaginates the document whenever you do any of the following:

• When you print the document.

• When you choose the Repaginate Now command from the Tools menu.

7

153

- When you choose the Page Layout command from the View menu.
- When you choose the Print Preview command from the File menu.
- When you compile a table of contents or an index.

Page Numbering

Word for Windows always inserts page numbers in a document as part of a header or footer. You can put page numbers in a document in two ways:

- By choosing the Page Numbers command from the Insert menu.
- By choosing the Header/Footer command from the View menu.

In this section you will learn how to put page numbers in a document by using the Page Numbers command. In the next section, which discusses headers and footers, you will learn how to put page numbers in a document by using the Header/Footer command.

When you use the Page Numbers command, you insert a page number on all pages except *the first page*. You can choose where the page numbers appear when printed, their alignment, their format, and the starting page number. By default, Word for Windows places an Arabic number (1, 2, 3, and so on) in a footer on the right side of the page. Word for Windows begins page numbering with page 1 and numbers the pages continuously.

To insert page numbers by using the Page Numbers command, follow these steps:

1. Position the insertion point where you want page numbering to begin.
2. Open the Insert menu.
3. Choose the Page Numbers command.

The Page Numbers dialog box enables you to choose the position, alignment, and format of page numbers.

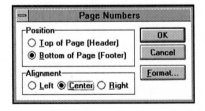

4. Choose the Top of Page (Header) or Bottom of Page (Footer) option button to specify the position of the page numbers.
5. Choose Left, Center, or Right alignment for the page numbers.

6. To change any default options, choose the Format button.

    The Page Number Format dialog box appears. After you make the changes, choose OK to return to the Page Numbers dialog box.

7. Choose OK in the Page Numbers dialog box to apply the page numbers to the document.

Creating Headers and Footers

You can store information that you want to repeat on each page of a document in headers and footers. Word for Windows enables you to create different headers and footers for the first page and the rest of the document and for odd and even numbered pages. You also can use the Header/Footer command to place page numbers in a document if you want to do any of the following:

- Place a page number on the first page.

- Include additional text with the number (for example, to include the word *Page* before the number).

- Create different headers or footers for odd and even numbered pages (for example, so that page numbers print in the outer corner on every page).

Word for Windows stores the header or footer information in the last paragraph mark of the document. If you accidentally delete the last paragraph mark, you lose the header or footer information, including the page numbers.

To place page numbers in a header or footer, make sure that you are in Normal View and then choose the Header/Footer command from the View menu.

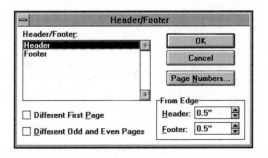

The Header/Footer dialog box appears.

The Header/Footer dialog box provides the following options:

- Choose the Different First Page check box if you want to use a different header or footer for the first page.

- Choose the Different Odd and Even Pages check box if you want to use different headers or footers for odd and even pages.

- From the Header/Footer list box, choose the location where you want the page number to appear (Header, Footer, First Header, First Footer, and so on).

- Use the From Edge box to move the vertical placement of the header or footer from the edge of the paper. (You also can move headers vertically by changing to Print Preview mode and dragging them.)

- To change the page numbering style from Arabic to Roman numerals or alphabetic characters or to change the starting page number, choose the Page Numbers button.

When you choose OK in the Header/Footer dialog box, the appropriate pane appears.

To insert a page number in a header or footer, follow these steps:

1. Position the insertion point where you want the page numbers to appear. If you want to center or right-align the page numbers, you can use the default tab stops Word for Windows provides. Press [Tab↔] one time to center the insertion point or two times to right-align it.

2. Choose the Page Number button.

In this example,
the page number
appears centered
in the footer.

Page Number
button

Data button

Time button

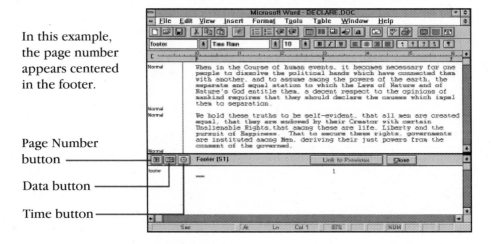

3. Add any other text (or formatting) you want to include in the header or footer.

4. Choose the Close button.

To place a page number in more than one header or footer, repeat these steps for each header and footer. To see the effect of your choices, choose the Page Preview command from the File menu.

You can insert the date (in MM/DD/YY format) in the header or footer by choosing the Date button. You can insert the time by choosing the Time button. If you insert the date or time, Word for Windows updates this information automatically.

You also can edit or delete a header or footer. To edit, first choose the header or footer from the Header/Footer dialog box. Then, edit the header or footer. You can apply formatting in headers and footers by using the Ribbon, the Ruler, the Toolbar, or the Character or Paragraph dialog box. When you finish editing, close the pane. To delete a header or footer, choose that header or footer from the Header/Footer list box and then delete everything from the pane. (To delete some items, you must select them and then press [Del].)

Creating Footnotes or Endnotes

7

If you include footnotes in a document, Word for Windows automatically reserves space at the bottom of each page and adjusts the text on the page so that a footnote and its reference (typically marked by a superscript number) appear on the same page. Word for Windows also automatically renumbers numbered footnotes if you move, add, or delete any footnotes. You also can change footnotes to endnotes, which appear at the end of the section or at the end of the document.

To add a footnote, make sure that you are in Normal View and then follow these steps:

1. Position the insertion point where you want the footnote reference mark to appear.

2. Open the Insert menu.

3. Choose the Footnote command.

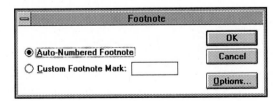

The Footnote dialog box appears.

If you accept the defaults, Word for Windows creates an automatically numbered footnote that appears at the bottom of the page with a short line separating it from the body of text.

4. To change the numbering scheme of the footnote, choose the Custom Footnote Mark option button and type a reference mark (such as *) in the text box.

5. To change the placement of the footnote so that it appears at the end of the text on the page or to change the footnote to an endnote that appears at the end of the section or the end of the document, choose the Options button.

   From the Footnote Options dialog box, you can change the starting number of the footnotes or restart the numbering at the beginning of each section. You can even change the separator that Word for Windows uses to separate document text from footnote text. After making any changes, choose the OK button to return to the Footnote dialog box.

6. Choose the OK button in the Footnote dialog box.

   The Footnote pane appears with a reference mark in it. (The footnote pane does not appear if you are in Page Layout View.)

7. Type the footnote text in the pane.

8. To close the Footnote pane and return to the document, choose the Close button.

   To return to the document, but leave the footnote pane open, press F6 or click anywhere in the text area of the document. (To switch back to the footnote pane, press F6 again or click anywhere in the footnote pane.) If you leave the footnote pane open, it scrolls to show the footnotes that correspond to the reference marks in the text.

To open the footnote pane at any time while you work on a document, you can double-click any automatically numbered footnote reference mark or choose the Footnotes command from the View menu.

To locate a specific footnote, follow these steps:

1. Open the Edit menu and choose the Go To command.

   Or

   Press F5, the Go To key, two times.

   The Go To dialog box appears.

2. Type one of the following characters in the text box:

Character	Effect
f	Goes to the next footnote.
f–	Goes to the preceding footnote.
f n	Goes to a specific footnote (footnote n).
f+n	Goes forward a specific number of footnotes (n footnotes).
f–n	Goes back a specific number of footnotes (n footnotes).

To edit footnote text, locate the footnote, open the footnote pane, and then change the text or apply character or paragraph formatting.

To copy footnote text, locate the footnote and then follow these steps:

1. In the document window, select the reference mark of the footnote you want to copy.
2. Open the Edit menu and choose the Copy command.

   Or

   Choose the Copy button on the Toolbar.
3. Position the insertion point where you want the new reference mark to appear.
4. Open the Edit menu and choose the Paste command.

   Or

   Choose the Paste button on the Toolbar.

   Word for Windows copies the footnote text and assigns the appropriate reference mark.

To delete a footnote, locate the footnote, select its reference mark in the text, and then do one of the following:

- Press Del.
- Choose the Cut command from the Edit menu.
- Choose the Cut button on the Toolbar.

Using Paragraph Numbering and Creating Bullets

In Chapter 6 you learned that you can indent paragraphs by using the Indentation buttons on the Toolbar. The Numbered List button and the Bullet button

7

on the Toolbar also indent text, but these buttons insert numbers or the default bullet (•) in front of each indented paragraph. When you choose either of these buttons, Word for Windows indents the text .25 inch from the left margin and inserts the special character at the left margin.

To create a numbered or bulleted list, follow these steps:

1. Type the text. Be sure to press ⏎Enter at the end of each phrase that you want Word for Windows to precede with a number or bullet.

2. Select the text you typed.

3. Choose the Numbered List button or the Bullet button from the Toolbar.

To add an item to an existing list, follow these steps:

1. Position the insertion point at the location where you want the new item to appear.

2. Type the text.

3. Select the text you typed.

4. Choose the Numbered List button or the Bullet button from the Toolbar.

Note: Depending on where you add a numbered item to the list, you may need to renumber the list by choosing the **Bullets** and Numbering command from the **Tools** menu.

To access additional options for customizing the appearance of bullets and numbered lists, open the **Tools** menu and choose the **Bullets** and Numbering command.

The Bullets and Numbering dialog box appears.

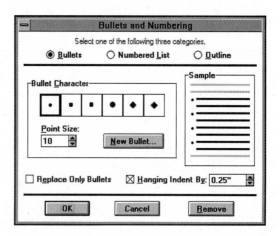

To set the bullet style, choose the **Bullets** option button (the default) at the top of the dialog box.

In the Bullet Character box, you can select a new bullet character. From the predefined bullet characters, you can choose a dot shape in one of four sizes or a diamond shape in one of two sizes. You can choose a different bullet size from the Point Size box by typing a point size or by clicking the arrows to increase or decrease the current size. You can choose a different bullet character by choosing the New Bullet button and then choosing a character from the symbol character set that Word for Windows displays.

To make Word for Windows change the bullet character for paragraphs with bullets, but not add new bullets to paragraphs without bullets, choose the Replace Only Bullets check box.

By default, the Hanging Indent check box is turned on so that Word for Windows formats paragraphs with bullets as hanging indents. You can control the amount of the indent by typing a measurement in the By text box or by clicking the arrows to increase or decrease the current measurement.

To remove bullets from selected text, choose the Remove command button.

If you want to create a numbered list rather than a bulleted list, choose the Numbered List option button at the top of the dialog box.

7

When you choose the Numbered List option button, the Bullets and Numbering dialog box changes to display numbering options.

From the Number box, you can choose a different format for the numbers (for example, Roman numerals or alphabetic characters), and you can change or delete the separator character. By default, Word for Windows adds a period (.) after each number the program inserts. You also can change the starting number. This feature is particularly useful if a numbered list is interrupted by text and then continues. You can change the starting number of the second part of the list to continue from the next number rather than starting with number 1 again.

To make Word for Windows change the numbers for paragraphs that already have numbers, but not add new numbers to unnumbered paragraphs, choose the Replace Only Numbers check box. This feature is useful when you want to renumber a document that contains a mixture of numbered and unnumbered paragraphs.

By default, the Hanging Indent check box is turned on so that Word for Windows formats paragraphs with numbers as hanging indents. You can control the amount of the indent by typing a measurement in the By text box or by clicking the arrows to increase or decrease the current measurement.

To remove numbers from selected text, choose the Remove command button.

If you want to create an outline rather than a bulleted or numbered list, choose the Outline option button at the top of the dialog box. The Outline feature is discussed in Chapter 10.

Inserting the Date and Time

7

Earlier in this chapter, you learned that you can insert the date and time into a header or a footer. You also can insert the date and time into document text by choosing the Date and Time command from the Insert menu.

Note: You cannot insert the date and time simultaneously.

To insert the date or time into a document, follow these steps:

1. Open the Insert menu.
2. Choose the Date and Time command.

The Date and Time dialog box appears.

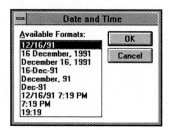

3. Choose a date or time format from the Available Formats list box.
4. Choose OK.

You can update the date or time in two ways:

- Print the document.
- Position the insertion point anywhere within the date or time and press F9.

If you don't want Word for Windows to update the date or time, position the insertion point anywhere within the date or time and press Ctrl + ⇧Shift + F9.

You cannot delete the date or time simply by pressing Del or ⬅Backspace; you must select the date or time and then press Del or ⬅Backspace. You can edit the date or time by positioning the insertion point where you want to edit and then backspacing and making changes.

Formatting Sections

Word for Windows enables you to divide a document into sections so that you can format different portions of the document in different ways. If you want the formatting for a document to be consistent throughout the document, you do not need to create any sections—the entire document is one large section. You must create a new section, however, if you want to change any of the following formatting for just part of a document:

- The margins, paper size, or page orientation.
- The format, position, or sequence of page numbers.
- The contents or position of headers and footers.
- The location of footnotes.
- The number of newspaper columns.
- The line numbering.

Inserting Section Breaks

To insert a section break, follow these steps:

1. Make sure that you are in Normal View.
2. Position the insertion point where you want to start the new section.
3. Open the Insert menu.
4. Choose the Break command.

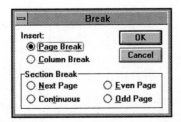

The Break dialog box appears.

The default option is **P**age Break. (Earlier in this chapter, you learned that you can place a hard page break in text by pressing Ctrl + ↵Enter or by using the Break dialog box.) You will learn about the **C**olumn Break option later in this chapter.

In the Section Break box, choose the page where you want the new section to begin and then choose the OK button.

Section breaks appear in the document as double dotted lines. These section marks do not print.

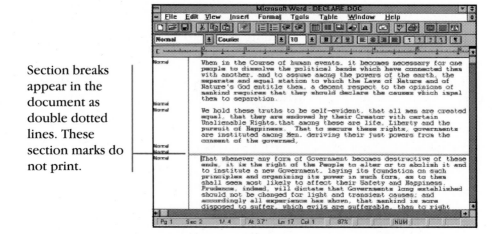

Word for Windows stores all section formatting in the section mark. If you delete a section mark, you delete all section formatting for the preceding section. The text then assumes the formatting of the next section.

To remove a section break, position the insertion point immediately before the section mark and press Del or immediately after the section mark and press ←Backspace .

You can format a section by positioning the insertion point anywhere in the section and then choosing any of the following commands:

- The Page Set**u**p command (from the F**o**rmat menu).
- The C**o**lumns command (from the F**o**rmat menu).
- The **S**ection Layout command (from the F**o**rmat menu).
- The Page N**u**mbers command (from the **I**nsert menu).
- The **H**eader/Footer command (from the **V**iew menu).

Setting Vertical Alignment

To set the vertical alignment of a section, open the Format menu and choose the Section Layout command.

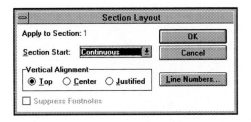

The Section Layout dialog box appears.

Changing the vertical alignment adjusts the spacing between paragraphs in a section. Word for Windows aligns the text in a section with the top or bottom margins of the page or centers it between the top and bottom margins. You can create a title page, for example, by centering the text vertically on the page. Although you cannot see the effect of your choice in Normal View, you can choose the Print Preview command from the File menu to see the alignment.

Turning on Line Numbering

To number the lines in a section, follow these steps:

1. Open the Format menu and choose the Section Layout command.
   The Section Layout dialog box appears.

2. In the Section Layout dialog box, choose the Line Numbers button.

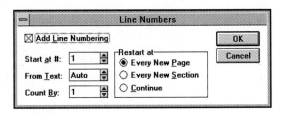

The Line Numbers dialog box appears.

3. Choose the Add Line Numbering check box.

Line numbers are particularly useful when proofreading, because reviewers can refer to specific line numbers in their comments. You can start the numbers over at the end of each page or section or have the numbers continue sequentially throughout the document. Later, when the document is finalized, you can turn off the line numbers by repeating these steps to remove the X from the Add **L**ine Numbering check box. For more details on line numbering options, see Chapter 10.

Working with Newspaper Columns

Word for Windows also can create text in newspaper columns. (To create parallel columns, see Chapter 11 for information about tables.)

When you use newspaper columns, text flows from the bottom of the first column to the top of the next column.

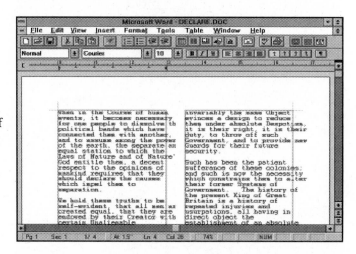

When you use parallel columns, text flows across the columns from left to right.

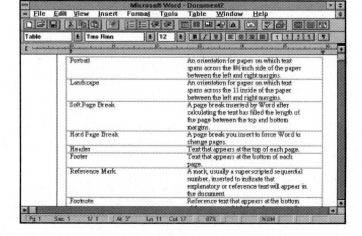

Although you can create up to 100 columns of text on a page, the actual number of newspaper columns you can produce depends on many factors, such as the size and orientation of the paper, the size of the columns, and the size of the fonts. From a practical perspective, a document becomes difficult to read if you use more than four columns on a page (using an average size font and portrait orientation). For landscape orientation, a document becomes difficult to read if you use more than six columns on a page (using an average size font).

You can adjust the margins, column widths, spacing between columns, and column breaks for newspaper columns.

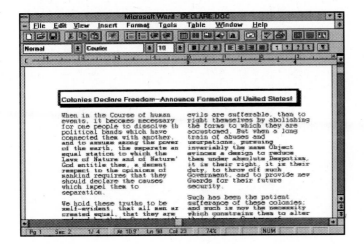

You also can format only part of a page in columns so that you can create, for example, a headline across the top of the page.

7

Each new document is a one-column document. If you create two or more columns, Word for Windows divides the document into sections. You can create documents with multiple sections and vary numbers of columns in each section.

Viewing Newspaper Columns

You can create multiple columns in any view of Word for Windows, but Normal View, Page Layout View and Print Preview are the most useful.

In Normal view, you can enter text quickly and make all formatting and editing adjustments. You also can see the section breaks, which appear as double dotted lines. The text, however, does not appear in "side-by-side" columns.

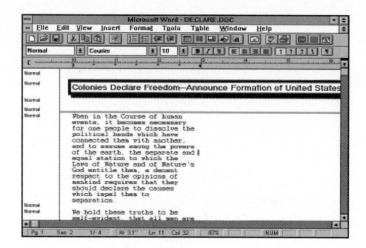

In Normal view, text appears in a single column.

In Page Layout View and Print Preview mode, the text does appear in side-by-side columns. In Page Layout View, you can read and edit the text, adjust the column widths, and insert column breaks, but the program works more slowly.

7

In Page Layout view, you can read and edit the text in side-by-side columns.

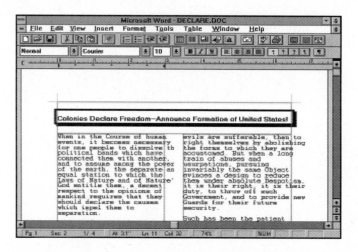

In Print Preview mode, you cannot read the text, but you can see the layout of text on the page and adjust the margins and page breaks.

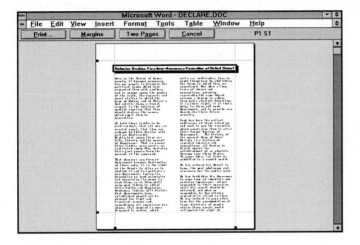

You can adjust only the margins and page breaks in Print Preview mode.

Creating Newspaper Columns

You can create newspaper columns in two ways:

- Use the Toolbar.
- Use the Columns command on the Format menu.

When you use the Toolbar to create newspaper columns, Word for Windows automatically places .5 inch of space between each column. To create newspaper columns by using the Toolbar, follow these steps:

1. Choose the Text Columns button on the Toolbar and hold down the left mouse button.
2. Drag the mouse pointer to the right.

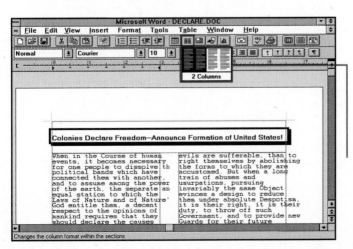

The Text Columns button displays various numbers of columns.

3. When you see the number of columns you want to create, release the mouse button.

   Word for Windows formats your text into the number of columns you chose.

To remove newspaper column formatting by using the Toolbar, position the insertion point anywhere in the section that has the column formatting you want to remove. Choose the Text Column button again, but choose only one column.

You can create newspaper columns before or after you type the text by using the Columns command on the Format menu. If you want to format only part of the text, select the text before you follow the steps.

To create newspaper columns by using the Columns command, follow these steps:

1. Open the Format menu.

2. Choose the Columns command.

The Columns dialog box appears. You can see the effect of your choices in the Sample box.

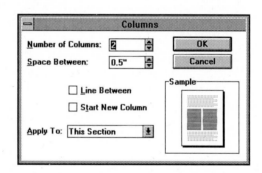

3. In the Number of Columns box, type a number of columns or click the arrows to increase or decrease the current number.

4. In the Space Between box, type an amount of space between columns or click the arrows to increase or decrease the current amount of space.

5. From the Apply To list box, choose whether you want to apply the column formatting to the entire document, the current section, or from the insertion point forward. If you selected text before opening the Columns dialog box, you also can choose to apply the column formatting to the selected text. If you choose to format the selected text, Word for Windows inserts section breaks before and after the text.

The Line Between and Start New Column check boxes are discussed later in this section.

Working with the Ruler

When you work with text in multiple columns, the Ruler displays settings for the column containing the insertion point. If you create two columns and then position the insertion point in the first column, you will see 0 at the left edge of the Ruler, which is also the left edge of the first column. If you position the insertion point in the second column, you will see 0 near the center of the Ruler, indicating the left edge of the second column. In this case, the numbers above the first column are negative.

To use the Ruler in newspaper columns, the Ruler should display the Margin scale.

Left column margins —

Right column margins

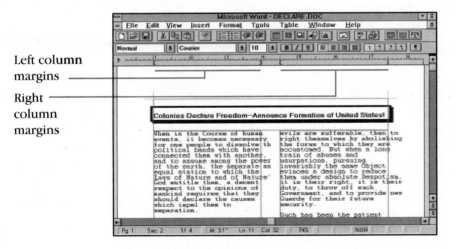

You set the Ruler to the Margin scale by clicking the scale symbol.

To change outside margins or column widths by using the Ruler, follow these steps.

1. Open the View menu.
2. Choose the Page Layout command.
3. Drag a column margin marker ([or]) on the Ruler to set a new margin or column width.

   Word for Windows automatically adjusts the other columns and the space between columns to accommodate your changes.

To keep the space between the columns uniform, but also change it from the default of .5 inch, you use the Columns dialog box. Follow these steps:

1. Open the Format menu.
2. Choose the Columns command.

    The Columns dialog box appears.

3. In the Space Between text box, type the amount of space you want between the columns or click the arrows to increase or decrease the current amount of space.

Controlling Breaks

With respect to the amount of text in a column or on a page, Word for Windows works in multiple columns just as it works in a single column. The program calculates the amount of space available and wraps to the next column or next page as needed. You can, however, influence where soft breaks occur by using the pagination features of paragraph formatting discussed in Chapter 6. You also can insert hard column and page breaks.

You can insert a column break in three ways:

Press Ctrl + ⇧Shift + ⏎Enter.

Or, follow these steps:

1. Open the View menu.
2. Choose the Page Layout command to see the columns side by side.
3. Position the insertion point where you want the new column to start.
4. Open the Insert menu.
5. Choose the Break command.
6. Choose the Column Break option button.
7. Choose OK.

Or, follow these steps:

1. Open the Format menu.
2. Choose the Columns command.
3. Choose the Start New Column check box.

You can insert a page break in two ways:

Press Ctrl + ⏎Enter.

172

Or, follow these steps:

1. Open the View menu and choose the Page Layout command.
2. Position the insertion point where you want the new page to start.
3. Open the Insert menu and choose the Break command.
4. Choose the Page Break option button.
5. Choose OK.

Balancing Text in Columns

You often find that the last page of a document is not a full page. Because Word for Windows fills each column before moving to the next, the last page of a document may have, for example, one long column and one short column. You can have Word for Windows evenly distribute the text between the two columns by inserting an extra continuous section break.

To balance text in columns on the last page of a document, follow these steps:

1. Position the insertion point at the end of the text you want to balance.
2. Open the Insert menu.
3. Choose the Break command.
4. In the Section Break box, choose the Continuous option button.
5. Choose OK.

Using Vertical Lines for Special Effects

You can create special effects in your columns by placing a vertical line between columns. You can apply vertical lines to the whole document or to only part of the document. The vertical lines are as long as the longest column on the page.

To place a vertical line between columns, follow these steps:

1. Position the insertion point in the section where you want to place vertical lines between columns.
2. Open the Format menu.
3. Choose the Columns command.
4. Choose the Line Between check box.

To see the vertical lines, choose the Print Preview command from the File menu.

Chapter Summary

In this chapter, you learned how to set up documents by using page and section formatting. Specifically, you learned the following information:

- You can set margins, paper size, paper orientation, and paper source by using the Page Setup command on the Format menu. You also can set margins by using the Ruler or the Print Preview command on the File menu.

- You can control pagination by using the Page Numbers command and the Breaks command on the Insert menu.

- You can create headers and footers by using the Header/Footer command on the View menu. You can insert page numbers, the date, the time, or text into a header or a footer.

- You can create footnotes or endnotes by using the Footnote command on the Insert menu. You can find a specific footnote by using the Go To command on the Edit menu or F5, the Go To key.

- You can number paragraphs and create bullets by using the Toolbar or the Bullets and Numbering command on the Tools menu.

- You can insert a date or time into a document by using the Date and Time command on the Insert menu. Word for Windows updates the date or time each time you print the document or update the field by pressing F9.

- You can create sections by using the Section Layout command on the Format menu. You can format a section just as you format a document. You also can set the vertical alignment and line numbering for the section by using the Section Layout command on the Format menu.

- You can create and work with newspaper columns by using the Toolbar or the Columns command on the Format menu.

In Chapter 8, you will learn how to manage and print your files.

Managing and Printing Your Files

As you work in Word for Windows, you will create many documents, some with information you want to reuse. As the number of documents grows, you will find it more difficult to identify specific documents or even to remember the contents of a particular document. You will find it harder to find the one document that contains the information you need for the current report.

Word for Windows provides some features specifically designed to help you manage documents. In this chapter, you will learn how to use these features to open, delete, copy, and print one or more documents. You also will learn how to specify print options so that you can print one page or several pages of a document.

Creating summary information

Finding files

Printing documents

Key Terms in This Chapter

Summary information	Information you supply to Word for Windows about a document. Word for Windows can use this information when searching for documents.
Keywords	One kind of summary information you can supply about a document. Word for Windows can search for all documents that have the keywords you specify.
Path	The DOS term that represents the location of a file. The path generally consists of a drive name (such as a:, b:, or c:) and directory name(s) separated by the backslash (\) character.
Active document	The document that contains the insertion point. Unless you have divided the screen into multiple windows, the active document is the document you are currently viewing on-screen.
Printer graphics resolution	A term that describes how clearly a document will print. Because resolution is based on the number of dots per inch (dpi), higher resolution numbers indicate better clarity.

Creating Summary Information

In the Summary Info dialog box, you can store information about a document that will help you to identify the document and to find that document later. You can save a title that is longer than the document name as well as subject information and keywords. You can record the author of the document and any comments about the document. In addition to the information you supply about a document, Word for Windows maintains certain statistics about each document: the date the document was created, the date it was last saved, the date it was last printed, and so on. Word for Windows automatically updates these statistics each time you open, save, or print a document; you also can choose to update the information at other times.

By default, Word for Windows displays the Summary Info dialog box the first time you save a document. Although entering the summary information takes a few extra moments initially, having this information can save you a great deal of time later (when you are trying to find a particular file).

Note: You can turn off this option by using Options command on the Tools menu. See Chapter 9 for more information.

Later, you may want to add to or change the summary information you supplied when you first saved the document. To edit the summary information or update the document statistics, you can open the Summary Info dialog box directly by choosing the Summary Info command from the File menu. You also can open the Summary Info dialog box by using the Find File command, but you cannot update the document statistics in this way.

To open the Summary Info dialog box, follow these steps:

1. Open the File menu.

2. Choose the Summary Info command.

The Summary Info dialog box appears.

At the top of the dialog box, you see the DOS file name and directory for the document. You cannot change this information in the Summary Info dialog box. (To change the name or directory of the document, you can use the Find File command on the File menu or use DOS).

You don't have to complete *every* text box in the Summary Info dialog box. The more information you include, however, the easier it will be to find the file later. In each text box, you can enter up to 255 characters of descriptive information.

Use the Title text box to enter a document name that is longer than the DOS file name. In the Subject text box, enter a description of the document. In the Author text box, Word for Windows automatically enters the name you supplied when you installed the program (see Appendix A for installation information), but you can change this name. In the Keywords text box, enter any words that represent important information or general topics in the document. You can, but don't have to, separate the words with commas; character case is not important. In the Comments text box, fill in any other information that might help you to locate this document later.

To see the statistics for this document, choose the Statistics button.

The Document Statistics dialog box appears.

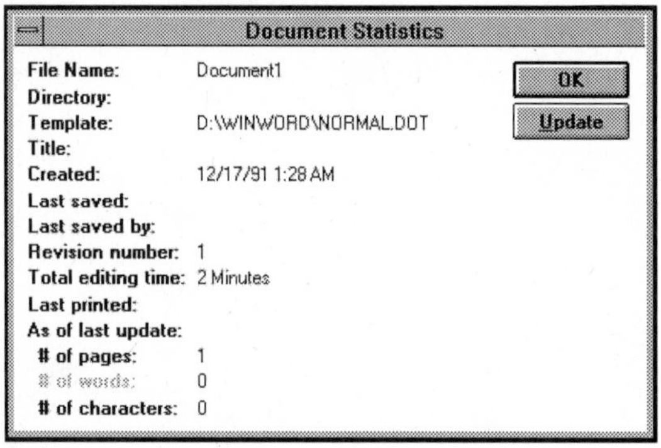
Document Statistics
File Name: Document1
Directory:
Template: D:\WINWORD\NORMAL.DOT
Title:
Created: 12/17/91 1:28 AM
Last saved:
Last saved by:
Revision number: 1
Total editing time: 2 Minutes
Last printed:
As of last update:
# of pages: 1
# of words: 0
# of characters: 0
OK
Update

You cannot enter or edit the document statistics. Word for Windows updates the statistics automatically (when you open, save, or print the document) or when you choose the Update button in the Document Statistics dialog box.

Most of the document statistics are self-explanatory. The Total editing time is the number of minutes the document has been open during all editing sessions. The Revision number is the number of times you saved the document. The Last printed information is the date and time you last printed the document *when the document was open*. Later in this chapter, you will learn that you can print a document without opening it. If you print the document without opening it, Word for Windows does not update the statistics. Also later in this chapter, you will learn how to print the summary information and document statistics with the document or separately.

Finding Files

By using the Find File command, you can view information about Word for Windows documents without opening them. You can search for documents and view and edit summary information. You also can open, print, delete, copy, and preview documents.

To open the Find File dialog box, follow these steps:

1. Open the **F**ile menu.
2. Choose the **F**ind File command.

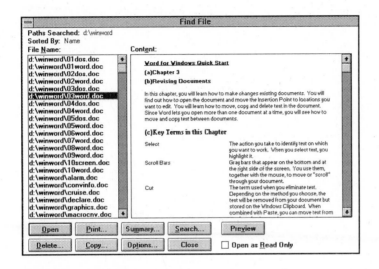

The Find File dialog box appears.

The first time you open the Find File dialog box, Word for Windows lists all documents stored in Word for Windows format on the current path. You can see the paths Word for Windows searched and the sort criteria at the top of the dialog box. In the File **N**ame list box, Word for Windows lists the complete DOS path name, including any directories, for each document (so that you can see the location of the documents). By default, Word for Windows highlights the first document in the File **N**ame list box and displays the highlighted document's contents in the Content box.

Note: If you display a document that is not in Word for Windows format and that contains graphics, choose the Preview command button to see the document accurately.

At the bottom of the dialog box are the **O**pen, **P**rint, **D**elete, and **C**opy command buttons you can use to manage documents and the Su**m**mary command button you can use to open the Summary Info dialog box.

The **O**pen command button performs the same function as the **O**pen command on the **F**ile menu and the Open button on the Toolbar. The **P**rint command button enables you to print one or more files. Printing is covered in detail later in this chapter.

8

Deleting a File

The **Delete** command button enables you to delete one or more files. When you choose a file and then choose the **Delete** button, Word for Windows opens a dialog box that displays that file's complete path and file name and asks you to confirm that you want to delete the file. To delete the file, choose the **Yes** button. If you don't want to delete the file, choose the **No** button or press Esc. If you are not sure why this dialog box appeared, you can choose the **Help** button.

Copying a File

The **Copy** command button enables you to copy one or more files to a different directory or drive. You can use this command button, for example, if you want to copy a document to a floppy disk in drive A.

When you use the **Copy** command button, you cannot enter a new name for a file. If you want to change the name of a file, open the file and then choose the **Save As** command from the **File** menu. Provide a new name for the file in the Save As dialog box and save the file. Then, close the original file (the one with the old name), and delete it by opening the Find File dialog box and following the directions for deleting a file.

Sorting Files

The Options command button in the Find File dialog box enables you to change the way Word for Windows sorts the File Name list and what information the program displays in the Content box.

When you choose the Options command button, the Options dialog box appears.

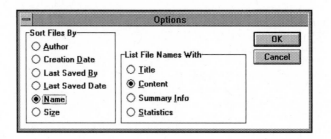

180

The Options dialog box is divided into two parts. In the Sort Files by box on the left, you can choose the method Word for Windows uses to order the files in the File Name list. In the List File Names With box on the right, you can choose what information Word for Windows displays in the Content box. If you choose Title, for example, the Content box displays *just the title of the highlighted file*. Word for Windows uses the summary information you enter to display any of the options in the List File Names With box.

Changing the Search Criteria

You can change the search criteria Word for Windows uses by choosing the Search command button.

If you choose the Search command button, the Search dialog box appears.

Most of the options in the Search dialog box are text boxes where you can type search information. In the File Name text box, you can specify the characters Word for Windows uses to search for file names. (You can use the DOS wild card characters * and ? to specify the file names.) In the Type list box, you can choose a specific type of document for which you want Word for Windows to search. If you choose to search for document templates, for example, Word for Windows automatically changes the information in the File Name text box to *.dot.

You also can change the location for the search by choosing a different drive from the Drives list box, by choosing the Edit Path command button, or by typing a DOS path name in the Path text box.

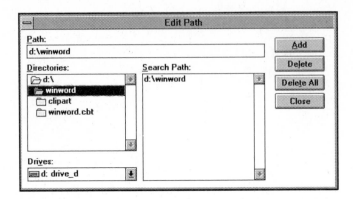

If you choose the Edit Path command button, the Edit Path dialog box appears.

Word for Windows can search more than one path for your criteria. To add or delete drives or directories you want Word for Windows to search, you use the Edit Path dialog box. After you choose the search paths, choose the Close button to return to the Search dialog box.

Word for Windows uses document summary information to search for any information you type in the Title, Subject, Keywords, Author, or Saved By text boxes or the Date Created or Date Saved boxes in the lower portion of the Search dialog box. Word for Windows searches the documents themselves for any text you type in the Any Text text box.

You use the Options list box to tell Word for Windows how to treat each additional search. If you choose Create New List, Word for Windows replaces the File Name list after each search. If you choose Add Matches to List, Word for Windows keeps all the files in the File Name list (the files that matched previous criteria) and adds the files that meet the current criteria. Adding matches to the list is effective if you want to carry out many searches with different search criteria and create one list of the results of all the searches. If you choose Search Only in List, Word for Windows searches the list of files that met the preceding criteria. Searching the list is effective when you want to narrow the number of files in order to find a particular file or a closely related group of files.

Printing Documents

You can print Word for Windows documents in many ways. You can print all of a document or part of a document. You can print more than one copy of a document. You can print more than one document at a time. You can print the summary information and statistics with the document or separately. In addition, you can print envelopes. The printing method you choose depends on what you want to print.

Note: If you have trouble printing, open and read the PRINTERS.DOC document that Microsoft shipped with Word for Windows. This document contains more than you probably want to know about printers, including common problems and their solutions.

Printing All of the Active Document

You can print all or part of the active document (the document that contains the insertion point). To print the entire document, simply choose the Print button on the Toolbar. If, however, you want to print only the current page, or just a few pages, or more than one copy of the document, use the Print dialog box.

Using the Print Dialog Box

You can print part of the active document (or print more than one copy of all or part of the active document) by choosing options in the Print dialog box. To open the Print dialog box, follow these steps:

1. Open the File menu.

2. Choose the Print command.

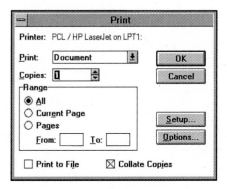

The Print dialog box appears.

Note: You also can open the Print dialog box from Print Preview mode by choosing the Print command button, but the Setup command button will not be available. For information on Print Preview mode, see Chapter 2.

8

In the Range box, you can specify the part of the document you want to print: All, Current Page or From and To. In the Copies box, you can type the number of copies you want to print or click the arrows to increase or decrease the current number.

By default, Word for Windows collates copies so that pages print in the correct order.

If you want to print the document to a file rather than to the printer, choose the Print to File check box. You may need to print to a file if you plan to send the document to a service bureau or to print the document at a computer that does not have Word for Windows. For more information about printing to a file, see *Using Word for Windows 2,* Special Edition.

Setting Print Options

If you choose the Options command button, Word for Windows displays the Print Options dialog box.

This dialog box displays the default print options set by using the Options command on the Tools menu.

The options in this dialog box are in effect every time you print a Word for Windows document. If you change these options, the new options remain in effect until you change them again. Because all the options are check boxes, you can choose more than one option at a time.

In the Printing Options box, you can choose Draft Output, which prints using the printer's draft mode. This option generally results in faster printing, but does not provide the best output quality. The Reverse Print Order option prints the pages from the last page to the first page. The Update Fields option updates any fields in your document (such as a date field) before printing.

In the Include with Document box, you can choose Summary Info to print the summary information whenever you print a document. You can choose Field Codes to print the codes instead of the results of the codes. You can choose Annotations to print any annotations in the document (see Chapter 10 for information on annotations). If you choose Hidden Text, Word for Windows prints any hidden text in the document, even if the hidden text does not appear on-screen.

In the Envelope Options box, choose the Printer's Envelope Feeder has been installed check box only if the printer has an envelope feeder.

In the Options for Current Document Only box, choose the Widow/Orphan Control check box to prevent widows and orphans. In Word for Windows, "widows" occur when the last line of a paragraph appears alone at the top of a page, and "orphans" occur when the first line of a paragraph appears alone at the bottom of a page.

When you finish choosing options, choose OK to return to the Print dialog box.

Choosing a Printer

If you have more than one printer available, you can choose a printer from the Print Setup dialog box. To open this dialog box, choose the Setup button in the Print dialog box.

Note: You can open the Print Setup dialog box directly by choosing the Print Setup command from the File menu.

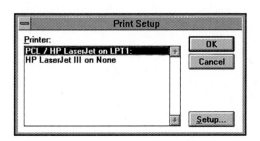

The Printer list box lists the printers you installed when you installed Windows.

Note: Installing a printer is not a Word for Windows function, but a Windows function. In Word for Windows, you can display and change printer settings, but you cannot install a printer. For more information on installing printers, see the *Windows User's Guide*.

To use a different printer, simply choose it from the Printer list box. To display or change the settings for the printer, choose the Setup command button.

Word for Windows displays a dialog box for the printer you choose.

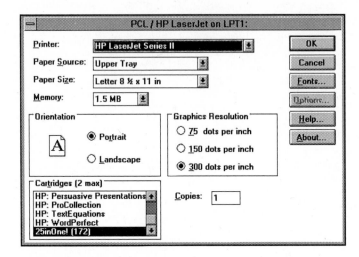

This dialog box contains all these settings established when you installed the printer in Windows. Typically, you will not change these settings.

Note: You do not need to change the printer's orientation if you changed the document's orientation by using the Page Setup command on the Format menu. If a conflict between orientation settings occurs, the Page Setup option takes precedence.

Many laser printers can use font cartridges. If you have a laser printer and a font cartridge, be sure the cartridge is highlighted in the Cartridges list box. Otherwise, you will not have access to all the fonts your printer can print.

The Graphics Resolution box enables you to determine the quality of graphics by choosing one of three resolutions. If you choose the Draft Output option in the Print Options dialog box, you should use 75 dpi. If you do not choose the Draft Output option, you should use 300 dpi. Note, however, that the higher the resolution, the longer it takes to print.

The Fonts command button enables you to install software fonts. If you purchase software fonts, follow the manufacturer's instructions for using the Printer Font Installer dialog box.

186

Printing Summary Information and Statistics

You can print summary information and statistics with the document or separately. If you choose the Annotations check box in the Print Options dialog box, Word for Windows prints summary information and statistics with every document you print. In this case, you don't need to take any special action to print the summary information and statistics whenever you print a document.

To print only the summary information for the active document, follow these steps:

1. Open the File menu.
2. Choose the Print command.

   The Print dialog box appears.
3. From the Print list box, choose Summary Info.

To print only the summary information for a document that is not open, use the Find File command on the File menu.

Printing by Using the Find File Command

8

You can print documents that are not open by using the Find File command on the File menu. You also can print more than one document at a time or print the summary information for one or more documents that are not open.

To print a document that is not open, follow these steps:

1. Open the File menu.
2. Choose the Find File command.
3. Choose the document you want to print.
4. Choose the Print button.

To print more than one document, you must choose all the documents you want to print before you choose the Print button.

To choose more than one document by using the mouse, hold down Ctrl and click the file names. If you make a mistake, hold down Ctrl and click the incorrect file name again. To choose documents listed sequentially, you also can click the first file name and then either drag the mouse pointer or hold down Shift and click the last file name to highlight the other file names.

To choose more than one document by using the keyboard, follow these steps:

1. Press ⇧Shift+F8.

2. Choose a document you want to print.

3. Press **space bar**. If you choose a document by mistake, press **space bar** again.

4. Repeat Steps 2 and 3 to choose all the documents you want to print.

5. Press ⇧Shift+F8 again.

Note: The processes for choosing multiple documents are the same for copying, deleting, and opening documents as for printing them.

Printing an Envelope

You can print envelopes easily by using the Envelope button on the Toolbar or the Create Envelope command on the Tools menu. You can, but do not have to, include a return address on the envelope. If you do include a return address, you need to type the address only the first time you print an envelope. Word for Windows stores the return address you type and uses it as the default for other envelopes.

To open the Create Envelope dialog box, do one of the following

• Choose the Envelope button on the Toolbar.

• Choose the Create Envelope command from the Tools menu.

The Create Envelope dialog box appears.

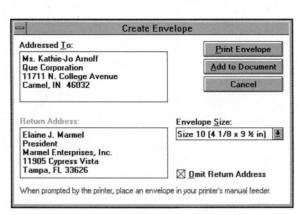

When you create an envelope, Word for Windows searches for an address in the active document and displays this address in the Addressed To box. If

Word for Windows cannot find an address, you can select the address in the document or type the name and address directly in the Addressed To box.

If you want to include a return address, type it in the Return Address box. If you want to include a return address on some (but not all) envelopes, type the address in the Return Address box now and choose the Omit Return Address check box whenever you don't want to include the return address.

If you will not be using a standard business envelope, choose the correct size from the Envelope Size list box. If you want to print the envelope now, choose the Print Envelope button. If you want to add the envelope to your document and print it later, choose the Add to Document button. When you add an envelope to a document, Word for Windows inserts the envelope at the beginning of the document (you can scroll down to see the document itself) and prints the envelope whenever you print the document.

Note: If you use a software font manager (such as Adobe Type Manager), the envelope goes through the printer, but nothing prints on the envelope. To print an envelope in Word for Windows, you must disable the software font manager and use a built-in printer font or one of the software fonts supplied with Word for Windows.

8

Chapter Summary

In this chapter, you learned how to use the Summary Info command, the Find File command, and the Print command to manage and print your documents. Specifically, you learned the following information:

- You can store a variety of information that describes your document by using the Summary Info command on the File menu.

- Word for Windows saves statistics about each document that include when it was created, when it was last printed, when it was last saved, and how many revisions have been made. You can display these statistics by choosing the Summary Info command from the File menu and then choosing the Statistics button in the Summary Info dialog box.

- You can use the Find File command on the File menu to search for, open, copy, delete, print, or preview one or more documents.

- You can print the entire active document by choosing the Print button on the Toolbar.

- You can print one or more copies of all or part of the active document by using the Print command on the File menu. You also can choose

189

whether to collate copies, print the document to a file, change the printer or printer setup, or adjust the print settings.

■ You can print the summary information and statistics whenever you print a document by choosing the Summary Info check box in the Options dialog box for printing. You can print summary information and statistics for the active document (without printing the document) by using the Print command on the File menu. You can print summary information and statistics for a document that is not open by using the Find File command on the File menu.

■ You can print Envelopes by using the Envelope button on the Toolbar or the Create Envelope command on the Tools menu.

In the next chapter, you will learn about customizing Word for Windows.

8

Customizing Word for Windows

9

To make your work easier and more efficient, you can customize Word for Windows in several ways. In this chapter, you will learn how to work with styles and document templates and how to set start-up defaults in Word for Windows.

Working with styles

Working with document templates

Choosing your start-up options

Key Terms in This Chapter

Style   A combination of character and paragraph formatting that you save in a style sheet. You can use a style, also called a *paragraph style*, to apply frequently used formatting more efficiently.

Style sheet   A collection of the different styles available in a document. You can create different style sheets for different documents.

Standard styles The styles provided by Microsoft in the template NORMAL.DOT.

Template   An empty document in which Word for Windows stores a particular style sheet and particular character, paragraph, and page settings. You can use a template, also called a *document template*, as a pattern to create similar documents.

Options   Default settings used by Word for Windows. The settings in the Options dialog box determine the way Word for Windows functions.

9

Working with Styles

In Chapter 5, you learned how to change specific character formatting. In Chapter 6, you learned how to change specific paragraph formatting. In some cases, however, you may want to use the same combination of character and paragraph formatting repeatedly. For example, you might always use 14-point, boldface, underlined Helvetica type for a certain level of heading in a document. You can copy the character and paragraph formatting, but Word for Windows provides an easier way to apply the entire combination: you can define a style to save the combination of formatting and then simply apply the style to new text whenever you need that combination.

Viewing the Standard Styles

Word for Windows provides several standard styles that are available in every document, ready for you to use.

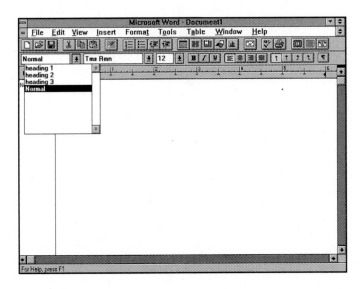

If you open the Style list box on the Ribbon (use the mouse or press Ctrl + S, ↓), you can see four standard styles.

You also can see the standard styles when you open the Style dialog box. To open the Style dialog box, follow these steps:

1. Open the Format menu.

2. Choose the Style command.

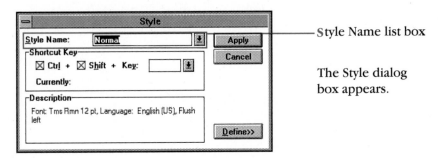

Style Name list box

The Style dialog box appears.

The collection of styles that appear in the Style Name list box (or in the Style list on the Ribbon) are the document's style sheet. If you define additional styles for the document, those styles become part of the document's style sheet. (Different documents can have different style sheets.)

To see additional standard styles in the Style dialog box, follow these steps:

1. Open the Style Name list box.

2. Press Ctrl + Y.

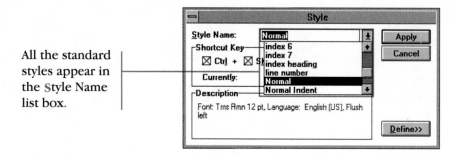

All the standard styles appear in the Style Name list box.

If you highlight different styles, you can see information about the styles in the Description box. As you become familiar with the standard styles, you may not need to define styles of your own.

Notice that the description of most standard styles begins Normal+ and then lists various formatting characteristics. This description means that the highlighted style is "based on" the Normal style, but adds some additional formatting.

Applying a Style

You can apply styles by using the Ribbon or the Style dialog box. You can type the text, select it, and then choose the style, or you can choose the style and then type the text.

To apply a style by using the Ribbon, open the Style list box and choose a style. To apply a style by using the Style dialog box, follow these steps:

1. Open the Format menu.
2. Choose the Style command.

   The Style dialog box appears.
3. Open the Style Name list box.
4. Choose a style.
5. Choose the Apply button.

Defining a New Style

The easiest way to define a style is to base the new style on text that has the formatting you want to save as a style. Word for Windows uses the formatted text as a "model" for the style.

To define a style based on formatted text, follow these steps:

1. In the document, type the text for which you want to define a style.
2. Apply all the character and paragraph formatting you want to define as the style.
3. Select the formatted text.
4. Position the insertion point in the Style list box on the Ruler (use the mouse or press Ctrl + S).
5. Type a name for the new style. The style name can have up to 24 characters, including spaces, but cannot include the backslash (\) character. Do not use a name that already exists in the Style list. (Word for Windows style names are not case-sensitive, so *Normal* and *normal* are the same name.)
6. Press ↵Enter.

You also can use the Style dialog box to create a new style before you type the text. To create a new style before you type the text, follow these steps:

1. Open the Format menu.
2. Choose the Style command.

   The Style dialog box appears.

3. Type a name for the new style in the Style Name text box. The style name can have up to 24 characters, including spaces, but cannot include the backslash (\) character. Do not use a name that already exists in the Style Name list. (Word for Windows style names are not case-sensitive, so *Normal* and *normal* are the same name.)

4. Choose the Define button.

9

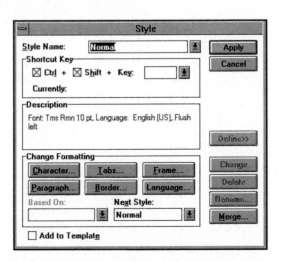

The second Style dialog box appears.

5. Use the buttons in the Change Formatting box to define the formatting for the new style:

   If you want the style to include character formatting, choose the Character button to open the Character dialog box (see Chapter 5 for more information on character formatting).

   If you want the style to include paragraph formatting, choose the Paragraph button to open the Paragraph dialog box (see Chapter 6 for more information on paragraph formatting).

   If you want the style to include tabs, choose the Tabs button to open the Tabs dialog box (see Chapter 6 for more information on tabs).

   If you want the style to include border formatting, choose the Border button to open the Border dialog box (see Chapter 6 for more information on borders).

   If you want the style to include a frame, choose the Frame button to open the Frame dialog box (see Chapter 12 for more information on frames).

   If you want the style to include foreign language formatting, choose the Language button to open the Language dialog box (see Chapter 4 for more information on foreign language formatting).

6. When you finish defining the formatting for the new style, choose one of the following buttons:

   Choose the Add button to add the new style to the list without applying its formatting to the paragraph containing the insertion point. Then, choose the Close button to close the Style dialog box.

   Choose the Apply button to add the new style to the list and apply its formatting to the paragraph containing the insertion point.

   Choose the Cancel button to ignore the formatting choices.

Assigning a Keyboard Shortcut to a Style

If you would prefer to apply styles by pressing key combinations rather than by choosing styles from the Style list, you can assign keyboard shortcuts to the styles.

To assign a keyboard shortcut to a style, follow these steps:

1. Open the Format menu.
2. Choose the Style command.

   The Style dialog box appears.

9

3. From the Style Name list box, choose the style to which you want to assign a keyboard shortcut.

4. In the Shortcut Key box, choose the key combination you want to assign to the style.

   If you leave the Ctrl and Shift check boxes turned on, you must press Ctrl + Shift + the key you type in the Key list box to apply the style. Alternatively, you can choose the Ctrl or Shift check box (to turn off the key) so that you press Shift + the key or Ctrl + the key in order to apply the style.

   Note: If the key combination you choose is already assigned to another function in Word for Windows, that function appears next to Currently. Choose another key combination.

5. Choose the Apply button.

To use the keyboard shortcut to apply the style, follow these steps:

1. Select the text to which you want to apply the style or position the insertion point where you want to type the text.

2. Press the key combination.

Modifying Styles

9

You can modify a style by using correctly formatted text as a model or by directly changing specific formatting characteristics of the style. If you use correctly formatted text as a model, you can use the Ribbon to modify the style. If you want to change the formatting characteristics of the style, you must use the Style dialog box.

To use the Ribbon to modify a style, follow these steps:

1. Apply the correct character and paragraph formatting to the text you want to use as a model.

   Note: If you want to modify one of the standard styles by using the Ribbon, you first must use that standard style in your document.

2. Select the correctly formatted text.

3. From the Ribbon's Style list box, choose the style you want to modify.

A dialog box asks
whether you want
to redefine the
style.

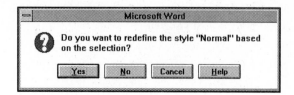

4. Choose Yes to modify the style.

You also can modify a style by choosing the Define button from the Style
dialog box and then choosing buttons in the Change Formatting box. To
modify a style by using the Style dialog box, follow these steps:

1. Open the Format menu.

2. Choose the Style command.

   The Style dialog box appears.

3. From the Style Name list box, choose the style you want to modify.

4. Choose the Define button.

   The second Style dialog box appears.

5. Use the buttons in the Change Formatting box to modify the style. For
   more information, see the steps for defining a new style.

6. Choose the Change button.

7. If you want to apply the modified style to all paragraphs formatted
   with that style and to the paragraph containing the insertion point,
   choose the Apply button.

   Or

   Choose the Close button.

Tip: In the Style dialog box, you can modify one of the standard styles by
pressing Ctrl+Y (to display all the standard styles in the Style Name list
box), choosing the style you want to change, and then following steps 4
through 8 in the preceding set of steps. When you choose the Change button,
a dialog box asks you to confirm the modification to a standard style.

Deleting Styles

You can delete a style from the style sheet list by using the Style dialog box.
Follow these steps:

1. Open the Format menu.

2. Choose the Style command.

The Style dialog box appears.

3. From the Style Name list box, choose the style you want to delete.

4. Choose the Define button.

The second Style dialog box appears.

5. Choose the Delete button.

A dialog box asks you to confirm the deletion.

6. Choose Yes.

7. Choose the Close button.

Any text formatted with the style you deleted reverts to Normal style.

Renaming Styles

If you don't want to change the formatting of a style, but you want to change the style name, follow these steps:

1. Open the Format menu.

2. Choose the Style command.

The Style dialog box appears.

3. From the Style Name list box, choose the style you want to rename.

4. Choose the Define button.

The second Style dialog box appears.

5. Choose the Rename button.

The Rename Style dialog box appears.

6. Type the new name in the New Style Name text box.

7. Choose OK.

8. Choose the Close button.

Printing the Style Sheet

To print a style sheet (the style names and the descriptions that appears in the Description box of the Style dialog box), follow these steps:

1. Open the File menu.

2. Choose the Print command.

3. From the Print list box, choose Styles.

9

4. Choose OK.

Word for Windows prints the style names and descriptions for the active document only.

Basing One Style on Another

Earlier in this chapter, you learned that the descriptions of most standard styles include the settings in the Normal style. Normal+ indicates that these styles are based on the Normal style. If you were to change the Normal style, Word for Windows would also change all styles based on the Normal style.

You can use this feature of Word for Windows to link styles by using a particular style as the "base style." Then, when you change the base style, Word for Windows changes all styles based on that style in exactly the same way. Suppose, for example, that you want all headings to appear in 14-point boldface Helvetica type and that you want to underline the first-level headings, but not the second-level headings. You create the style for the first-level headings just as you create any style. Then, for the second-level headings, you create another style based on the style for the first-level headings.

To create a style based on an existing style, follow these steps:

1. Position the insertion point in a paragraph formatted with the "base style." In the example, you position the insertion point in a first-level heading.
2. Open the Format menu.
3. Choose the Style command.

   The Style dialog box appears.
4. Type a name for the second style in the Style Name list box.
5. Choose the Define button.

   The second Style dialog box appears. In the Based On list box, you can see the name of the first style.
6. Modify the style by using the buttons in the Change Formatting box. For the example, you choose the Character button and then remove the underlining.
7. Choose the Add button.
8. Choose the Close button.

You have now created one style based on another. If you later decide to make the same change to both styles, you simply modify the base style. In the

9

example, if you decide to change all the headings to 16-point type, you modify the style for the first-level heading. Word for Windows changes the base style and all styles based on that style in exactly the same way.

Making One Style Follow Another

Word for Windows also enables you to make one style immediately follow another style. For example, when you type a letter, you type the date, then the inside address, and then the salutation. You can tell Word for Windows to make your address style follow your date style and to make your salutation style follow your address style.

To make one style automatically follow another, follow these steps:

1. Position the insertion point in a paragraph formatted with the style that appears first.

2. Open the Format menu.

3. Choose the Style command.

   The Style dialog box appears.

4. Choose the Define button.

   The second Style dialog box appears.

5. From the Next Style list box, choose the style you want to follow the style of the paragraph containing the insertion point.

6. Choose the Apply button.

   A dialog box asks you to confirm the change.

7. Choose Yes.

Note: You will find that you use some styles, such as Normal style, more continuously than other styles, such as Heading 1. For this reason, the Normal style is its own Next Style.

Adding Styles to a Template

When you create a new style, you are creating that style for the active document. When you save the active document, you save the style *for that document only*. You may find that you want some styles you create to be available whenever you use the current template. To accomplish this, you can add your styles to the template's style sheet.

9

To add a style to the current template, follow these steps:

1. Open the Format menu.
2. Choose the Style command.

   The Style dialog box appears.
3. From the Style Name list, choose the style you want to add to the template's style sheet.
4. Choose the Define button.

   The second Style dialog box appears.
5. Choose the Add to Template check box.

The Add to Template check box is at the bottom of the second Style dialog box.

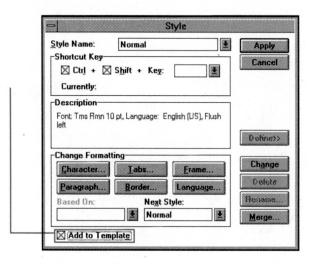

6. Choose the Change button.
7. Choose the Close button.

Merging Styles between Templates and Documents

As you create a document, you may change existing styles as well as add new styles. You then may decide that you want to record your changes in the template for the document. In the preceding section, you learned to add styles to the current template. Now, you will learn how to update the template with the changes you make.

When you change a style and then save the document, Word for Windows stores the changes with the document, not with the template. Word for Windows does, however, enable you to store modified styles in the current template or in another document by "merging" the styles. At the end of this section, you will learn how to merge styles between documents. First, you need to learn how to merge styles between the active document and its template.

You can merge styles in two directions: to the template or from the template. When you merge styles from the active document *to* its template, Word for Windows copies the styles of the active document into the template. If any styles exist both in the document and in the template, the document's version *replaces* the version in the template. In addition, Word for Windows adds to the template any styles from the active document that do not exist in the template. Word for Windows does not alter any styles in the template that have unique style names.

Note: Remember, style names are not case-sensitive, so *normal* and *Normal* are the same style. Word for Windows will *replace* one with the other.

To merge styles from a document to its template, follow these steps:

1. Open the document whose style sheet you want to merge to its template.
2. Open the Format menu.
3. Choose the Style command.

   The Style dialog box appears.
4. Choose the Define button.

   The second Style dialog box appears.
5. Choose the Merge button.

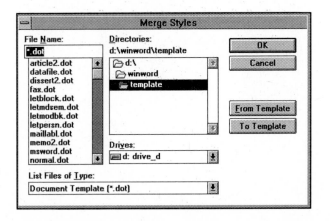

The Merge Styles dialog box appears.

6. Select the template to which the document is attached.

7. Choose the To Template button.

   A dialog box asks you to confirm that you want to replace the styles in the template with the styles from the active document.

8. Choose Yes to continue.

9. Choose the Close button.

If you want to merge the styles of a document to a different template, you must first attach the document to that template or create a new template. See the later sections of this chapter for more information on document templates.

When you merge *from* the template, Word for Windows copies the styles of the template into the active document. If any styles exist in the template *and* in the document, the template's version *replaces* the version in the active document. In addition, Word for Windows adds to the active document's style sheet any styles from the template that do not exist in the document. Word for Windows does not alter any styles in the active document that have unique style names.

Note: Remember, style names are not case-sensitive, so *normal* and *Normal* are the same style. Word for Windows will *replace* one with the other.

To merge styles to a document from a template, follow these steps:

1. Make sure that the document to which you want to merge styles is active.

2. Open the Format menu.

3. Choose the Style command.

   The Style dialog box appears.

4. Choose the Define button.

   The second Style dialog box appears.

5. Choose the Merge button.

   The Merge Styles dialog box appears.

6. Choose the template from which you want to copy styles. You can merge styles from the document's template or from another template.

7. Choose the From Template button.

   A dialog box asks you to confirm that you want to replace styles of the same name.

8. Choose Yes to continue.

9. Choose the Close button.

To merge styles between documents, follow these steps:

1. Make sure that the document *to* which you want to merge styles is active.

2. Open the Format menu.

3. Choose the Style command.

   The Style dialog box appears.

4. Choose the Define button.

   The second Style dialog box appears.

5. Choose the Merge button.

   The Merge Styles dialog box appears.

6. From the List Files of Type list box, choose Word Document (*.doc).

7. From the File Name list box, choose the document *from* which you want to copy styles.

8. Choose the From Template button.

   A dialog box asks you to confirm that you want to replace styles of the same name.

9. Choose Yes to continue.

10. Choose the Close button.

9

Manual v. Automatic Formatting

The formatting techniques you learned in Chapters 5 and 6 are examples of "manual formatting." In this chapter, you have been learning to use "automatic formatting" by using styles. You can combine automatic and manual formatting, but be aware that you may create inconsistencies within the document.

If you apply a style and then apply manual formatting to the same paragraph, the manual formatting essentially "overrides" the formatting of the style. For example, if the style does not include indentation but you add indentation, you are adding indentation to the appearance of the paragraph, but you are not affecting the style definition.

If you apply a style to a paragraph that already contains manual formatting, the style "overrides" the manual formatting in the paragraph; that is, the paragraph loses the manual formatting and assumes the characteristics of the style.

Character attributes such as boldface and underlining behave as toggle switches—choosing the character attribute one time turns it on and choosing the same attribute a second time turns it off. If you combine manual character formatting with automatic character formatting, the results will vary. The amount of manually formatted text in the paragraph determines the effect of applying a style that contains character formatting.

If you manually apply a character format such as underlining to a small part of a paragraph and then apply a style that contains underlining, the text you manually formatted with underlining loses its underline, but the other text becomes underlined. If, however, you manually apply underlining to a large part of the paragraph and then apply a style that contains underlining, all text in the paragraph becomes underlined.

To remove manual formatting from a paragraph, select the paragraph and press [Ctrl]+space bar.

Working with Document Templates

When you installed Word for Windows, you had the option of installing the templates provided by Microsoft. If you chose to install these templates, you have available more than a dozen templates that can provide the basis for many different kinds of documents, including reports, letters, and memos. These templates can save you time when you format documents. Table 9.1 provides a list of the templates and of the description Microsoft supplied for each template in its summary information.

Table 9.1
Document Templates

Name	Description
ARTICLE2	Create an article manuscript for publication.
DATAFILE	Print Merge Data/Header File Template.
DISSERT2	Create an academic dissertation.
FAX	Create a cover sheet for a fax.
LETBLOCK	Create a block letter.
LETMDSEM	Create a modified semi-block letter.

9

Name	Description
LETMODBK	Create a modified block letter.
LETPERSN	Create a personal letter.
MAILLABL	(No description supplied—creates mailing labels.)
MEMO2	Create a business memo.
MSWORD	Word for DOS key mappings.
NORMAL	Default template for new documents.
OVERHEAD	Create a set of slides for an overhead projector presentation.
PRESS	Create a press release.
PROPOSAL	Create a business proposal.
REPLAND	Create a business report with the pages in landscape orientation (wider than they are tall).
REPSIDE	Create a business report with sideheads (headings which are printed to the left of the text).
REPSTAND	Create a business report with the pages in standard, portrait orientation (taller than they are wide).
TERM2	Create an academic term paper.

9

Just as Word for Windows documents have the default extension DOC, Word for Windows templates have the default extension DOT.

If you chose not to install the templates supplied by Microsoft, you still installed a template called NORMAL.DOT. As you learned in Chapter 2, Word for Windows bases all new documents on the NORMAL.DOT template unless you choose a different template. NORMAL.DOT is a special template in which Word for Windows stores items that are "globally" available—that is, items that are available for all documents, regardless of the template on which a document is based. These items include Toolbar options (discussed later in this chapter) and macros (see Chapter 13 for more information on macros).

Choosing a Template for a New Document

Whenever you create a document, you base it on a template. If you don't choose a template, Word for Windows chooses NORMAL.DOT for you. You can choose a template other than NORMAL.DOT by using the New command on the File menu.

In the New dialog box, the available templates appear in the Use Template list box.

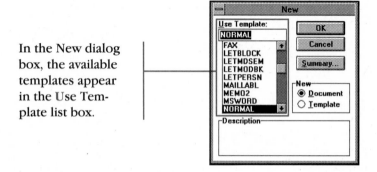

Choose the template you want to use from the Use Template list box. If you highlight a template before you choose it, a brief description of that template appears in the Description box.

Attaching a Document to a Different Template

Sometimes, you may start a document based on one template (such as NORMAL.DOT), then later decide that you want to use a different template. You can change the template by following these steps:

1. Open the File menu.
2. Choose the Template command.

   The Template dialog box appears.
3. Open the Attach Document To list box.
4. Choose a different template for the document.

Modifying a Template

You can modify a template just as you can modify a document. You open the template, make changes to it, and then save it. Just be aware that if you type text while working in a template, you are adding that text to the template. In other words, that text becomes *boilerplate text*, which appears whenever you use the template to create a new document.

To modify a template, follow these steps:

1. Open the File menu.
2. Choose the Open command.

   The Open dialog box appears.
3. From the List Files of Type list box, choose Document Templates.

   In the File Names list box, Word for Windows displays only those files that have the extension DOT.
4. Choose the template you want to modify.
5. Choose OK.
6. Make changes to the template as you would change any document.
7. Save the template (by using the Toolbar or the File menu).

You also can change the character, page setup, or language formatting in a template by modifying a document based on the template. The Character, Page Setup, and Language dialog boxes each include a Use as Default command button. To modify the character, page setup, or language formatting of a template, open a document on which that template is based. Then, open the appropriate dialog box, make the changes, and choose the Use as Default button. When you choose this button, Word for Windows displays a dialog box asking you to confirm that you want to change the document template. Choose Yes.

Creating a New Template

You can create a new template in two ways:

- You can modify an existing template and then save the modified template under a new name.
- You can convert a document to a template and then save the template.

9

To create a new template by modifying an existing template, follow the steps for modifying a template (in the preceding section), but choose the Save As command from the File menu the first time you save the new template. Type a name for the new template and choose OK. Word for Windows displays the Summary Info dialog box. You can use summary information for templates just as you use summary information for documents, so take a few minutes to complete the information.

You also can choose to create a new template based on an existing template. This process is very similar to modifying an existing template. Follow these steps:

1. Open the File menu.
2. Choose the New command.

    The New dialog box appears.

3. From the Use Template list box, choose the existing template on which you want to base the new template.
4. In the New box, choose Template.
5. Choose OK.
6. Make any changes to the existing template.
7. Open the File menu again.
8. Choose the Save or Save As command.

    Word for Windows displays the Save As dialog box.

9. Type a name for the new template.
10. Choose OK.

To convert an existing document to a template, follow these steps:

1. Open the document on which you want to base the new template.
2. Make any changes, including deleting any text you don't want to include in every new document based on the template.
3. Open the File menu.
4. Choose the Save As command.
5. Type a name for the new template.
6. From the Save File as Type list box, choose Document Template (*.dot).
7. Choose OK.

9

Choosing Start-Up Options

The last way in which you can customize Word for Windows is by using the Options command on the Tools menu. These options enable you to set program defaults—the way Word for Windows behaves and appears every time you use the program. You can decide, for example, how your screen looks, what buttons appear on the Toolbar, and what options Word for Windows uses when saving your documents.

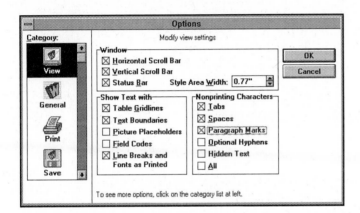

When you choose the Options command from the Tools menu, the Options dialog box appears.

9

From the Category box, you choose the aspect of Word for Windows for which you want to set defaults. From the rest of the dialog box, you choose default options (and then choose OK to save your choices). These choices remain in effect until you change them again.

This book does not cover setting options for all categories, but focuses on the options you probably will use most frequently. For example, you learned in Chapter 2 about setting the options Word for Windows uses when saving documents. You learned in Chapter 8 about setting the options Word for Windows uses for printing. In this chapter, you will learn about setting options for the following categories:

- View
- General
- Spelling
- User Info
- Toolbar

See *Using Word for Windows 2,* Special Edition, or the *Word for Windows User's Guide* for information on options not covered here.

Setting View Options

You use the View options to set defaults for displaying text and the window area. When Word for Windows first opens the Options dialog box, the View category is highlighted and the View options appear in the rest of the dialog box.

In the Window box, you use the Horizontal Scroll Bar or Vertical Scroll Bar check boxes to display or hide the scroll bars at the bottom and right side of each window. You use the Status Bar check box to display or hide the status bar. Normally, you display both scroll bars and the status bar. You also can determine the width of the style area—choosing 0 inches in the Style Area Width box eliminates the display of the style area.

In the Show Text with box, you use the Table Gridlines check box to display or hide each cell's borders (see Chapter 11 for more information on tables). You use the Text Boundaries check box to display or hide the lines around page margins in Page Layout View. Normally, you display the table gridlines and, in Page Layout View, the text boundaries.

If you choose the Picture Placeholders check box, Word for Windows displays a box instead of the graphic whenever you insert a graphic into a document. This option can make moving around in a document faster. If you choose the Field Codes check box, Word for Windows displays the formulas (field codes) rather than the results of the fields.

Choosing the Line Breaks and Fonts as Printed check box ensures that what you see on-screen matches what will print as closely as possible. Choosing this option helps to eliminate surprises when you choose, for example, a font that your printer can't print. Word for Windows displays the text and breaks in an available font that is similar to the font you chose.

In the Nonprinting Characters box, you can choose to display characters that represent Tabs, Spaces, Paragraph Marks, Optional Hyphens, Hidden Text, or All (of the above). Displaying some or all of these options can make editing easier.

9

Setting General Options

You use the General options to set defaults for general editing features.

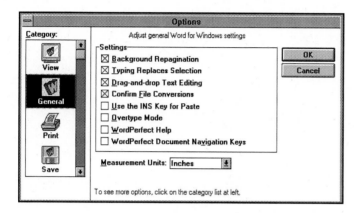

To display the General options, choose the General category.

You use the **B**ackground Repagination check box to tell Word for Windows whether to repaginate documents as you type. You use the **T**yping Replaces Selection check box to tell Word for Windows whether to delete selected text as soon as you start to type. The **D**rag-and-drop Text Editing check box determines whether Word for Windows enables you to move text by dragging it from one location to another.

Whenever you open a document that was not created in Word for Windows, the program converts that document to Word for Windows format. If you choose the Confirm **F**ile Conversions check box, Word for Windows enables you to verify the original file type before the program converts the file.

Choosing the **U**se The INS Key for Paste check box enables you to copy the contents of the Clipboard into your document by pressing [Ins] as well as by choosing the Paste button on the Toolbar or the **P**aste command from the **E**dit menu.

As you learned in Chapter 2, Word for Windows automatically inserts text at the insertion point and moves any existing text to the right. You also learned that you can make Word for Windows replace existing text rather than move it to the right by pressing [Ins] to switch to Overtype mode. Choosing the **O**vertype Mode check box makes **O**vertype mode the default mode.

Choosing the **W**ordPerfect Help check box makes WordPerfect Help available (see Chapter 1 for more information on WordPerfect Help). Choosing the

9

WordPerfect Document Navigation Keys check box makes the directional keys
(⬆, ⬇, ⬅, ➡, Home, End, PgUp, PgDn, and Esc) operate as they do in
WordPerfect.

From the Measurement Units list box, you can choose the default unit of
measure that appears in dialog boxes and on the Ruler. You can choose
Inches, Centimeters, Picas, or Points. The initial Word for Windows default is
Inches.

Setting Spelling Options

You use the options in the Spelling category to tell Word for Windows how to
check spelling.

To display the
Spelling options,
choose the
Spelling category.

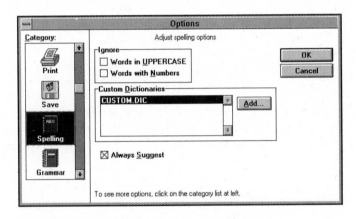

You can choose the Words in UPPERCASE or Words with Numbers check box
to make Word for Windows always ignore words in all uppercase letters (such
as acronyms) or words that include numbers (such as 1st). In the Custom
Dictionaries list box, you can tell Word for Windows to always use certain
custom dictionaries. Also, you can use the Always Suggest check box to choose
whether Word for Windows suggests alternative spellings whenever it encounters a misspelled word.

Setting User Information Options

You established certain User Info when you installed Word for Windows. You
can use the User Info category to change the name or initials of the user and
to enter a mailing address.

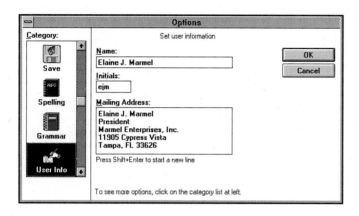

To display the User Info options, choose the User Info category.

The Name text box contains the name that appears in the Summary Info dialog box (see Chapter 8 for more information). The Initials text box contains the initials that appear in annotations (see Chapter 10 for more information). The Mailing Address text box contains the return address that appears on envelopes (if you choose to print a return address).

Setting Toolbar Options

You use the Toolbar category to customize the Toolbar. You can decide what buttons appear on the Toolbar and what commands or macros those buttons execute. To display the Toolbar options, choose the Toolbar category.

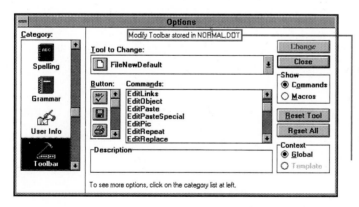

Word for Windows stores any changes you make to the Toolbar options in the active template.

9

215

When you are working with the Normal template, the Template option in the Context box is unavailable. (When you work in the Normal template, the changes you make are automatically *global*—available in all documents.) When you are working in any other template, you can choose the Template option in order to make your changes affect only the documents attached to that template.

You can change the tool that appears on a certain Toolbar button or you can change the action Word for Windows performs when you choose the Toolbar button. You also can add Word for Windows commands or macros to the Toolbar (see Chapter 13 for more information on macros).

To undo your last action, choose the Reset Tool command button. To undo all your actions and return the Toolbar to its original state (as it appeared when you first installed Word for Windows), choose the Reset All command button.

To change the tool that appears on a Toolbar button, follow these steps:

1. Open the Tool to Change list box.

   Word for Windows lists the buttons currently on the Toolbar and the commands they perform. The first button, for example, opens a new document based on the NORMAL.DOT template. Next to that button, you see FileNewDefault, which identifies the menu, the command, and the template that Word for Windows uses when you choose this button.

2. From the Tool to Change list box, choose the tool you want to replace.

3. From the Button list box, choose the button you want to substitute for the tool you chose in step 2.

4. Choose the Change command button.

5. When you finish making changes, choose the Close command button.

Before you change the action Word for Windows performs when you choose a Toolbar button, you need to understand that you can assign two kinds of actions to the Toolbar: commands and macros. You will learn more about macros in Chapter 13. When you first install Word for Windows, all buttons on the Toolbar represent Word for Windows commands.

To change the command that Word for Windows performs when you choose a Toolbar button, follow these steps:

1. In the Show box, choose Commands.

   All the Word for Windows menu commands appear alphabetically in the Commands list box.

9

2. From the Tool to Change list, choose the tool you want to change.

3. From the Commands list, choose the command you want that tool to execute.

4. If you also want to change the button, choose a new button for the tool from the Button list.

5. Choose the Change button.

6. When you finish making changes, choose the Close button.

If you want to *add* a button to the Toolbar, follow these steps:

1. In the Show box, choose Commands.

2. Open the Tools to Change list. Notice that the list contains several options called [space]. Each corresponds to a space that currently exists on the Toolbar.

3. Choose the [space] option closest to the location where you want to add the button.

4. From the Button list, choose a button to represent the tool you want to add.

5. From the Commands list, choose the command you want Word for Windows to execute when you choose that button.

6. Choose the Change button.

7. When you finish making changes, choose the Close button.

Chapter Summary

In this chapter, you learned how to customize Word for Windows by using styles, document templates, and default options. Specifically, you learned the following information:

■ You can view the standard styles in the Ribbon's Style list box or the Style dialog box's Style Name list box by pressing Ctrl + Y.

■ You can apply styles by using the Ribbon or the Style command on the Format menu. You can type the text, select it and then choose the style, or you can choose the style and then type the text.

■ You can define, modify, delete, and rename styles by using the Style command on the Format menu. You also can assign a key combination to a style and then use the key combination as a shortcut for applying that style.

■ You can print the style sheet for the active document by using the Print command on the File menu.

■ You can use one style as a base for other styles. Using this technique to link styles can help you to create or modify related styles.

■ You can make one style automatically follow another style by using the Style command on the Format menu.

■ You can add styles to the template by using the Style command on the Format menu. You also can merge styles between documents and templates.

■ You can change the template to which a document is attached. You also can modify a template or create a new template.

■ You can set and change default options that determine the way Word for Windows operates by using the Options command on the Tools menu.

In the next chapter, you will learn about working with document notation.

9

Working with Document Notation

Often, when you work on a long document, several people are involved in writing, reviewing, and updating. Each reviewer makes comments and suggests changes, and each writer may want to approve those changes.

Word for Windows has several features that make on-line reviewing and updating easy. Rather than printing, distributing, and collecting several copies of the document and then trying to collate all the comments and incorporate the changes, you can use Word for Windows features to review, annotate, revise, and update the document at the computer. In addition to these notation features, Word for Windows has three features that help you to manage the construction of a long document: Outline, Table of Contents, and Index.

In this chapter, you will learn about bookmarks, line numbers, revision marks, and annotations—the Word for Windows document notation tools. You also will learn how to use outlining to maintain the structure of a document and how to create a table of contents and an index.

Using bookmarks and cross-references

Using line numbers

Using revision marks

Using annotations

Outlining

Creating a table of contents

Creating an index

Key Terms in This Chapter

Annotations	Comments that reviewers insert directly into a Word for Windows document. Word for Windows identifies each annotation by the initials of the reviewer and a number. The annotations appear in a separate pane so that they do not interrupt the document text.
Bookmarks	Place holders that enable you to mark locations or blocks of text in a Word for Windows document.
Cross-reference	A Word for Windows feature that enables you to use bookmarks to link references to text or page numbers.
Line numbers	A Word for Windows feature that enables you to insert (and later remove) line numbers in the left margin of a document. Reviewers then can refer to specific line numbers in their annotations.
Revision marks	Marks that you place in text to identify new or changed text or to suggest deletion of existing text.

10   Using Bookmarks and Cross-References

You can use bookmarks to mark locations or blocks of text in a Word for Windows document. Later, you can use the bookmarks to go directly to a specific location or block of text or to move or copy marked text. You also can combine bookmarks with cross-references to create references to other parts of the document. You can cross-reference text or page numbers.

Inserting a Bookmark

You can insert up to 450 bookmarks in a document. To insert a bookmark, follow these steps:

1. To mark a location, position the insertion point at that location. To mark a block of text, select that text.

2. Open the Insert menu.

3. Choose the Bookmark command.

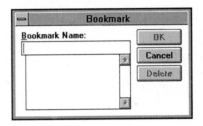

The Bookmark
dialog box
appears.

4. Type a name in the Bookmark Name text box. The bookmark name can have up to 20 characters, cannot include spaces, and must begin with a letter.

5. Choose OK.

Deleting a Bookmark

To delete a bookmark, follow these steps:

1. Open the Insert menu.

2. Choose the Bookmark command.

   The Bookmark dialog box appears.

3. From the Bookmark Name list box, choose the bookmark you want to delete.

4. Choose the Delete button.

5. Choose the Close button.

Note: If the bookmark marked a block of text, this procedure deletes only the bookmark—*not* the text.

Going to a Bookmark

After you insert a bookmark, you can return to its location or block of text by using the Go To key (F5) or the Go To command on the Edit menu.

When you go to a bookmark that marks a location, Word for Windows positions the insertion point at that location. When you go to a bookmark that marks a block of text, Word for Windows goes to that location and selects the text.

10

To go directly to a bookmark by using the Go To key, press F5. The prompt Go To appears on the status bar. Type the name of the bookmark at the prompt.

If you use the **G**o To command on the **E**dit menu, you don't have to remember the bookmark name—you can choose from a list of bookmarks. To go directly to a bookmark by using the **G**o To command, follow these steps:

1. Open the **E**dit command.
2. Choose the **G**o To command.

   The Go To dialog box appears.
3. From the **G**o To list box, choose the bookmark to which you want to go.
4. Choose OK.

Moving or Copying Text Marked with Bookmarks

When you go to a bookmark that marks a block of text (by using the Go To key or the **G**o To command), Word for Windows selects that text. You then can perform any Word for Windows action that you can perform on selected text; for example, you can add character or paragraph formatting, or you can move or copy the text.

As you learned in Chapter 2, moving or copying text involves cutting or copying the text and then pasting it into a new location. The bookmark remains with the *pasted* text. If you move the text, Word for Windows moves the bookmark with the text. If you copy the text, Word for Windows attaches the bookmark to the text in the *new* location (the text in the original location no longer has a bookmark). If you paste a block of text containing a bookmark into a different document, however, Word for Windows attaches the bookmark to the text in *both* documents.

To paste marked text into a different document, you first must define a bookmark that contains the text you want to paste. You then can paste the marked text into a different document in two ways; the method you use depends on whether both documents are open.

If both documents are open, follow these steps to paste marked text from one document to another:

1. In the document that contains the bookmark (the source document), use the Go To key or the **G**o To command to locate and select the text.

10

2. Cut or copy the selected text (by using the Toolbar or the Edit menu), depending on whether you want to move or copy the bookmark.

3. Open the Windows menu and choose the other document (the receiving document).

4. Position the insertion point at the location where you want the text to appear.

5. Paste the text into the document (by using the Toolbar or the Edit menu).

To paste marked text from a closed source document to an open receiving document, follow these steps:

1. Position the insertion point at the location where you want the text to appear.

2. Open the Insert menu.

3. Choose the File command.

   The File dialog box appears.

4. From the File Name list box, choose the source document that contains the bookmark.

5. In the Range text box, type the name of the bookmark.

6. To be able to update the text in the receiving document with subsequent changes in the source document's text, choose the Link to File check box.

7. Choose OK.

If your default options include viewing field codes, an {INCLUDE} statement that identifies the source file appears in the receiving document. If your default options do *not* include viewing field codes, the pasted text appears in the receiving document.

If you linked the documents and later change the text in the source document, you can update the text in the receiving document by using the Go To key or the Go To command to select the text and then pressing F9.

Creating a Cross-Reference to Text

Text cross-references are very useful when you refer to certain text in a document more than one time and you want to ensure that the references are consistent. In addition, if you change the text in the bookmark, Word for Windows updates the references when you print the document.

10

To create a text cross-reference, follow these steps:

1. Define a bookmark that includes the reference text. The cross-reference will insert the contents of the bookmark (the reference text) at the location you specify.

2. Position the insertion point where you want the reference text to appear.

3. Open the Insert menu.

4. Choose the Field command.

   The Field dialog box appears.

5. In the Insert Field Type list box, choose Reference. (You can press R to choose Reference).

A list of bookmarks appears in the Instructions list box.

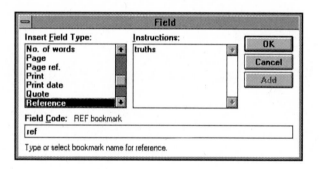

6. From the Instructions list box, choose the bookmark name.

7. Choose the Add button.

8. Choose OK.

If your default options include viewing field codes, a {REF} statement that identifies the bookmark appears in the document. If your default options do *not* include viewing field codes, the referenced text appears in the document.

Creating a Cross-Reference to a Page Number

To direct the reader's attention to text on a particular page, you can use page number cross-references. Suppose, for example, that you need to include a phrase such as "See Page 36 for more information on guppies" in a document. You can create a page cross-reference instead of typing *36*. Word for Windows inserts *36* as long as the bookmark that marks the information on guppies remains on page 36. If the bookmark moves to page 37, Word for Windows updates the reference to *37* when you print.

10

Page number cross-references are particularly useful when you must refer to several blocks of text that appear on different pages. By using page cross-references, you can have Word for Windows track all the references for you.

To create a page cross-reference, follow these steps:

1. Define a bookmark that marks the reference text. The cross-reference will insert the page number of the bookmark (the reference text) at the location you specify.

2. Position the insertion point where you want the page number of the bookmark to appear.

3. Open the Insert menu.

4. Choose the Field command.

   The Field dialog box appears.

5. From the Insert Field Type list box, choose Page ref. (You can press $\boxed{P}$ two times to choose Page ref.)

6. From the Instructions list box, choose the bookmark name.

7. Choose the Add button.

8. Choose OK.

If your default options include viewing field codes, a {pageref} statement that identifies the bookmark appears in the document. If your default options do *not* include viewing field codes, the page number of the referenced text appears in the document.

Using Line Numbers

You can use the Word for Windows line numbering feature to print line numbers in the left margin (or between columns) of a document. Then, reviewers can use the line numbers to identify text about which they are commenting.

You can add numbers to every line or according to some increment you specify. Because line numbering is a section layout feature, you also can number an entire document or only certain sections. You can number lines sequentially from one page to the next, or you can restart the numbers at the beginning of each page or section. When you no longer need the line numbers, you can remove them.

Line numbers appear only in the printed document or in Print Preview mode.

10

To open the Line Numbers dialog box and set up line numbering, follow these steps:

1. Open the Format menu.

2. Choose the Section Layout command.

   The Section Layout dialog box appears.

3. Choose the Line Numbers button.

   The Line Numbers dialog box appears.

4. Choose the Add Line Numbering check box.

The options in
the Line Numbers
dialog box
become available.

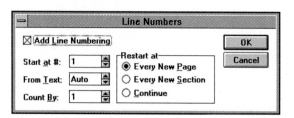

5. Choose any of the following line numbering options:

   In the Start at # box, you can change the starting line number.

   In the From Text box, you can change the physical placement of the number in relation to the text. Auto (the default setting) places a line number .25 inch from the text (for single columns) or .13 inch from the text (for multiple columns).

   In the Count By box, you can change the interval at which Word for Windows adds line numbers. If you choose 2, for example, Word for Windows adds line numbers every other line. If you begin numbering with 1, Word for Windows numbers only the odd-numbered lines.

   In the Restart at box, you can choose Continue to number the entire document sequentially (from the number in the Start at # box), or you can choose Every New Page or Every New Section to restart the numbers at the beginning of every page or section.

6. Choose OK two times to save your choices and return to the document.

To remove line numbers, you can open the Line Numbers dialog box, choose the Add Line Numbering check box again to remove the X, and then choose OK two times. If the document has more than one section, you must remove line numbers from each section.

10

You also can leave line numbering turned on, but conceal the numbers for selected paragraphs. Follow these steps:

1. Select the paragraphs for which you want to conceal the line numbers.

2. Open the Format menu.

3. Choose the Paragraph command.

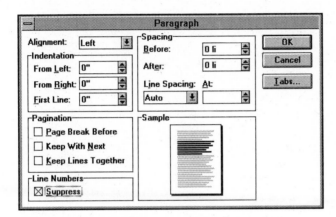

The Paragraph dialog box appears.

4. In the Line Numbers box, choose the Suppress check box to conceal line numbers for the selected paragraphs.

Word for Windows does not print the line numbers for the selected paragraphs.

Using Revision Marks

Revision marks help readers to identify text that has changed since the last time they reviewed the document. Word for Windows provides two ways to insert revision marks:

- Word for Windows can mark revisions as you make changes.

- Word for Windows can compare two versions of the same document after you make all the changes. If you use this method, Word for Windows does not identify the text you deleted from the original version.

10

Inserting Revision Marks

By default, Word for Windows adds bars in the margin next to text you change, adds strikethrough character formatting to text you delete, and underlines text you add.

To mark revisions as you edit, follow these steps:

1. Open the document you want to edit.
2. Open the Tools menu.
3. Choose the Revision Marks command.

The Revision Marks dialog box appears.

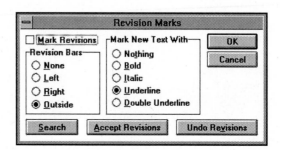

4. To turn on revision marks, choose the Mark Revisions check box. To turn off revision marks, choose the check box again.

5. In the Revision Bars box, specify where you want revision bars to appear:

   If you choose None, Word for Windows does not display or print revision bars.

   If you choose Left or Right, Word for Windows displays and prints revision bars in the left or right margin (in Normal View, however, revision bars always appear on the left).

   If you choose Outside, and the document has facing pages, Word for Windows displays and prints revision marks in the outside margin (the left margin for even-numbered pages and the right margin for odd-numbered pages).

6. In the Mark New Text With box, choose the type of character formatting you want Word for Windows to apply to new text.

7. Choose OK to accept your choices.

10

As you edit the document, Word for Windows inserts the appropriate revision marks. MRK appears on the status bar as long as the Mark Revisions check box contains an X.

If you prefer, you can make all the changes to the text and then mark the revisions by comparing the edited document to a previous version. Because the Compare Versions command compares documents paragraph-by-paragraph rather than word-by-word, however, this method can produce unexpected results.

If you mark the revisions by comparing the edited document to a previous version, Word for Windows does not identify text that appears in the older version of the document, but not in the edited version. In other words, when you use the Compare Versions command, Word for Windows does not identify text you deleted. Also, if you add any information to a paragraph (even a single word), Word for Windows marks the entire paragraph as an addition, indicating only that something in the paragraph has changed.

To insert revision marks by comparing documents, follow these steps:

1. Open the newer version of the document.

2. If you want to change the default revision marks, open the Revision Marks dialog box (by choosing the Revision Marks command from the Tools menu) and choose revision bar and character formatting options, but do not turn on the Mark Revisions option. Choose OK to return to the document.

3. Open the Tools menu.

4. Choose the Compare Versions command.

   The Compare Versions dialog box appears.

5. From the File Name list box, choose the older version of the document.

6. Choose OK.

   In the status bar, you can see the percentage of the documents Word for Windows has compared.

When the program finishes the comparison, you can print the document with the revision marks. Reviewers then can easily identify which paragraphs have changed.

Note: Because this method marks only those paragraphs that have changed, using it to reject revisions can produce unexpected results (see the next section for more information).

10

Accepting or Rejecting Revisions

Regardless of the method you use to mark revisions, you eventually must accept or reject the revisions and remove the revision marks. You can accept or reject revisions for the entire document, or you can accept or reject specific revisions. (You can find specific revisions quickly by opening the Revision Marks dialog box and choosing the Search button.)

To accept or reject revision marks, follow these steps:

1. Select the text for which you want to accept or reject revisions. To accept or reject revisions for the entire document, do not select any text.

2. Open the Tools menu.

3. Choose the Revision Marks command.

   The Revision Marks dialog box appears.

4. To accept the revisions, choose the Accept Revisions button. To reject the revisions, choose the Undo Revisions button.

If you marked revisions as you edited the document, Word for Windows does the following:

- If you accept revisions, Word for Windows makes the indicated changes (deleting text marked for deletion, adding new text, or replacing changed text) and removes the revision bars and revision character formatting. New or changed text assumes the formatting of the paragraph in which it appears.

- If you reject revisions, Word for Windows removes all revision marks, does *not* delete text marked for deletion, does *not* add new text, and does *not* replace changed text.

If you marked revisions by comparing documents, Word for Windows does the following:

- If you accept revisions, Word for Windows removes the revision marks and each paragraph remains exactly as it appears on-screen.

- If you reject revisions, however, Word for Windows *deletes each changed paragraph* (because you chose not to add text marked for addition).

Using Annotations

Traditionally, reviewers provide comments or revisions by writing notes on a printed copy of the document. In the preceding sections of this chapter, you

10

learned about line numbering and revision marks, Word for Windows features that can help reviewers to work in this traditional way. Now, you will learn how reviewers can use annotations to insert comments directly into a Word for Windows document.

To comment on a specific part of the text, a reviewer can insert an annotation mark into a document and then type a comment or suggested revision in the Annotations pane. Word for Windows identifies each annotation with the initials of the reviewer and a number.

Using annotations helps to maintain the flow of text on-screen and in the printed document. Word for Windows formats annotation marks as hidden text, so these marks do not appear on-screen unless you set the default options to display hidden text. Annotation marks do appear in the printed document, but all the annotation comments print on a separate page. (The annotation comments appear in a list, identified by their corresponding annotation marks.)

You can incorporate annotations directly into the document. You can edit or apply formatting to annotations. You also can copy annotation text if you want to use an annotation in more than one place.

As the author, you can lock your document so that you control all revisions. If you lock a document, reviewers can insert annotations, but not modify the document. To lock the document, follow these steps:

1. Open the File menu.
2. Choose the Save As command.
3. If you want to keep the original version of the document unchanged and lock a second version of the document, type a different name in the File Name text box.
4. Choose the File Sharing button.
5. Choose the Lock File for Annotations check box.
6. Choose OK two times to return to the document.

Inserting an Annotation

To insert an annotation, follow these steps:

1. Position the insertion point at the location where you want to insert the annotation.
2. Open the Insert menu.
3. Choose the Annotation command.

10

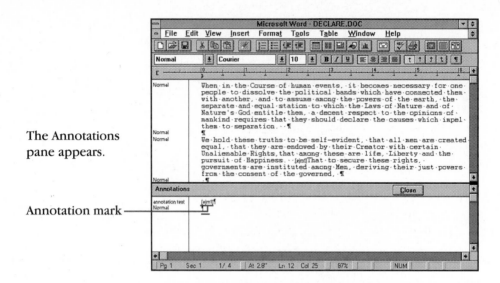

The Annotations pane appears.

Annotation mark ———

Word for Windows inserts the user initials and a number in the document window *and* the Annotations pane. Word for Windows numbers annotation marks sequentially for each set of user initials. (For information on changing the user initials, see Chapter 9.)

4. Type the comment.

5. To close the Annotations pane and return to the document, choose the Close button.

   You do not have to close the Annotations pane. To keep the Annotations pane open and return to the document, press F6 or click anywhere in the text area of the document.

If you are displaying the style area, a new style appears in the Annotation pane—the annotation text style. Word for Windows automatically applies this style, one of the standard styles, to any text you type in the Annotation pane. Word for Windows applies another style, the annotation reference style, to the annotation reference mark that appears in the document. If you open the Style list box on the Ribbon, you now see the annotation reference style and the annotation text style.

Deleting an Annotation

To delete an annotation, select the annotation mark in the document and then press Del (or choose the Cut button on the Toolbar or the Cut

10

command from Edit menu). Word for Windows deletes the annotation mark and its associated text. If the document contains subsequent annotations, Word for Windows automatically renumbers them.

Viewing Annotations

Annotation text scrolls in the Annotations pane as the text of the document scrolls in the document window. If an annotation mark appears in the document window, and you open the Annotations pane, the annotation text for that annotation mark appears in the Annotations pane. If an annotation mark is not in view in the document window, the annotation text is not in view in the Annotations pane.

If you closed the Annotations pane, but want to see a particular annotation, you can double-click the annotation mark to open the Annotations pane and display the corresponding text. You also can use the menus to open the Annotations pane. Follow these steps:

1. In the document, select the annotation mark for which you want to view the annotation text.

2. Open the View menu.

3. Choose the Annotation command.

Going to an Annotation

You can use the Go To key (F5) or the Go To command on the Edit menu to move the insertion point to specific annotations. After pressing F5 or choosing the Go To command, type one of the following codes to move the insertion point:

Table 10.1
Going to an Annotation

Code	Effect
a	Goes to the next annotation.
a–	Goes to the preceding annotation.
ax	Goes to annotation number x.
a+x	Goes forward x number of annotations.
a–x	Goes back x number of annotations.

continues

10

	Table 10.1 (continued)
Code	*Effect*
p*y*a*x*	Goes to annotation number *x* on page *y*. If you type **p2a3**, for example, Word for Windows goes to the third annotation mark on Page 2 (which might actually be annotation number 6).
s*z*a*x*	Goes to annotation number *x* in section *z*.

Copying Annotations

To copy the annotation text and use it for another annotation mark, follow these steps:

1. Select the annotation mark for the annotation text you want to copy.
2. Choose the Copy button on the Toolbar or the **C**opy command from the **E**dit menu.
3. Move the insertion point to the location for the new annotation mark.
4. Choose the Paste button on the Toolbar or the **P**aste command from the **E**dit menu.

   Word for Windows inserts another annotation mark at the new location and copies the annotation text from the original annotation mark. Word for Windows also renumbers the annotation marks if necessary.

Printing Annotations

You can print annotations with the document or separately. To print annotations with the document, follow these steps:

1. Open the **F**ile menu.
2. Choose the **P**rint command.

   The Print dialog box appears.
3. Choose the **O**ptions button.

   The Options dialog box appears.
4. In the Include with Document box, choose the **A**nnotations check box.

   If you did not already choose the **H**idden Text check box, Word for Windows automatically chooses this option when you choose the **A**nnotations check box.

10

5. Choose OK to return to the Print dialog box.

6. Set any other printing options.

7. Choose OK.

   The annotations print on a separate page at the end of the document.

To print the annotations only, follow these steps:

1. Open the File menu.

2. Choose the Print command.

   The Print dialog box appears.

3. From the Print list box, choose Annotations.

4. Choose OK.

Making an Annotation Comment Part of the Document

After reviewing the annotations, you may want to include some of the comments in the document. You do not need to retype the annotation text to
make it part of your document. Instead, follow these steps:

1. Open the Annotations pane so that you can see the text you want to
   include in your document.

2. Select the annotation text. Do *not* include the annotation mark or the
   paragraph mark at the end of the annotation text.

3. Choose the Cut button on the Toolbar or the Cut command from the
   Edit menu.

4. In the document window, position the insertion point where you want
   the annotation text to appear.

5. Choose the Paste button on the Toolbar or the Paste command from
   the Edit menu.

   Word for Windows inserts the text and formats it with the Normal
   style.

6. Delete the annotation mark in the document window by selecting it
   and pressing Del.

10

Outlining

Traditionally, when you begin to work on a long document, you prepare an
outline to help you organize your thoughts. Then, you begin to write, refer-
ring to your outline as you work. From time to time, you may find that you
need to adjust both the outline and the document.

Word for Windows enables you to build an outline on-screen and then to work in the outline to create a document. As you work, you can switch back and forth between Outline View, which focuses on the headings and structure of the document, and the traditional view of the document (Normal View or Page Layout View).

Normal View focuses on the printed appearance of the document.

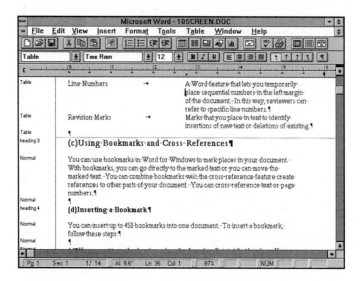

Outline View focuses on the headings and structure of the document.

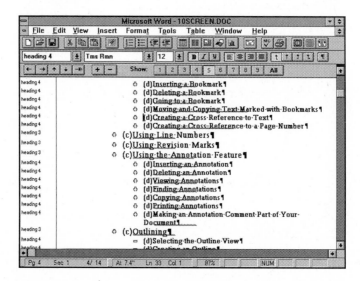

Beyond these basic capabilities, the Word for Windows outlining feature makes adjusting *both* the outline and the document simple. Word for Windows automatically applies to the document any structural changes you make to the outline.

Word for Windows outlining is based on using the standard styles for headings. The program provides nine heading styles, each corresponding to a different level in an outline. If you use the standard styles when you create long documents, you can create an outline "automatically."

Note: If you don't like the formatting of the standard heading styles, you can modify them to suit your needs. See Chapter 9 for more information.

Changing to the Outline View

Displaying your document in Outline View is simply a matter of choosing the Outline command from the View menu.

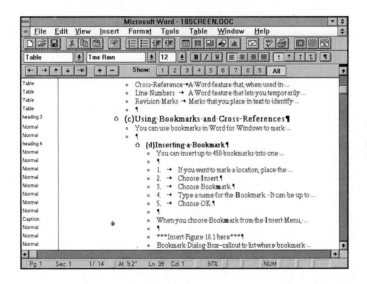

Here is the same document in Outline View.

10

Notice that each entry in the outline is preceded by a plus sign, a minus sign, or a small square. Plus or minus signs precede headings; the small squares precede text. A plus sign indicates that the heading is followed by text or subordinate headings. A minus sign indicates that the heading has no text or subordinate headings.

237

In Outline View, the Outline View icon bar appears at the top of the text area (where the Ruler appears in Normal View). Table 10.2 lists the icons that appear on this bar.

Table 10.2
Outline View Icons

Icon	Effect
←	Promote; promotes a heading and its subordinate text one level.
→	Demote, demotes a heading and its subordinate text one level.
↑	Up; moves a heading and its subordinate text up in the outline.
↓	Down; moves a heading and its subordinate text down in the outline.
⇥	Body Text; demotes a heading to body text.
+	Displays the next lower level of headings or body text below the currently displayed level(s).
–	Hides the lowest level of headings or body text currently displayed.
1 - 9	Displays the corresponding number of heading levels.
All	All; shows all headings and their subordinate text.

You will learn more about using the buttons on the Outline View icon bar (or substituting keystrokes) later in this chapter.

Note: To switch back to Normal View, choose Normal from the View menu.

Creating an Outline

The easiest and most effective way to work with the outlining feature is to switch to Outline View and start typing the outline. You do *not* need to indent the headings; instead, you use three buttons on the Outline View icon bar to tell Word for Windows the level of each heading. Follow these guidelines to assign headings levels:

- Type the first heading and press `↵Enter` at the end of the line.
- To make the next heading the same level as the heading you just typed, simply type the next heading and press `↵Enter`.
- To make the next heading one level *lower* than the heading you just typed, choose the Demote button (or press `Alt`+`⇧Shift`+`→`), type the next heading, and then press `↵Enter`.
- To make the next heading one level *higher* than the heading you just typed, choose the Promote button (or press `Alt`+`⇧Shift`+`←`) type the next heading, and then press `↵Enter`.
- Sometimes, as you create an outline, you have an idea you don't want to lose. Choose the Body Text button (or press `5` on the numeric keypad) and then type the information as text rather than as a heading.

Word for Windows formats and indents the headings according to the standard styles. In Outline View, Heading 1 appears at the left margin, Heading 2 is indented .5 inch from the left margin, Heading 3 is indented 1 inch from the left margin, and so on. These indentations appear in only Outline View. In Normal View, the headings appear according to the standard styles.

Adjusting the Outline Structure and Appearance

In the previous section, you learned how to create an outline in Word for Windows—you learned to use three buttons on the Outline View icon bar to create a document structure. You also can use these and other buttons to adjust the structure of the outline *and* the document.

Promoting and Demoting Headings

You can promote or demote a heading to a different level. When you change the level of a heading, Word for Windows moves any subordinate headings and body text accordingly. In addition, Word for Windows automatically reformats the heading according to its new level.

Note: If you move a heading to a different *location* without changing its *level*, Word for Windows moves only the subordinate body text, not the subordinate headings.

10

You can promote or demote existing headings and their subordinate text in three ways:

- Use the Promote or Demote buttons on the Outline View icon bar.
- Use key combinations.
- Drag the symbol preceding the heading or paragraph.

To promote or demote a heading by using buttons on the Outline View icon bar or their key combinations ([Alt]+[⇧Shift]+[→] or [Alt]+[⇧Shift]+[←]), follow these steps:

1. Position the insertion point anywhere in the heading.
2. Choose the Promote or Demote button or press [Alt]+[⇧Shift]+[→] or [Alt]+[⇧Shift]+[←].

You also can promote or demote a heading (and its subordinate text) or a paragraph of body text by dragging. To drag body text or a heading and its text, follow these steps:

1. Position the mouse pointer on the symbol preceding the item you want to promote or demote.

   The mouse pointer's shape changes to arrows pointing in four directions.

2. Hold down the left mouse button and drag the item to the left or right to promote or demote it.

   When you move the mouse, the mouse pointer's shape changes to an arrow pointing in two directions. A vertical line (with a small square attached) extends from the top to the bottom of the text area and moves to the next level in the direction you drag.

3. Release the mouse button when the line is in the correct position.

   Word for Windows automatically reformats the item according to its new level.

Note: To change a heading to body text, you must drag the line to the right through all nine heading levels. The vertical line then jumps to the *left*. When you release the mouse button, the heading becomes body text.

Expanding and Contracting the View

You can use the Outline View icon bar (or a key combination) to expand and contract the view of a document so that you can see more or less of the document. You use the buttons on the right end of the Outline View icon bar

10

to identify the number of levels you want to see. If you want to see everything (headings and body text) in Outline View, choose the All button or press Alt + Shift + A.

When you are viewing headings and body text, you can view all the body text or only the first line. If you choose to view just the first line, Word for Windows displays one line of the text followed by an ellipsis (...). To display only the first line of body text, press Alt + Shift + F. This key combination is a toggle switch; to display all the body text again, simply press Alt + Shift + F again.

You also can specify the number of heading levels you want to view by pressing Alt + Shift + n (where n is the number of levels).

Moving Sections of Text

When you discover that you need to reorganize a document by moving a heading and all its subordinate text to another part of the document, use Outline View. You can use the Outline View icon bar buttons, the direction keys on the keyboard, or the mouse to move that section of text.

To use the Outline View icon bar to move a heading and its subordinate text, follow these steps:

1. Contract the view to display only the headings.
2. Position the insertion point anywhere in the heading whose subordinate text you want to move.
3. Choose the Up or Down button on the Outline View icon bar.

   Word for Windows selects the heading and all its subordinate body text (but not its subordinate headings) and moves them up or down in the structure.

To use the keyboard to move a heading and its subordinate text, follow these steps:

1. Contract the view to display only the headings.
2. Position the insertion point anywhere in the heading whose subordinate text you want to move.
3. Press Alt + Shift + ↑ or Alt + Shift + ↓.

   Word for Windows selects the heading and all its subordinate body text (but not its subordinate headings) and moves them up or down in the structure.

10

To move a heading and its subordinate text to a new location by dragging, follow these steps:

1. Contract the view to display only the headings.

2. Position the mouse pointer on the icon preceding the heading whose subordinate text you want to move.

    The mouse pointer shape changes to arrows pointing in four directions.

3. Drag the heading up or down.

    When you move the mouse, the mouse pointer's shape changes to an arrow pointing in two directions. A horizontal line (with an arrowhead) extends across the text area and moves in the direction you drag.

4. Release the mouse when the heading is in the correct position.

You can move a sequential group of headings (or body text) in any direction (that is, you can change their level or their location) by using the Outline View icon bar or the keyboard. First, you must select the group you want to move. Be sure that you use the selection bar on the left side of the screen (do not use the plus, minus, or square symbols that appear to the left of the items). Then, use the Up or Down button on the Outline View icon bar or press Alt + ⇧Shift + ↑ or Alt + ⇧Shift + ↓.

Numbering an Outline

You can number a Word for Windows outline with four different numbering schemes:

- Legal
- Sequence
- Outline
- Outline All

You also can devise your own numbering scheme, which Word for Windows applies according to an example.

To apply numbers to an outline, follow these steps:

1. Open the View menu.

2. Choose the Outline command.

3. Expand or contract the outline to display only the items you want to number.

10

4. Select all the outline items you see.

5. Open the Tools menu.

6. Choose the Bullets and Numbering command.

   The Bullets and Numbering dialog box appears.

7. Choose the Outline option button at the top of the dialog box.

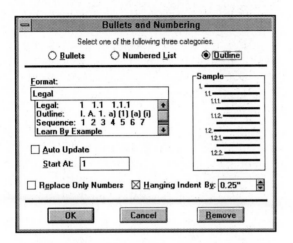

When you choose the Outline option button, the Bullets and Numbering dialog box changes to display outlining options.

8. Choose numbering options from the dialog box:

   From the Format list box, you can choose one of the Word for Windows numbering formats or Learn By Example.

   In the Start At box, you can choose a starting outline number.

   By default, Word for Windows formats paragraphs to have a hanging indent of .25 inch. You also can turn off the Hanging Indent check box or change the indention in the By box.

   Watch the Sample box to see the effects of your choices.

9. Choose OK.

If you already numbered an outline and then moved information, you can renumber the outline by following the same steps. If, however, you want to use the outline numbering feature without changing to Outline View, you can choose the Replace Only Numbers check box (in the Bullets and Numbering dialog box) to renumber only the paragraphs that currently contain numbers.

Another way to renumber an outline is to choose the Auto Update check box. Then, Word for Windows inserts a field rather than a number. If you move a

10

heading (its location or its level), Word for Windows automatically updates its number as well as its formatting. If you choose the Auto Update check box, however, you cannot choose Learn by Example or Outline All from the Format list box and you cannot set a starting number.

Creating a Table of Contents

Because the headings you use in a document are usually the entries you want to include in a table of contents, Word for Windows enables you to create a table of contents from your document without retyping the headings.

By using the Table of Contents command on the Insert menu, you can create a table of contents based on the outline of the document. Word for Windows generates a table of contents which, by default, uses the heading styles in your document to determine the placement of the corresponding table of contents entries: headings formatted with the Heading 1 style appear at the left margin, headings formatted with the Heading 2 style are indented .5 inch from the left margin, and so on. Word for Windows places dot leaders after all table of contents entries and then adds the page number for the heading at the right margin.

10

Here is a sample table of contents.

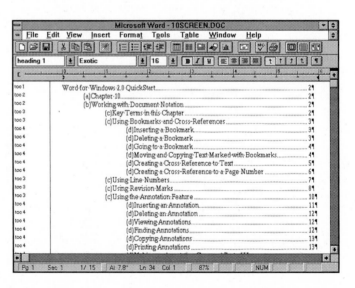

If you have special requirements for your table of contents, you cannot use the basic procedure described in this section. If, for example, you don't want to use the headings in your document as the table of contents, or you need to create another list (such as tables of figures), or you want to include chapter numbers in the page number, you must create a more complex table of contents by using Table Entry fields. For details on compiling a complex table of contents, see *Using Word for Windows 2,* Special Edition, or the *Word for Windows User's Guide*.

Tip: If you intend to create an index for the document, you may want to generate the index before you generate the table of contents. Then, the page numbers for the index also appear in the table of contents. See the next section for information on creating a basic index.

To generate a basic table of contents, follow these steps:

1. Apply heading styles to all the items you want to include in the table of contents.

2. Position the insertion point where you want the table of contents to appear.

   If you want the table of contents to appear on a separate page before page 1, position the insertion point at the beginning of the document, insert a hard page break (press [Ctrl] + [↵Enter]), and then position the insertion point on the new, empty page 1.

3. Turn off the display of hidden text and field codes because these features can affect pagination. (You turn off hidden text and field codes by using the **O**ptions command on the **T**ools menu).

4. Open the **I**nsert menu.

5. Choose the Table of **C**ontents command.

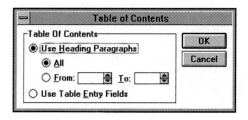

The Table of Contents dialog box appears.

6. Choose the **H**eading Paragraphs option button to create a basic table of contents or choose the Table **E**ntry Fields option button to create a complex table of contents.

10

7. If you use heading paragraphs, choose All to include all headings or use the From and To boxes to include only certain heading levels.

8. Choose OK.

Typically, you create a table of contents after you finish the document. Some-times, however, you must make additional changes, and those changes make the table of contents inaccurate. You can regenerate the table of contents by following the preceding set of steps. Word for Windows highlights the existing table of contents and displays a dialog box that asks whether you want to replace it. Choose OK.

After you create the table of contents, the document has some new styles—toc styles. If you don't like the appearance of the table of contents, simply modify the toc styles. (If you manually format the table of contents, you will lose that formatting if you regenerate the table of contents.)

Creating an Index

When you create an index, you usually want to include special terms and the headings and subheadings that appear in the document. Although you need to plan the items that appear in your index, Word for Windows can help you create the index.

When you create a basic index in Word for Windows, you can choose from two formats: single level entries or entries with subentries.

The following is a sample index that has a number of single entries:

Tab key, 79, 437, 472
Table key, 39, 437
TABLE macro key name, 437
Templates, 290, 296

The following is a sample index that has multilevel entries (*Reports* and *Setting up printer* are the index entries):

Printing
Reports
commands, 477
one-page, 214-216
Setting up printer, 230

In either basic index format, Word for Windows lists each item followed by a comma and a space and separates the page numbers of different references with commas. You can include page ranges in an index entry by using book-marks (described earlier in this chapter).

As with the Table of Contents feature, you can create a basic index or a more complex index. If you have any special requirements, you cannot use the basic procedure described in this section. If, for example, you want to create index entries with text references (such as Reports, *See Printing*) or you want to include chapter numbers in the page number reference, you must create a more complex index by using fields. For details on compiling a complex index, see *Using Word for Windows 2,* Special Edition, or the *Word for Windows User's Guide*.

If you want to specify a range of pages for an index entry, follow these steps to create a bookmark for the range before you create the index entry:

1. Select all of the text you want the index entry to cover.
2. Open the Insert menu.
3. Choose the Bookmark command.
4. Type a name for the bookmark. This name does *not* appear in the index.
5. Choose OK.

To create an index entry, follow these steps:

1. If the text you want to use as an index entry appears in the document, select that text. Otherwise, position the insertion point at the location to which Word for Windows should refer when creating the page number index reference.
2. Open the Insert menu.
3. Choose the Index Entry command.

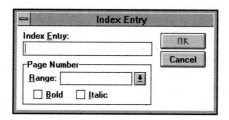

The Index Entry dialog box appears.

You must complete the Index Entry dialog box for each entry you want to appear in the index.

4. If you selected text for the index entry, that text appears in the Index Entry text box. Otherwise, type the text you want to appear in the index. (This text *does* appear in the index.)

5. If you want the entry to list a range of pages, choose the bookmark entry for that range from the **R**ange list box.

6. If you want the index entry to have special formatting, choose **B**old or **I**talic.

7. Choose OK.

To create subentries, follow these steps for each subentry:

1. Position the insertion point at the location to which Word for Windows should refer when creating the page number index reference.

2. Open the **I**nsert menu.

3. Choose the Index **E**ntry command.

4. In the Index **E**ntry text box, type the main heading, a colon (:) and then the subentry.

5. If you created a bookmark, choose it from the **R**ange list.

6. If you want the index entry to have special formatting, choose **B**old or **I**talic.

7. Choose OK.

To create the subentry in the second example, you would type **Printing:Reports:commands** in the Index Entry text box. This subentry has three levels (*commands* appears under *Reports*, which appears under *Printing*). A subentry can have up to seven levels. Do not confuse subentry *levels* with subentries. In the example, the Reports entry has two subentries (*commands* and *one-page*).

Tip: To create a main entry with no page numbers, you do not create an Index Entry. Instead, you include the main heading in the subentries.

After you create all your index entries, you are ready to compile the index. You can compile a normal index or a "run-in" index. A run-in index places subentries on the same line as the main heading. The preceding examples show a normal index. The following example shows a run-in index for the same entries:

Printing: Reports: commands, 477; one-page, 214-216; Setting up printer, 230.

You also can choose a heading separator. The sections of the index appear alphabetically, regardless of the heading separator.

10

Follow these steps to compile the index:

1. Turn off the display of hidden text and field codes because these features can affect pagination. (You turn off hidden text and field codes by using the Options command on the Tools menu.)

2. Position the insertion point where you want the index to appear.

    If you want the index to begin on a separate page at the end of the document, position the insertion point at the end of the document and insert a hard page break (press [Ctrl]+[↵Enter]).

3. Open the Insert menu.

4. Choose the Index command.

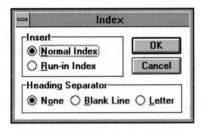

The Index dialog box appears.

5. In the Insert box, choose Normal Index or Run-in Index.

6. In the Heading Separator box, choose None, Blank line, or Letter.

    If you choose Letter, Word for Windows adds the first letter of the section's main entries at the beginning of each index section. If you choose Blank line, Word for Windows adds a blank line at the beginning of each index section. If you choose None, Word for Windows does not indicate the beginning of each index section.

7. Choose OK.

    Word for Windows generates the Index.

Now, if you display hidden text, you can see field entry codes (enclosed in {}) that start with XE. These codes are the index entries.

Typically, you create an index after you finish the document. Sometimes, however, you must make additional changes, and those changes make the index inaccurate. You can regenerate the index by following the preceding set of steps. Word for Windows highlights the existing index and displays a dialog box that asks whether you want to replace it. Choose OK.

10

After you create the index, the document has some new styles—index styles. The index style names include numbers, which indicate the number of index levels you created. If you don't like the appearance of the index, simply modify the index styles. (If you manually format the index, you will lose that formatting if you regenerate the index.)

Chapter Summary

In this chapter, you learned to work with document notation. Specifically, you learned the following information:

- You can insert and delete bookmarks by using the Bookmark command on the Insert menu.

- You can go to a bookmark by using the bookmark name and ⬆Shift + F5 or the Go To command on the Edit menu.

- You can use bookmarks to select text you want to move or copy.

- You can create cross-references to text or page numbers by using bookmarks and the Field command on the Insert menu.

- You can add or remove line numbering by using the Section Layout command on the Format menu.

- You can use the Revision Marks or Compare Versions command on the Tools menu to identify inserted, deleted, or changed text.

- You can use the Annotation feature to insert comments directly into a document and then review those comments. You can print annotations with the document or separately.

- You can create and manage the structure and organization of your document by using the Outline command on the View menu.

- You can generate a table of contents or index for a document by using the Table of Contents or Index command on the Insert menu.

In Chapter 11, you will learn how to work with tables.

10

Working with Tables

In Chapter 7, you learned how to format text in newspaper columns, in which text flows down one column and then continues from the top of the next column. In some situations, however, you may want to format text in columns in which the information in one column relates to the information in the next column. If you are defining terms, for example, you may want to type each term in Column 1 and the corresponding definition in Column 2. You can create this type of columns by setting tabs, but using Word for Windows' table feature is much easier. In this chapter, you will learn how to work with tables in Word for Windows.

11

Creating a Table

When you create a table in Word for Windows, you specify the number of rows and columns you want to include in the table. You can change these settings later by adding or deleting rows or columns. Word for Windows names each cell with the combination of its column letter and row number (for example, A1 or C3) and provides nonprinting gridlines to help you identify the cell in which you are working. You can choose to hide or display the table gridlines. If you set your View options to show paragraph marks (see Chapter 9), Word for Windows also displays end-of-cell and end-of-row marks.

Table button

Row

Cell

Column

Gridlines

End-of-cell marker

End-of-row marker

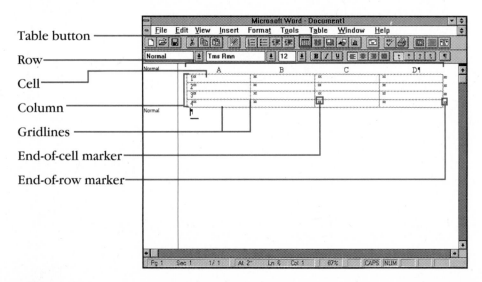

11

Note: The row numbers and column letters in the illustration were inserted to help you identify the rows and columns.

You can create a table by choosing the Table button on the Toolbar or the Insert Table command from the Table menu. When you create a table by using the Insert Table command, you can specify the initial width of the columns. When you use the Toolbar, Word for Windows automatically sets the initial column width so that the table fills all available space between the left and right margins. If necessary, you can change the column width after you create the table.

To use the Toolbar to insert a table, follow these steps:

1. Position the insertion point where you want the table to appear.

2. Choose the Table button on the Toolbar.

    Word for Windows displays a table grid.

3. Drag the mouse across the table grid to highlight the number of rows and columns you want to include in the table.

    Word for Windows displays the number of rows and columns in the box at the bottom of the grid. (If you change your mind, drag the mouse pointer back to the Toolbar to cancel your action.)

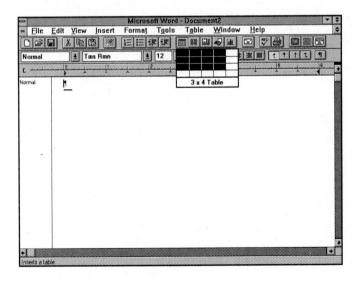

3 x 4 Table indicates that Word for Windows will insert a table of 3 rows and 4 columns.

4. Release the mouse button to insert the table.

11

To specify the initial width of the columns, follow these steps:

1. Position the insertion point where you want the table to appear.
2. Open the Table menu.
3. Choose the Insert Table command.

The Insert Table
dialog box
appears.

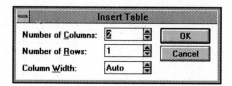

4. Specify the number of rows, the number of columns, and the column width for the table.
5. Choose OK.

Typing in a Table

To type in any cell, simply position the insertion point in that cell and begin typing. A cell can contain more than one line of text. As you type, text wraps to the next line within the cell. You also can press ←Enter to begin a new line within a cell.

The height of a row depends on the height of the largest cell in the row. You can create rows of different heights (discussed later in this chapter), but you cannot create cells of different heights within the same row. Suppose, for example, that you enter three lines of text in cell A1 and two lines of text in cell B1. The height of Row 1 is then three lines; cell B1 appears to contain a blank line.

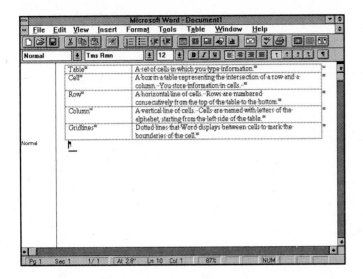

In this example, different amounts of text in the two columns of each row causes a blank line to appear in the cells of the first column.

Tip: Usually, when you press Tab, you move from cell to cell. You can type a tab character in a cell by pressing Ctrl + Tab.

Moving and Selecting in a Table

In this section, you will learn how to move the insertion point around a table and how to select text in a table.

Table 11.1 describes the actions you can use to move the insertion point around a table.

Table 11.1
Moving around a Table

Action	Effect
Click a cell	Moves the insertion point to the cell you click.
Tab	Moves the insertion point from left to right (forward) across a row one cell at a time.
← or →	When the cells are empty, moves the insertion point from cell to cell. When the cells contain text, moves the insertion point one character at a time within a cell.

continues

11

Table 11.1 (continued)

Action	*Effect*
⦿Shift + Tab⇆ (Back Tab)	Moves the insertion point from right to left (backward) across a row one cell at a time.
↑ or ↓	Moves the insertion point up or down one column.

When you move forward from the last cell in the row, the insertion point moves to the first cell of the next row. When you move backward from the first cell in the row, the insertion point moves to the last cell of the preceding row.

When you move the insertion point from cell to cell by pressing Tab⇆ or ⦿Shift + Tab⇆, Word for Windows automatically selects any text in the active cell. Word for Windows also provides selection bars for each row, column, and cell. You can use any of the following methods to select all the text in a cell, a row, a column, a block of adjoining cells, or the entire table.

To select all the text in a cell, do either of the following:

- Click in the cell's selection bar at the left edge of the cell. (The mouse pointer changes to an arrow pointing up and slightly to the right when it is in the cell's selection bar.)

- Position the insertion point at the left edge of the cell and then press ⦿Shift + End.

To select all the text in a row of cells, do one of the following:

- Click in the row's selection bar (outside the table to the left of the first cell in the row).

- Double-click the selection bar of any cell in the row.

- Position the insertion point in the row and then choose the Select Row command from the Table menu.

To select all the text in a column of cells, do one of the following:

- Click in the column's selection bar at the top of the column. (The mouse pointer changes to an arrow pointing down when it is in the column's selection bar.)

- Position the mouse pointer in any cell in the column and then click the *right* mouse button.

- Position the insertion point in the column and then choose the Select Column command from the Table menu.

To select all the text in adjoining cells in a table, do either of the following:

- Click in the selection bar of the first cell you want to select and then drag the mouse pointer to highlight the adjoining cells. If the adjoining cells you want to select are entire rows or columns, you also can click in the selection bar of the first row or column and then drag to select adjoining rows or columns.
- Hold down ⬆Shift and press ↑, ↓, ←, or →.

To select all the text in an entire table, do either of the following:

- Choose the Select Table command from the Table menu.
- Press Alt + 5 (on the numeric keypad). The Num Lock light on the keyboard must be off.

Editing in a Table

Within a table, you can insert, delete, move, copy, and format text just as you do outside a table. Later in this chapter, you also will learn how to modify the structure of the table by inserting or deleting rows and columns.

Deleting Text in a Table

You can delete characters within a table by using ⬆Backspace or Del just as you do outside a table. To delete single characters, position the insertion point at the appropriate location and press ⬆Backspace or Del. To delete entire words, position the insertion point at the appropriate location and press Ctrl + ⬆Backspace or Ctrl + Del.

If you select an entire row or column, pressing ⬆Backspace deletes only the text in the first cell of the row or column (the first cell is then blank). Pressing Del deletes all text in the row or column (all the cells are then blank).

Moving Text within a Table

To move text within a table, you can use the Cut and Paste commands on the Edit menu or the Cut and Paste buttons on the Toolbar. Do not confuse moving text within a table and changing the structure of the table by moving rows or columns. When you move text within a table, you move the *contents* of the cell. When you change the structure of a table, you move the *actual cell and its contents*.

11

Whether you move text or a cell in a Word for Windows table depends on whether you include the end-of-cell marker in your selection. If you *don't* include the end-of-cell marker, Word for Windows moves the *contents* of the cell without moving the actual cell. If you *do* include the end-of-cell marker, Word for Windows moves the *actual cell and its contents*. See the "Moving Rows, Columns, or Cells" section later in this chapter to learn how to move the actual cell and its contents.

To move the contents of one cell to another cell without moving the actual cell, follow these steps:

1. Select the text you want to move to another cell. If you want to move all the text in the cell, be sure that you highlight *only* the text. Do not include the end-of-cell marker in the selection.

2. Choose the Cut command from the Edit menu or the Cut button on the Toolbar.

3. Position the insertion point in the cell to which you want to move the text. If that cell already contains text, position the insertion point where you want to add the cut text.

4. Choose the Paste command from the Edit menu or the Paste button on the Toolbar.

   Word for Windows moves the text from the original cell to the cell that contains the insertion point.

Copying Text within a Table

To copy text from one cell and add the copied text to another cell without copying the actual cell, follow these steps.

1. Select the text you want to copy. If you want to copy all the text in the cell, be sure that you highlight *only* the text. Do not include the end-of-cell marker in the selection.

2. Choose the Copy command from the Edit menu or the Copy button on the Toolbar.

3. Position the insertion point in the cell to which you want to copy the text. If that cell already contains text, position the insertion point where you want to add the copied text.

4. Choose the Paste command from the Edit menu or the Paste button on the Toolbar.

   Word for Windows copies the text from the original cell to the cell that contains the insertion point.

258

You also can copy a cell or cells so that the same text appears in more than one place in the table. In this case, you are copying the actual cell(s) as well as the text.

To copy cells and *replace* the destination cells, follow these steps:

1. Select the cell(s) you want to copy and *include* the end-of-cell marker in the selection.
2. Choose the Copy command from the Edit menu or the Copy button on the Toolbar.
3. Position the insertion point anywhere in the first destination cell.
4. Choose the Paste command from the Edit menu or the Paste button on the Toolbar.

   Word for Windows replaces the destination cells with the copied cells.

Note: Remember that you can create tables in which some rows are longer than others. Suppose, for example, that you are working in a 4 x 4 table. If you copy cells A2 and B2 and then choose D2 as the first destination cell, you will create Cell E2. Row 2 will be the only row that has a fifth column.

Formatting Text in a Table

You can format text that appears in a table with the same types of formatting you use in other parts of a document. You can select text and apply character formatting such as boldface or underlining. You also can set tabs within a table. You can, in general, add all character and paragraph formatting in the same ways you learned in Chapters 5 and 6: by using the Ruler, the Ribbon, the Toolbar, or the menus. You can, for example, use the Alignment buttons on the Ribbon to center text within a cell.

Adding Borders and Shading to a Table

Sometimes, you may want to print a table with lines that represent the gridlines. You also may want to highlight certain portions of a table to call the reader's attention to those cells. To create lines or highlighting, you can apply borders and shading to the table.

Adding Border Gridlines

11

Table gridlines do not print, but appear only on-screen. To print lines around all or part of a table and its cells, you use the **B**order command on the Format menu. Follow these steps:

1. Select the table (or the part of the table) for which you want to print lines.

2. Open the Format menu.

3. Choose the **B**order command.

The Border Table dialog box appears. **G**rid appears in the Preset box.

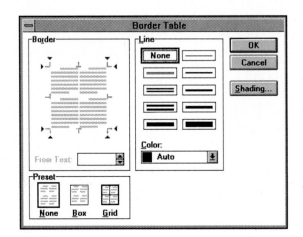

4. In the Preset box, choose **G**rid.

5. Choose OK.

Adding Shading

To emphasize certain cells or a certain table, you can shade some or all cells in the table. To apply shading, follow these steps:

1. Select the cells you want to shade.

2. Open the Format menu.

3. Choose the **B**order command.

    The Border Table dialog box appears.

4. Choose the **S**hading button.

    The Shading dialog box appears.

11

5. From the Pattern list box, choose the amount of shading you want to apply. (The higher the percentage, the darker the shading. If the shading is too dark, however, the reader cannot see the shaded text. Five percent or ten percent is usually the darkest shading you will need.)

6. Choose OK two times.

Modifying the Table Structure

You can modify the structure of a table in a number of ways:

- Hide or display gridlines.
- Size columns or rows.
- Insert or delete rows, columns, or cells.
- Move rows, columns, or cells.
- Merge and split cells.
- Split the table into two tables.

Hiding or Displaying Gridlines

If you don't want to see the gridlines on-screen, you can hide them. Hiding or displaying gridlines involves a "toggle" switch—follow these steps one time to turn off gridlines. Follow the steps again to turn on the gridlines again.

In Word for Windows, you can hide or display gridlines in two ways:

1. Open the Table menu.
2. Choose the Gridlines command.

Or

1. Open the Tools menu.
2. Choose the Options command.
3. From the Category options, choose View.
4. Choose the Table Gridlines check box.

When you are displaying gridlines, a check mark appears next to the Gridlines command on the Table menu and an X appears in the Table Gridlines check box in the View category options.

261

11

Sizing Columns

When you insert a table by using the Table button on the Toolbar, Word for Windows bases the column width on the available space between the left and right margins and reserves a small amount of space between columns. If you insert a table by using the Insert Table command on the Table menu, you can choose the column width. In either case, however, all the columns initially have the same width.

After you insert a table, you can change the width of its columns and the spacing between the columns. You can change the width of table columns in three ways:

- Drag column borders.
- Drag column markers on the Ruler.
- Use the Column Width command on the Table menu.

Unless you have very precise measurements for your columns, using one of the dragging methods is easiest.

Dragging Column Borders

You can adjust the width of an individual column by dragging its column border.

The column borders are the gridlines that appear between columns.

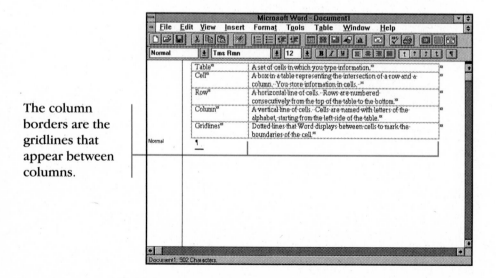

If you do not select any cells in the table or you select an entire column, Word for Windows changes the width of the entire column. If you select a cell or group of cells in the column, Word for Windows changes only those cells. Be aware that you will create a table with uneven column widths if you select only some of the cells in a column.

To adjust column widths by dragging the column borders, follow these steps:

1. Position the mouse pointer on the right column border of the column for which you want to adjust the width.

   The mouse pointer changes shapes when you position it on the column border.

2. Drag the column border to the left to make the column narrower. Drag the column border to the right to make the column wider.

3. Release the mouse button.

   Word for Windows adjusts the column width accordingly.

When you change the width of a column by dragging its column border, you do not affect the size of the other columns, so you *do* affect the overall size of the table.

If you prefer, you can adjust the width of one column but maintain the overall size of the table by adding or removing space from the next column to the right. Hold down ⇧Shift as you drag the column border. Drag the column border to the right to make the current column wider and the column to its right narrower. Drag the column border to the left to make the current column narrower and the column to its right wider.

You also can adjust the width of one column but maintain the overall size of the table by equally adjusting the size of all columns to the right. Hold down Ctrl as you drag the column border. Drag the column border to the right to make the current column wider and all the columns to its right narrower. Drag the column border to the left to make the current column narrower and all the column to its right wider.

Dragging Column Markers on the Ruler

When you position the insertion point anywhere in a table, the Table scale appears on the Ruler.

11

Column markers —

Ruler scale —
symbol

Each column
marker on the
Table scale
represents the
right edge of a
column.

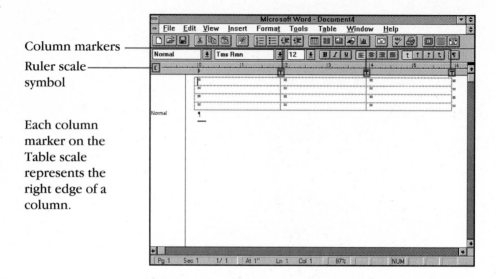

You can adjust the width of a column by dragging its column marker. Drag the column marker to the right to make the column wider. Drag the column marker to the left to make the column narrower. When you release the mouse button, Word for Windows adjusts the column width accordingly.

When you change the width of a column by dragging its column marker, you do not affect the size of the other columns, so you *do* affect the overall size of the table.

If you prefer, you can adjust the width of one column but maintain the overall size of the table by adding or removing space from the next column to the right. Hold down ⇧Shift as you drag the column marker. Drag the column marker to the right to make the current column wider and the column to its right more narrow. Drag the column marker to the left to make the current column narrower and the column to its right wider.

You also can adjust the width of one column but maintain the overall size of the table by equally adjusting the size of all columns to the right. Hold down Ctrl as you drag the column marker. Drag the column marker to the right to make the current column wider and all the columns to its right narrower. Drag the column marker to the left to make the current column narrower and all the columns to its right wider.

When the insertion point is in a table, you still can change the Ruler scale to the Margin scale or Indent scale by clicking the Ruler scale symbol. The Margin scale has no special uses for working with tables, but you can use the Indent

11

scale just as you did for paragraphs. For example, you can use the Indent scale to indent text in a cell (see Chapter 6 for more information).

Using the Column Width Dialog Box

If you need to set precise widths and spacing for the columns in a table, you must use the Column Width dialog box. To adjust column widths and spacing by using the Column Width dialog box, follow these steps:

1. Select the first column you want to adjust. (If you do not select an entire column, Word for Windows will adjust only the selected cells or the cell that contains the insertion point, creating uneven columns.)

2. Open the Table menu.

3. Choose the Column Width command.

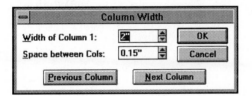

The Column Width dialog box appears.

4. In the Width of Column *x* box, specify the width for the column you selected. In the Space between Cols box, specify the space between columns. (Word for Windows takes this space from both sides of the cells.)

5. To adjust another column, choose the Next Column or Previous Column button to move the insertion point and then repeat step 4. (If you selected any combination of cells other than an entire column, choosing the Next Column or Previous Column button moves the insertion point to the next or preceding *cell*.)

6. Choose OK.

Note: When you specify a width in the Width of Column *x* box, you are actually adjusting the width of the selected cells. When you specify an amount of space in the Space between Cols box, you are adjusting the amount of usable space in the selected cells. If, for example, you make a cell 2 inches wide and the space between columns .15 inch, you can type text in only 1.85 inches of the cell.

11

Sizing Rows

When you insert a table, Word for Windows bases the row height and spacing on the font and point size of the Normal style. You can change the row height, the spacing between rows, and the alignment of rows within a table.

Changing Row Height

The height of a row depends on the height of the largest cell in the row. You can create rows of different heights, but—unlike columns, for which you can create uneven widths—you cannot create a row with cells of different heights. Although Row 1 can have a different height than Row 2, *all* cells in Row 1 must be the same height and *all* cells in Row 2 must be the same height.

The height of a row depends on the maximum number of lines you want to type in a cell in that row. When you insert a table, Word for Windows uses Auto row height, which enables you to type any amount of text in a cell. Word for Windows automatically adjusts the row height to accommodate the maximum number of lines you type in a cell in that row.

To adjust row height after you insert a table, you use the Row Height dialog box. To adjust the height of one or more rows, follow these steps:

1. Position the insertion point anywhere in the row you want to adjust. If you want to adjust more than one row, select the rows you want to adjust.
2. Open the Table menu.
3. Choose the Row Height command.

The Row Height dialog box appears.

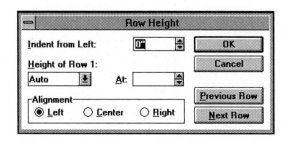

4. From the Height of Row *x* list box, choose At Least (to specify a minimum number of rows) or Exactly.
5. In the At box, specify the minimum or exact number of lines for the row height.

6. To adjust the height of another row, choose the **P**revious Row or **N**ext Row button to move the insertion point and then repeat steps 4 and 5.

7. Choose OK.

Indenting a Row

You also can change the placement of a table between the left and right margins. You may want to indent the table (particularly a small table) so that it aligns with some other portion of the document. You can use the Ruler or the Row Height dialog box to adjust the indentation of a table.

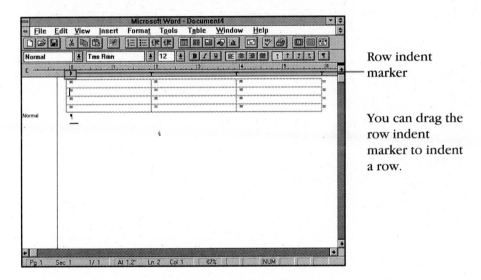

Row indent marker

You can drag the row indent marker to indent a row.

To indent one or more rows by using the Ruler, follow these steps:

1. Select the row you want to indent. If you want to indent more than one row, select those rows.

2. Drag the row indent marker to indent the row(s).

You also can use the Row Height dialog box to specify indentation. Follow these steps:

1. Position the insertion point anywhere in the row you want to indent. If you want to indent more than one row, select those rows.

2. Open the T**a**ble menu.

3. Choose the Row **H**eight command.

11

The Row Height
dialog box
appears.

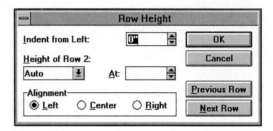

4. In the Indent from Left box, specify the distance (in inches, by default) you want to indent the row(s).

5. To indent another row, choose the Previous Row or Next Row button to move the insertion point and then repeat step 4.

6. Choose OK.

Aligning a Row

You also can align a table relative to the margins. To align one or more rows, you use the Row Height dialog box. Follow these steps:

1. Position the insertion point anywhere in the row you want to align. If you want to align more than one row, select those rows.

2. Open the Table menu.

3. Choose the Row Height command.

   The Row Height dialog box appears.

4. From the Alignment box, choose Left, Center, or Right.

5. To align another row, choose the Previous Row or Next Row button to move the insertion point and then repeat step 4.

6. Choose OK.

Changing Spacing between Rows

To add space between rows of a table, you add lines to those rows. Follow these steps:

1. Position the insertion point anywhere in the row to which you want to add lines. If you want to add lines to more than one row, select those rows.

2. Open the Format menu.

3. Choose the Paragraph command.

11

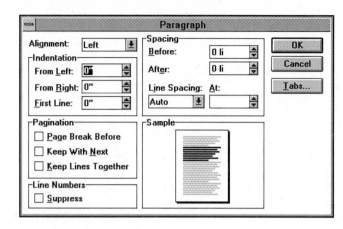

The Paragraph
dialog box
appears.

4. In the Spacing box, specify the number of lines you want to add before or after each row in the Before or After box.

5. Choose OK.

Note: If you changed the Row Height from Auto to Exactly, the number of lines you choose in the Paragraph dialog box must fit within the constraints you defined for Row Height.

Inserting or Deleting Rows, Columns, or Cells

You can modify the size or structure of a table by inserting or deleting rows, columns, or cells anywhere in the table.

Inserting or Deleting Rows

To insert one new row at the end of a table, position the insertion point in the last cell of the table and press Tab↹.

To insert more than one new row at the end of a table, follow these steps:

1. Position the insertion point outside the table in the line immediately below the table.

2. Open the Table menu.

3. Choose the Insert Rows command.

11

The Insert Rows
dialog box
appears.

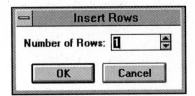

4. Type the number of rows you want to insert.

5. Choose OK.

To insert one or more rows within a table, follow these steps:

1. Position the insertion point in the row you want to appear immediately below the new rows.

2. Select same number of rows (from the insertion point toward the end of the table) as the number of rows you want to insert.

3. Open the Table menu.

4. Choose the Insert Rows command.

   Word for Windows inserts the new rows immediately above the rows you selected.

You can insert one or more rows within a table and simultaneously duplicate an existing row or rows by copying. Follow these steps:

1. Select the rows you want to copy, including the end of row markers.

2. Choose the Copy command from the Edit menu or the Copy button on the Toolbar.

3. Position the insertion point in Column A of the row you want to appear immediately below the new rows.

4. Choose the Paste command from the Edit menu or the Paste button from the Toolbar.

   Word for Windows inserts the new rows above the row that contains the insertion point and inserts the copied text.

To delete rows, follow these steps:

1. Select the rows you want to delete.

2. Open the Table menu.

3. Choose the Delete Rows command.

Inserting or Deleting Columns

You can insert one or more columns at the right side of the table, or you can insert columns within the table. Before you begin this process, you should display the gridlines and end-of-cell marks.

To insert one column at the right edge of the table, follow these steps:

1. Position the insertion point at the right edge of the table and click the right mouse button to select all the end-of-row marks.
2. Open the Table menu.
3. Choose the Insert Columns command.

    Word for Windows inserts one new column at the right side of the table.

To insert more than one column at the right side of the table, follow these steps:

1. Select the same number of columns as the number of columns you want to insert.
2. Choose the Copy command from the Edit menu or the Copy button on the Toolbar.
3. Position the insertion point immediately before the end-of-row marker for the first row.
4. Choose the Paste command from the Edit menu or the Paste button on the Toolbar.

To insert one or more columns within a table, follow these steps:

1. Position the insertion point in the column you want to appear immediately to the right of the new columns.
2. Select the same number of columns (from the insertion point toward the right side of the table) as the number of columns you want to insert.
3. Open the Table menu.
4. Choose the Insert Columns command.

    Word for Windows inserts the new columns to the left of the selected columns.

11

To delete columns, follow these steps:

1. Select the columns you want to delete.
2. Open the Table menu.
3. Choose the Delete Columns command.

   Word for Windows deletes the columns you selected.

Inserting or Deleting Cells

Although you can use the following steps to insert cells, rows, or columns into a table, all references in the steps are to cells. When you insert one or more cells within a table, you select the number of cells you want to insert. Word for Windows places the new cells immediately to the left of or above the selected cells.

To insert cells into a table, follow these steps:

1. Position the insertion point in the cell to the right or below the location for the new cells.
2. Select the same number of cells (from the insertion point toward the right side or end of the table) as the cells you want to insert.
3. Open the Table menu.
4. Choose the Insert Cells command.

   Word for Windows displays the Insert Cells dialog box.
5. Choose Shift Cells Right or Shift Cells Down to specify the direction in which you want to shift the cells you selected. You also can choose Insert Entire Row or Insert Entire Column to insert an entire row or column at that location.
6. Choose OK.

To delete cells from a table, follow these steps:

1. Select the cells you want to delete.
2. Open the Table menu.
3. Choose the Delete Cells command.

   Word for Windows displays the Delete Cells dialog box.
4. Choose Shift Cells Left or Shift Cells Up to specify the direction in which you want to shift the remaining cells. You also can choose Delete Entire Row or Delete Entire Column to delete an entire row or column at that location.
5. Choose OK.

Moving Rows, Columns, or Cells

11

You can move rows, columns, or cells from one area in a table to another. When you move a cell or group of cells by cutting and pasting, Word for Windows replaces the cells in the "receiving" location. When you move cells by dragging, Word for Windows replaces the cells at the "receiving" location and, if necessary, inserts additional rows. When you move rows by dragging, Word for Windows does *not* replace the cells; instead, the program inserts the rows above the receiving location and moves preceding rows up. With either method, the cells you move must maintain their relative table structure—that is, you can move cells A1, A2, and A3 to cells B3, B4, and B5, but you cannot move cells A1, A2, and A3 to cells B2, C2, and D2.

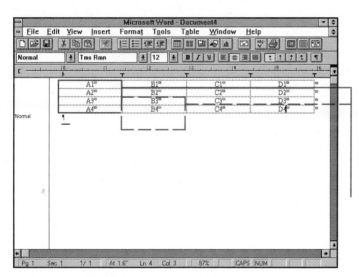

You can move adjacent cells to another location in the table as long as you don't change their relative positions.

Moving Rows, Columns, or Cells by Cutting and Pasting

You can move rows, columns, or cells by cutting and pasting. (You also can move a cell or a row by dragging; this method is discussed in the next section.) Unless you want to replace existing information, you may need to insert new cells at the "receiving" location before you move any combination of cells by cutting and pasting. See the "Inserting or Deleting Rows, Columns, or Cells" section earlier in this chapter for more information.

11

To move rows, columns, or cells by cutting and pasting, follow these steps:

1. Select the rows, columns, or cells you want to move. Be sure that you include the end-of-cell markers in the selection.

2. Choose the Cut command from the Edit menu or the Cut button on the Toolbar.

3. Position the insertion point in the upper left cell of the "receiving" location.

    Or

    Select the "receiving" cells.

4. Choose the Paste command from the Edit menu or the Paste button on the Toolbar.

    Word for Windows inserts the selected rows, columns, or cells in the new location and replaces any existing information in the "receiving" cells.

Tip: You can move an entire table from one location in a document to another by cutting and pasting. Simply select the entire table and then cut and paste as usual.

Moving Cells or Rows by Dragging

You also can move cells and rows by dragging. When you move cells by dragging, Word for Windows replaces the "receiving" cells, and, if necessary, inserts additional rows. When you move rows by dragging, Word for Windows does *not* replace the "receiving" rows; the program inserts the rows above the location you specify and moves preceding rows up. (If you move a row to the top of the table, however, Word for Windows inserts the row *at* the location you specify and moves subsequent rows down.) If you move more than one row, Word for Windows moves the rows in the same order as they originally appeared.

To move one or more cells by dragging, follow these steps:

1. Use the selection bar to select the cells you want to move.

2. Drag the selected cells to the first cell you want to replace.

    Word for Windows inserts the selected cells at the new location, replacing the "receiving" cells and, if necessary, inserting additional rows.

To move one or more rows by dragging, follow these steps:

1. Use the selection bar or the Select Row command on the Table menu to select the rows you want to move.

274

11

2. Drag the selected rows to the first cell of the row you want to appear below your selection.

   Word for Windows inserts the selected rows in the new location and moves preceding rows up.

Note: You cannot move columns by dragging. To move a column, follow the steps in the preceding section for cutting and pasting.

Combining and Splitting Cells

After you create a table, you may want to combine cells within the table. For example, you may want to create a heading that spans several columns (or the entire width of the table), but resides in only one cell. To create such a heading, you can merge cells so that the heading fits in a single cell. (To center the heading in the table, you can merge all the cells in the row and then center the heading in the resulting cell.)

You can merge empty cells or cells that contain text. After you merge cells, you can split them apart again. (You cannot, however, split cells you have not merged.)

To merge cells, follow these steps:

1. Select the cells you want to merge, including their end-of-cell markers.

2. Open the Table menu.

3. Choose the Merge Cells command.

   Word for Windows merges the selected cells and combines any paragraph marks you entered.

After Word for Windows merges cells, you can delete the extra paragraph marks. Also, if you want the text in the merged cell to serve as a heading, you can center the text in that cell or apply other formatting.

To split a merged cell, follow these steps:

1. Select the merged cell.

2. Open the Table menu.

3. Choose the Split cells command.

Note: The Split cells command is available only if you selected merged cells.

Word for Windows splits a merged cell into its original cells. For example, if a table originally had four columns and you merged Row 1 into one cell, splitting the cell in Row 1 produces four cells in Row 1. If you deleted

275

11

paragraph marks, reinsert the paragraph marks before you split the cell; otherwise, all the text will appear in the first cell of the row.

Splitting One Table into Two

Occasionally, you may want to split a table—for example, to insert regular text in the middle of the table. Word for Windows can split a table above the insertion point. Follow these steps:

1. Position the insertion point in the row you want to be the first row of the new table.
2. Open the Table menu.
3. Choose the Split Table command.

Tip: If you need to insert text before a table at the beginning of a document, you cannot simply position the insertion point before the table and type. You must first position the insertion point in the first row of the table and split the table.

Sorting Table Entries

You can change the order of the rows in a table by sorting the table entries. By default, Word for Windows sorts a table alphabetically based on the entries in Column 1. You can, however, specify a different column and sorting method.

Note: Save the document before you sort, in case you get unexpected results.

Follow these steps to sort the entries in a table:

1. Select the entire table.

   You also can sort the entries in one column without regard for the other columns in the table. To sort only one column, select that column. Exercise great care when using this option, particularly if the information across a row is related. You can destroy the accuracy of your table.

2. Open the Tools menu.
3. Choose the Sorting command.

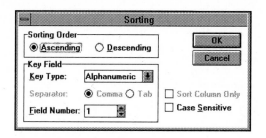

11

The Sorting dialog box appears.

4. In the Sorting Order box, choose Ascending or Descending.

   If you choose Ascending, Word for Windows sorts from the beginning of the alphabet, from the lowest number, or from the earliest date. If you choose Descending, Word for Windows sorts from the end of the alphabet, from the highest number, or from the latest date.

   Note: If you want to sort dates, you must format the information as dates so that Word for Windows can recognize them. See Chapter 7 for information on dates.

5. From the Key Type list box, choose Alphanumeric, Numeric, or Date. (If the column by which you want to sort the table contains numbers and text or numbers and special characters (such as hyphens), choose Alphanumeric.)

   If you choose Alphanumeric, Word for Windows sorts special characters and punctuation, then letters, then numbers, then dates. If you choose Numeric, Word for Windows sorts numbers only (and treats dates as numbers). If you choose Date, Word for Windows sorts only text formatted as dates.

6. In the Field Number box, enter the number of the column by which you want Word for Windows to sort the rows of the table.

7. If you choose Alphanumeric from the Key Type list box, the Case Sensitive check box is available. To list words with uppercase first letters before words with lowercase first letters, choose the Case Sensitive check box.

8. If you selected only one column, choose the Sort Column Only check box.

   Warning: Exercise great care when using this option, particularly if the information across a row is related. You can destroy the accuracy of your table.

9. Choose OK.

11 Creating a Table from Existing Text

You can convert existing text to a table as long as you separate the text with commas, tabs, or paragraph marks. Word for Windows enables you to establish cells based on any one of these three separators.

To create a table from existing text, follow these steps:

1. Select the text you want to convert to a table.

2. Open the Table menu.

3. Choose the Convert Text to Table command.

If more than one of the separators appears in the selected text, Word for Windows displays the Convert Text to Table dialog box.

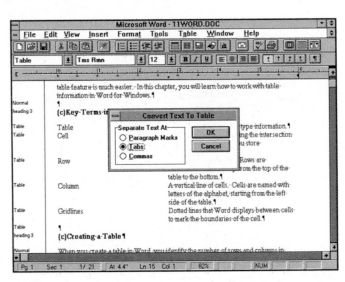

4. If the Convert Text to Table dialog box appears, choose the separator you want Word for Windows to use to divide the text into cells.

5. Choose OK.

You may have to remove extra paragraph marks, commas, or tab characters to get the table design you want. If characters appear in a long vertical string in a column, change the paragraph formatting so that you have no indentations. You also can "undo" your action if you don't like the table layout.

Creating Text from an Existing Table

11

You also can convert all or part of a table into text. You can choose to separate the text from each cell with commas, tabs, or paragraph marks.

To create text from an existing table, follow these steps:

1. Select the rows of the table you want to convert. To convert the entire table, select the entire table.

2. Open the Table menu.

3. Choose the Convert Table to Text command.

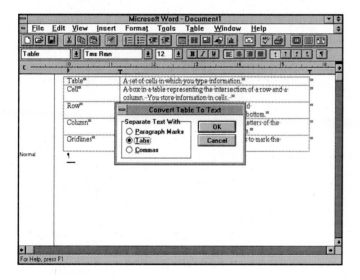

The Convert Table to Text dialog box appears. Notice that, except for its name, the Convert Table to Text dialog box looks exactly like the Convert Text to Table dialog box.

4. Choose Paragraph Marks, Tabs, or Commas to separate the text from each cell.

5. Choose OK.

You may have to reformat the text after you convert it. You also can "undo" your action if you don't like the appearance of the text.

11

Chapter Summary

In this chapter you learned how to work with tables. Specifically, you learned the following information:

- You can insert a table by using the Table button on the Toolbar or the Insert Table command on the Table menu.

- You can move the insertion point around a table by using the mouse or by pressing Tab ⇥ or ⇧Shift + Tab ⇥. You can select text within a table by dragging, by using the cell's selection bar, or by pressing ⇧Shift + End.

- You can delete, move, or copy text in a table by using the Copy, Cut, and Paste buttons on the Toolbar or the Copy, Cut, and Paste commands on the Edit menu. You can format text in a table by using the Ribbon or the commands on the Format menu.

- You can print lines around all or part of a table or shade all or some of the cells in a table by using the Border command on the Format menu.

- You can display or hide gridlines by using the Gridline command on the Table menu.

- You can change the size of columns by dragging or by using the Column Width command on the Table menu. You can change the size of a row by using the Row Height command on the Table menu.

- You can add or delete rows by using the Insert Rows or Delete Rows command on the Table menu. You can add or delete columns by using the Insert Columns or Delete Columns command on the Table menu.

- You can move cells or rows by dragging, by using the Toolbar, or by using the Cut and Paste commands on the Edit menu. You can move columns by using the Toolbar or the Cut and Paste commands on the Edit menu.

- You can combine or split cells by using the Merge Cells or Split Cells command on the Table menu. You can split a table into two parts by using the Split Table command on the Table menu.

- You can sort rows in a table (or the entries in one column of a table) by using the Sorting command on the Tools menu.

- You can create a table from existing text by using the Convert Text to Table command on the Table menu. You can covert a table into text by using the Convert Table to Text command on the Table menu.

In the next chapter, you will learn how to work with pictures and frames.

Working with Frames and Pictures

You can use frames and pictures in a Word for Windows document to create effects that capture the reader's attention and add interest to the document. In this chapter, you will learn how to insert a frame into a document and then place text or a picture in the frame. You also will learn about your options for displaying text around graphics. You will learn how to size, move, align, remove, and delete a frame. You also will learn how to insert pictures that come with Word for Windows or that you create by using other programs. You will learn how to change the size or appearance of a picture by scaling and cropping. You will learn how to place and move framed information on the page.

Working with frames and pictures in Word for Windows is easiest when you use a mouse. Also, because you can see the effects of changes, working with frames and pictures is easiest in Page Layout View. Unless otherwise stated, all procedures in this chapter work in Page Layout View (rather than Normal View). To change to Page Layout View, open the View menu and choose the Page Layout command.

12

Key Terms in This Chapter

Frame	A box that surrounds a picture or text. You can use a frame to highlight or position its contents. You can, but do not have to, print a frame.
Picture	Any graphic image in a variety of art formats. Word for Windows comes with a collection of clip art pictures. You also can use images you create in a drawing program or charts you create in a spreadsheet program as pictures.
Scaling	Changing the size of a picture. You can use scaling to make a picture larger or smaller or to stretch or shrink it.
Cropping	Changing the amount of a picture that appears in the document. You can use cropping to remove unwanted portions of a picture.

Understanding Frame Basics

A frame is a box you use to surround text or a picture in a Word for Windows document. The primary purpose of a frame is to help you control the size and placement of the item inside the frame. When you frame an item, Word for Windows automatically wraps text around the frame. Later in this chapter, you will learn how to adjust the text flow.

Views and Frames

Frames appear differently in different Word for Windows views. Working with frames is easiest in Page Layout View because the framed item appears in the document where it will print, but you still can modify the frame.

12

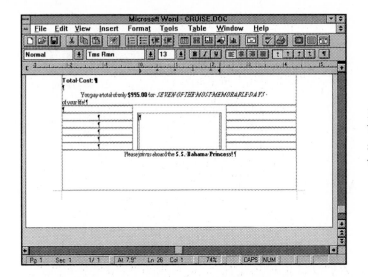

In Page Layout
View, a frame
appears where it
will print.

In Normal View or Outline View, frames do not appear at their actual size or
in the locations where they will print. Still, you may prefer to use Normal View
or Outline View when you are working on other elements of the document.

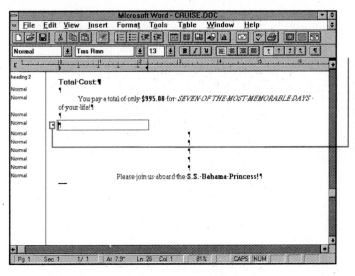

In Normal View, a
frame marker
appears at the left
side of the frame
but does not
print.

12

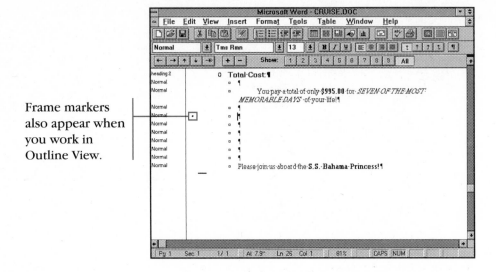

Frame markers also appear when you work in Outline View.

In Print Preview, the frame appears where it will print, but you cannot modify the frame.

Mouse Pointer Shapes and Frames

When you use a mouse to work with frames, you will see one of two mouse pointer shapes. When you position the mouse pointer anywhere over an *unselected* frame, the mouse pointer appears as a four-headed arrow. When the mouse pointer has this shape, you can select the frame by clicking the left mouse button. When you position the mouse pointer over the outside edge of a *selected* frame, the mouse pointer appears as a four-headed arrow or a two-headed arrow. When the mouse pointer has the four-headed arrow shape, you can move the frame; when the mouse pointer has the two-headed arrow shape, you can change the size of the frame.

Inserting an Empty Frame

A frame can surround text or a picture. You can insert a frame into a document before or after you type the text or insert the picture you want the frame to surround. Each frame you place in a document has a border. If you print the border, you effectively print the frame. You also can remove the border so that you do not print the frame.

Using the Mouse To Insert an Empty Frame

You can insert a frame in two ways:

- Use the Frame button on the Toolbar.
- Use the Frame command on the Insert menu.

12

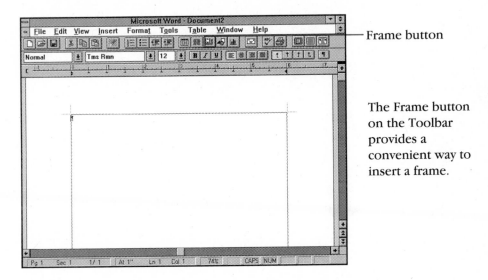

Frame button

The Frame button on the Toolbar provides a convenient way to insert a frame.

To insert an empty frame by using the mouse, change to Page Layout View (by choosing the Page Layout command from the View menu) and then follow these steps:

1. Choose the Frame button on the Toolbar.

   Or

   Open the Insert menu and choose the Frame command.

   The mouse pointer changes to a plus shape.

2. Position the mouse pointer where you want the upper left corner of the frame to appear.

3. Click and hold down the left mouse button to anchor the upper left corner of the frame.

4. Drag the mouse pointer down and to the right until the frame is approximately the correct size.

5. Release the mouse button to anchor the frame.

Word for Windows positions the insertion point inside the frame (so that you can type any text in the frame). To move the insertion point outside the frame, click anywhere in the document outside the frame.

Using the Keyboard To Insert an Empty Frame

To insert an empty frame by using the keyboard, change to Page Layout View (by choosing the Page Layout command from the View menu) and then follow these steps:

1. Open the Insert menu.

2. Choose the Frame command.

    The mouse pointer changes to a plus shape.

3. Press ←, →, ↑, or ↓ to position the insertion point where you want the upper left corner of the frame to appear.

4. Press ↵Enter to anchor the upper left corner of the frame. (If you change your mind and don't want to anchor the frame, press Esc.)

5. Press ↑, ↓, ⇧Shift+↑, or ⇧Shift+↓ until the frame is approximately the correct size.

    When you press ↑ or ↓, Word for Windows adjusts the size of the frame in small increments. When you press ⇧Shift+↑ or ⇧Shift+↓, Word for Windows adjusts the size of the frame in larger increments.

6. Press ↵Enter to anchor the frame.

Word for Windows positions the insertion point inside the frame (so that you can type any text in the frame). To move the insertion point outside the frame, press ←, →, ↑, or ↓.

Placing a Frame around Existing Text

You also can place a frame around existing text. Word for Windows automatically wraps the text to fit the size of the frame. If the text around which you place a frame appears in a long vertical string, you may need to remove or adjust indentations in the text. (You use the Paragraph command on the Format menu to remove or adjust the indentations. See Chapter 6 for more information.)

To place a frame around existing text, make sure that you are in Page Layout View and then follow these steps:

1. Select the text. To frame a paragraph, be sure to include the paragraph mark in your selection.
2. Choose the Frame button on the Toolbar.

   Or

   Open the Insert menu and choose the Frame command.

12

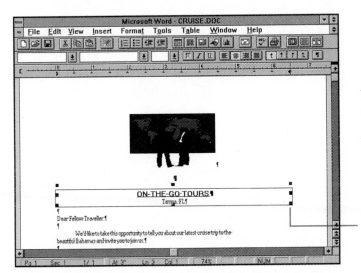

Word for Windows inserts and selects a frame. When a frame is selected, eight handles appear around the frame.

— Handle

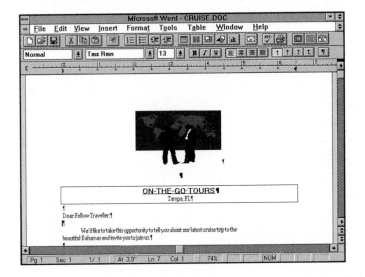

When a frame is not selected, the handles do not appear.

Changing the Frame Size

12

You can change the size of a frame after you insert it in a document. The steps you follow to change the size of a frame depend on whether you use a mouse or the keyboard. If you use a mouse, you can drag the handles to change the frame's size. If you use the keyboard, you must use the Frame dialog box.

Using the Mouse To Size a Frame

If you do not need a frame of precise measurements, using the mouse to size the frame is easy and convenient. To size a frame by using the mouse, make sure that you are in Page Layout View and then follow these steps.

1. Position the mouse pointer over the frame you want to size.

   The mouse pointer changes to the four-headed arrow shape.

2. Click the mouse button to select the frame.

   Eight handles appear around the frame.

3. Position the mouse pointer over the handle you want to use to size the frame.

   The mouse pointer changes to the two-headed arrow shape.

4. Drag the handle in the direction you want to change the size of the frame.

   A dotted outline of the frame indicates the changing size.

   Warning: Do *not* drag when the mouse pointer has the four-headed arrow shape. When the mouse pointer has this shape, dragging moves the frame rather than changing its size.

5. Release the mouse button when the frame is the correct size.

Using the Keyboard To Size a Frame

To size a frame by using the keyboard, you must use the Frame dialog box. You also can use the Frame dialog box to specify precise measurements for a frame.

To open the Frame dialog box, you first position the insertion point inside the frame. If the insertion point is not inside the frame, the Frame command is not available and appears gray on the Format menu. You can position the insertion point in a frame in Normal View or Page Layout View. (In Normal View, a frame marker appears in front of the frame.)

To see the effects of your changes, you must work in Page Layout View or switch to Page Layout View after you size the frame.

Follow these steps to adjust the size of a frame by using the Frame dialog box:

1. Press ←, →, ↑, or ↓ to position the insertion point inside the frame.

2. Open the Format menu.

3. Choose the Frame command.

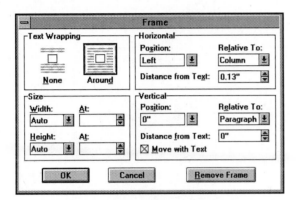

The Frame dialog box appears.

4. In the Size box, specify the width and height of the frame:

   From the Width box, choose Auto or Exactly. If you choose Auto, Word for Windows adjusts the width of the frame to fit its contents. If you choose Exactly, type a specific measurement in the At box.

   From the Height box, choose Auto, At Least, or Exactly. If you choose Auto, Word for Windows adjusts the height of the frame to fit its contents. If you choose At Least, type a minimum height in the At box. If you choose Exactly, type a specific height in the At box.

5. Choose OK.

Adjusting the Flow of Text around a Frame

When you insert a frame into a document, Word for Windows automatically wraps text around the outside of the frame. You can change the flow of text by using the Frame dialog box. To see the effects of your changes, you must work in Page Layout View.

12

To open the Frame dialog box, follow these steps:

1. Position the insertion point inside the frame or select the frame. If you select the frame, eight handles appear around the frame.

2. Open the Format menu.

3. Choose the Frame command.

The Frame dialog box appears. In the Text Wrapping box, you can choose None or Around.

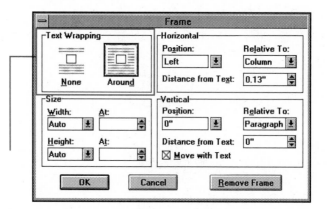

If you choose Around (the default), Word for Windows wraps the text around the frame.

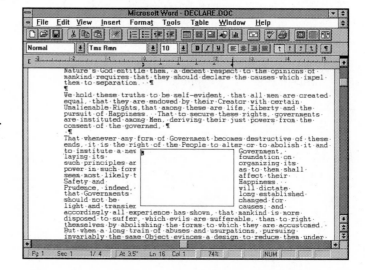

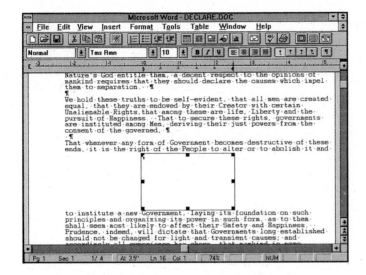

12

If you choose None, the same document looks like this.

Moving a Frame

You can use the mouse to drag a frame to another location. To move a frame by using the mouse, follow these steps:

1. Position the mouse pointer over the frame you want to move.

    The mouse pointer changes to the four-headed arrow shape.

2. Click the mouse button to select the frame.

    Eight handles appear around the frame.

3. Position the mouse pointer over the outside edge of the frame.

    The mouse pointer changes to the four-headed arrow shape.

4. Drag the edge of the frame to the correct location.

    Warning: Do *not* drag when the mouse pointer has the two-headed arrow shape. When the mouse pointer has this shape, dragging changes the frame's size rather than its position.

You also can move a frame (and set the distance between the frame and the text) by using the Frame dialog box. Use the Frame dialog box if you need to make precise changes, if you want to set the distance between the frame and the text, or if you do not have a mouse.

Aligning a Frame Horizontally

12

Word for Windows horizontally aligns a frame relative to the width of the page and places the frame .13 inch from the surrounding text. You can specify a different horizontal position in the Frame dialog box.

To change the horizontal alignment of a frame, follow these steps:

1. Position the insertion point in the frame or select the frame.

2. Open the Format menu.

3. Choose the Frame command.

    The Frame dialog box appears.

4. Specify the horizontal position by typing a number (in inches, by default) in the Position list box or by choosing Left, Right, Center, Inside, or Outside from the Position list box. (Inside and Outside are positions on facing pages. Inside, for example, is the left side of an odd-numbered page, but the right side of an even-numbered page.)

5. From the Relative To list box, choose Margin, Page, or Column.

    Word for Windows aligns the frame relative to the left or right margin, the left or right edge of the page, or the left or right column margin.

    If you align a frame to the left or right edge of the page, Word for Windows places the frame in the margin.

If you choose Left from the Position list box and Page from the Relative To list box, the document looks like this.

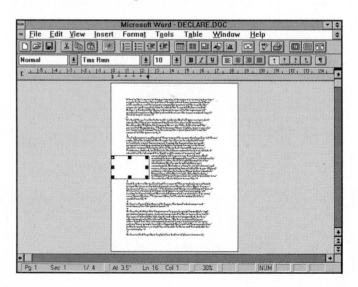

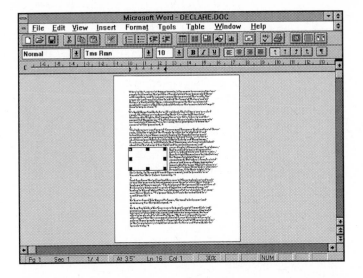

12

If you choose Left from the Position list box and Margin from the Relative To list box, the document looks like this.

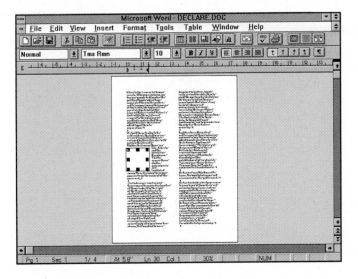

If you choose Left from the Position list box and Column from the Relative To list box, the document looks like this.

6. In the Distance from Text text box, specify the horizontal distance you want to place the frame from the surrounding text.

7. Choose OK.

Aligning a Frame Vertically

By default, Word for Windows vertically aligns a frame immediately after the preceding paragraph mark. You can specify a different vertical position in the Frame dialog box.

To change the vertical alignment of a frame, follow these steps:

1. Position the insertion point in the frame or select the frame.

2. Open the Format menu.

3. Choose the Frame command.

   The Frame dialog box appears.

4. Specify the vertical position by typing a number (in inches, by default) in the Position text box or by choosing Top, Bottom, or Center from the Position list box.

5. If you typed a number in the Position text box, choose Paragraph, Margin, or Page from the Relative To list box. If you choose Paragraph, Word for Windows places the frame that distance from the preceding paragraph mark. If you choose Margin or Page, Word for Windows places the frame that distance from the top margin or the top of the page.

   If you chose Top, Bottom, or Center from the Position list box, choose Margin or Page from the Relative To list box. Word for Windows aligns the frame relative to the top or bottom edge of the page or relative to the top or bottom margin. (Although Paragraph is available in the Relative to list box, you cannot use this option with Top, Bottom, or Center.)

   If you align a frame at the top or bottom of the page, Word for Windows places the frame in the margin.

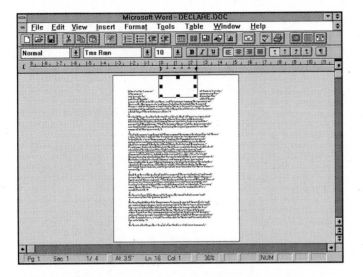

12

If you choose Top from the Position list box and Page from the Relative To list box, the document looks like this.

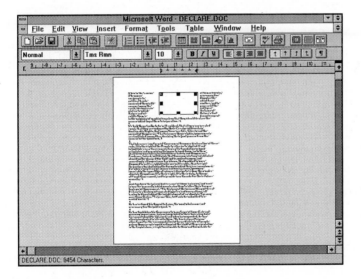

If you choose Top from the Position list box and Margin from the Relative To list box, the document looks like this.

6. In the Distance from Text text box, specify the vertical distance between the frame and the surrounding text (the default is 0 inches).

7. To make Word for Windows move the frame with its associated text, choose the Move with Text check box. (If you do not choose this check box, Word for Windows keeps the frame in a fixed position on the page regardless of any editing changes that move the associated text.)

295

12

If the contents of the frame are related to the text in the document, you typically choose the Move with Text check box. If the contents of the frame are not related to the text in the document (for example, if the frame contains a letterhead), you typically do *not* choose the Move with Text check box.

8. Choose OK.

Deleting a Frame, Removing a Frame, or Suppressing Frame Borders

When you *delete* a frame, you remove the frame and its contents. To delete a frame, follow these steps

1. Position the insertion point in the frame or select the frame.
2. Press Del.

When you *remove* a frame, you remove the frame but do not remove its contents. Rather, you remove the outline that represents the border of the frame (and, therefore, the shape of the frame. If the frame contained text, the text flows in line with the text that preceded it.

To remove a frame, follow these steps:

1. Position the insertion point in the frame or select the frame.
2. Open the Format menu.
3. Choose the Frame command.

   The Frame dialog box appears.
4. Choose the Remove Frame button.

Sometimes, you simply don't want to print the border that Word for Windows places around a frame. If you want to maintain the frame's contents, size, shape, and position, but do not want to print the border, follow these steps:

1. Position the insertion point in the frame or select the frame.
2. Open the Format menu.
3. Choose the Border command.

   The Border Paragraphs dialog box appears.
4. In the Preset box, choose None.
5. Choose OK.

   Word for Windows leaves the frame intact, but removes the frame's outline.

296

Using Pictures in Word for Windows

You can incorporate pictures into a Word for Windows document. One source of pictures is the collection of clip art images that comes with Word for Windows. If you followed the standard installation procedures (see Appendix A for more information), these clip art images are available in the CLIPART directory on the drive that contains Word for Windows.

You also can incorporate charts you create in a spreadsheet program or in Microsoft Graph, a charting package that comes with Word for Windows (see Chapter 15 for more information). And, you can incorporate images you create in a drawing program or in Microsoft Draw, a drawing package that comes with Word for Windows (see Chapter 16 for more information). If you want to use spreadsheet and drawing programs other than Microsoft Graph and Microsoft Draw, you must answer questions during installation about the types of files you plan to import into Word for Windows (see Appendix A for more information).

The remainder of this chapter explains how to import pictures into a Word for Windows document and then adjust the imported pictures. The pictures in the examples are clip art images that come with Word for Windows. For more information on creating charts and graphs by using Microsoft Graph, see Chapter 15. For more information on creating drawings by using Microsoft Draw, see Chapter 16.

Inserting a Picture without Using a Frame

Although Microsoft provides examples of the types of charts and graphs you can create with Microsoft Graph in the Graph documentation, it does not provide samples of the clip art images. You can, however, view a clip art image on-screen before you import it into a document. If you followed the standard installation procedures (see Appendix A), all the clip art images are stored in the CLIPART directory. Their file names end with the extension WMF, which stands for Windows Metafile and indicates their file type.

You can insert a picture with or without using a frame. If you insert a picture without using a frame, you can add a frame later. If you think you might need to move the picture, however, you probably should import the picture into a frame (because a frame helps you to position the picture).

You can insert a picture into a document by using Word for Windows commands, the Clipboard, or Microsoft Draw. Use Word for Windows commands if you are currently working in Word for Windows and want to import a Word

12

for Windows clip art image or an image from another drawing or charting program. Use the Clipboard if you are currently working in another program and want to make the image easily available when you open Word for Windows. Use Microsoft Draw if you need to modify the image or select additional options for importing certain graphic file formats (see Chapter 16 for more information).

Note: If you decide to modify a picture *after* you import it, you can open Microsoft Draw and edit the picture. If you want to be able to modify an image in the original program and then update the picture in the Word for Windows document without importing it again, choose the **L**ink to File option when you first import the picture.

To insert a clip art image from the CLIPART directory (the clip art supplied with Word for Windows) by using Word for Windows commands, follow these steps:

1. Position the insertion point where you want the picture to appear.
2. Open the **I**nsert menu.
3. Choose the **P**icture command.

The Picture dialog box appears.

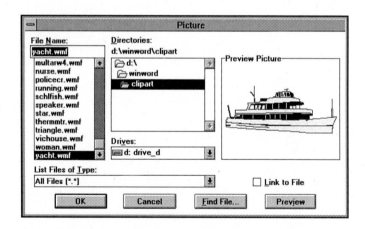

4. From the **D**irectories list box, choose clipart.
5. From the File **N**ame list box, choose the clip art image you want to import to the Word for Windows document.
6. To view the image, choose the Preview button.

   Word for Windows displays the image in the Preview Picture box.

7. If you want to be able to modify the image in the original program and then update the picture in Word for Windows without importing it again, choose the **L**ink to File check box.

If you later modify the image in the original program, you can transfer the modifications to Word for Windows automatically by using the Links command on the Edit menu.

8. Choose OK to insert the picture into the document.

12

When you insert a picture into a Word for Windows document without using a frame, the picture appears in the document, but is not selected and does not have any handles. The insertion point appears immediately to the right of the picture.

If you want to use Word for Windows commands to insert an image not stored in the Word for Windows CLIPART directory (for example, an image supplied by another vendor), follow these steps:

1. Position the insertion point where you want the picture to appear.

2. Open the Insert menu.

3. Choose the Picture command.

   The Picture dialog box appears.

4. Choose the Find File button.

   The Find File dialog box appears.

5. Choose the Search button.

   The Search dialog box appears.

6. In the Path text box, type the path to the image files from which you want to choose.

7. From the Type list box, choose the correct image file format.

8. Choose the Start Search button.

9. From the File Name list box, choose the image you want to import into the Word for Windows document.

10. To view the image, choose the Content button.

    Word for Windows displays the image in the Content box.

11. Choose the Insert button to return to the Picture dialog box.

    The name of the file you just inserted now appears in the File Name list box.

12. Choose OK to import the picture into the document.

If you are working in another program and want to make a picture available to Word for Windows, follow these steps:

1. In the other program, copy the picture to the Clipboard.

2. In Word for Windows, position the insertion point where you want the picture to appear.

12

3. Choose the Paste button on the Toolbar.

Or

Open the **E**dit menu and choose the **P**aste command.

To use Microsoft Draw to import an image, follow these steps:

1. Position the insertion point where you want the picture to appear.

2. Choose the Microsoft Draw button on the Toolbar.

Microsoft Draw button

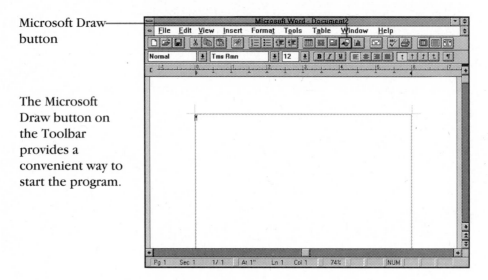

The Microsoft Draw button on the Toolbar provides a convenient way to start the program.

The Microsoft Draw window appears.

3. Open the **F**ile menu on the Microsoft Draw menu bar.

Note: If you open the **F**ile menu on the Word for Windows menu bar, you will hide the Draw window. Use the Switch to command on the Word Control menu to switch back to the Draw window.

4. Choose the **I**mport Picture command.

5. From the **D**irectories list box, choose the directory that contains the image you want to import.

6. From the **F**iles list box, choose the image you want to import into the Word for Windows document.

7. Choose OK.

The image appears in the Microsoft Draw window. For information on using Microsoft Draw tools to modify the image, see Chapter 16.

8. When you finish any modifications, open the **F**ile menu on the Microsoft Draw menu bar.

9. Choose the Exit and Return to *document1* command.

   A dialog box asks whether you want to update the document.

10. To update the document, choose Yes. If you change your mind and don't want to import the image, choose No. If you want to return to Microsoft Draw, choose Cancel.

Adding a Frame to a Picture

In the preceding section, you learned how to insert a picture into a document without using a frame. When you insert a picture without using a frame, no handles appear around the picture, and the insertion point appears immediately to the right of the picture. If you later want to move the picture, you must add a frame.

To add a frame to a picture you already inserted, follow these steps:

1. Select the picture.

   To select the picture by using the mouse, position the mouse pointer over the picture and click the left mouse button. (Note that the mouse pointer does not change to the four-headed arrow shape as it does when you position the mouse pointer over a frame.)

   To select the picture by using the keyboard, position the insertion point in the text immediately above or below the picture and then press ⇧Shift + the arrow key that moves the insertion point toward the picture.

   Eight handles appear around the picture.

2. Choose the Frame button on the Toolbar.

   Or

   Open the Insert menu and choose the Frame command.

   Word for Windows adds a frame to the picture and, if necessary, moves the frame and its contents to the left margin, but does *not* select the frame and its contents.

Inserting a Picture into a Frame

Although you do not have to use a frame when you insert a picture into a Word for Windows document, moving a picture is easier if you insert the picture into a frame when you insert the picture into the document.

Follow these steps to insert a picture into a frame:

1. Insert a frame by using Frame button on the Toolbar or the Frame command on the Insert menu. Size the frame to the approximate size you want the picture to appear in your document.

2. Open the Insert menu.

3. Choose the Picture command.

4. Choose the image you want to insert. (For more information, see the "Inserting a Picture without Using a Frame" section of this chapter.)

   Word for Windows inserts the picture into the frame and positions the insertion point next to the frame, but does not select it.

When you position the mouse pointer over the framed picture, the mouse pointer does change to the four-headed arrow shape (so you can select the frame *and* its contents).

Adjusting a Picture

When you insert a picture into a frame, Word for Windows automatically sizes the picture to fit the frame. You may find, therefore, that the picture is now too small or too large. You can change the size of the picture by scaling the picture, or you can crop the picture to display only the part you need. You also may want to move the picture. For any of these tasks, using the mouse is much easier than using the keyboard.

When you import an image into Word for Windows, you are working with a copy of the image stored on the hard disk. Any changes you make affect only the copy. The original image still appears as it did before you inserted the copy into the document.

Scaling a Picture

When you scale a picture, you change its size. As you change the size of a picture in Word for Windows, you may distort the image; however, because changes you make to the picture affect only the copy of the picture on-screen, Word for Windows can adjust the picture to correspond with the original image on disk.

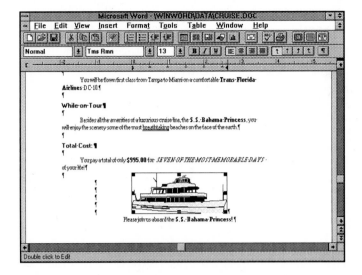

Here is a picture
before scaling.

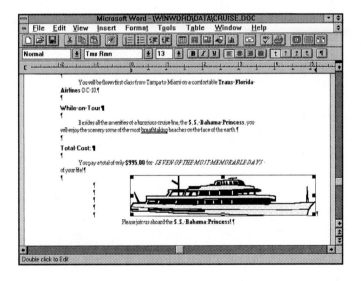

Here is the same
picture after
scaling.

To scale a picture by using the mouse, follow these steps:

1. Position the mouse pointer over the picture you want to scale.

   The mouse pointer changes to the four-headed arrow shape.

2. Click the left mouse button to select the picture.

   Eight handles appear around the picture.

303

12

3. Position the mouse pointer over the handle you want to use to scale the picture.

   The mouse pointer changes to the two-headed arrow shape.

4. Drag the handle in the direction you want to scale the picture.

   A dotted outline indicates the changing size.

   Warning: Do *not* drag when the mouse pointer has the four-headed arrow shape. When the mouse pointer has this shape, dragging moves the picture rather than changing its size.

5. Release the mouse button when the picture is the correct size.

To scale a picture by using the keyboard, you use the Picture dialog box. To open the Picture dialog box, you first must select the picture you want to scale. If you do not select the picture, the Picture command is not available and appears gray on the Format menu.

Follow these steps to scale a picture by using the keyboard:

1. Position the insertion point in the text immediately above or below the picture you want to scale.

2. Press the ⇧Shift + the arrow key that moves the insertion point toward the picture.

   Eight handles appear around the picture.

3. Open the Format menu.

4. Choose the Picture command.

The Picture dialog box appears. You use the options in the Scaling and Size boxes to scale a picture.

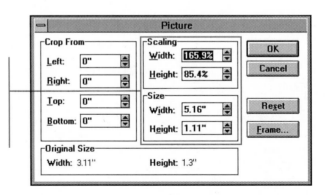

5. In the Scaling box, adjust the percentages in the Width and Height boxes.

   Or

   In the Size box, adjust the measurements in the Width and Height boxes.

304

Note: Scaling options are not independent of Size options. For example, if you adjust the scaling width or height, you also adjust the size width or height.

6. Choose OK.

If you distort the image during scaling (whether you are using the mouse or the Picture dialog box), you can return the image to its original dimensions by choosing the Reset button in the Picture dialog box.

Cropping a Picture

If you want to change the amount of a picture that appears in the document, you can crop the picture by using the mouse or the Picture dialog box.

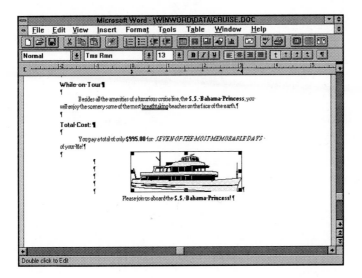

Here is a picture before cropping.

12

Here is the same picture after cropping.

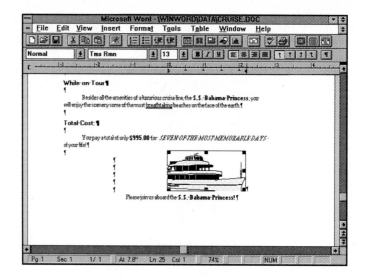

To crop a picture by using the mouse, follow these steps:

1. Position the mouse pointer over the picture you want to crop.

   The mouse pointer changes to the four-headed arrow shape.

2. Click the left mouse button to select the picture.

   Eight handles appear around the picture.

3. Position the mouse pointer over the handle you want to use to crop the picture.

   The mouse pointer changes to the two-headed arrow shape.

4. Hold down ⇧Shift and drag the handle in the direction you want to crop the picture.

   A dotted outline indicates the changing size.

   Warning: Do *not* drag when the mouse pointer has the four-headed arrow shape. When the mouse pointer has this shape, dragging moves the picture rather than changing its size.

5. Release the mouse button when the dotted outline displays only those portions of the picture that you want to include in the document.

   Word for Windows redraws the screen to incorporate the changes.

To crop a picture by using the keyboard, you use the Picture dialog box. To open the Picture dialog box, you first must select the picture you want to crop. If you do not select the picture, the Picture command is not available and appears gray on the Format menu.

Follow these steps to crop a picture by using the keyboard:

1. Position the insertion point in the text immediately above or below the picture you want to scale.
2. Press ⇧Shift + the arrow key that moves the insertion point toward the picture.

   Eight handles appear around the picture.
3. Open the Format menu.
4. Choose the Picture command.

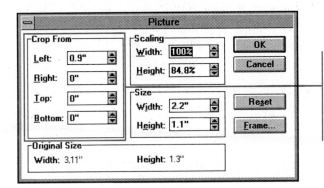

The Picture dialog box appears. You use the options in the Crop From box to crop a picture.

5. In the Crop From box, specify the amounts you want to crop from the edges of the picture in the Left, Right, Top, and Bottom boxes.
6. Choose OK.

If you distort the image during cropping (whether you are using the mouse or the Picture dialog box), you can return the image to its original dimensions by choosing the Reset button in the Picture dialog box.

Moving a Picture

To move a picture from the position where you inserted it, you must place a frame around the picture. Then, you can move the picture in the same ways you can move a frame.

To move a framed picture by dragging, follow these steps:

1. Position the mouse pointer over the picture (and frame) you want to move.

   The mouse pointer changes to the four-headed arrow shape.
2. Click the left mouse button to select the framed picture.

   Eight handles appear around the framed picture.

12

3. Position the mouse pointer over the edge of the framed picture.

   The mouse pointer changes to the four-headed arrow shape.

4. Drag the edge of the framed picture to the correct location.

   Warning: Do *not* drag when the mouse pointer has the two-headed arrow shape. When the mouse pointer has this shape, dragging changes the size of the picture (and frame) rather than changing their position.

You also can change the vertical and horizontal position of a picture and frame (and set the distance between the picture and frame and the text) by using the Frame dialog box. Use the Frame dialog box if you need to place the framed picture precisely or if you do not have a mouse. For detailed information, see the sections in this chapter about aligning a frame vertically or horizontally.

Chapter Summary

In this chapter, you learned how to work with frames and pictures in Word for Windows. You learned that working with frames and pictures is easiest when you use a mouse and when you work in Page Layout View. You learned that the mouse pointer changes shape as you work with frames and pictures. You also learned that you can insert pictures with or without using frames, but that you must use frames for moving pictures. Specifically, you learned that you can do the following:

- You can insert an empty frame by using the Frame button on the Toolbar or the Frame command on the Insert menu.

- You can place text in a frame simply by positioning the insertion point in the frame and then typing the text.

- You can insert a frame around existing text by selecting the text and then choosing the Frame command from the Insert menu.

- You can change the size of the frame after you insert it by selecting the frame and then dragging its handles (when the mouse pointer is a two-headed arrow shape) or by using the keyboard.

- You can decide how text flows around the frame by selecting the frame and then using the Frame command from the Format menu.

- You can move a frame by selecting the frame and then dragging its edge (when the mouse pointer is a four-headed arrow shape). You can align a frame vertically or horizontally by using the Frame dialog box. (To open the Frame dialog box, you select the frame and then choose the Frame command from the Format menu.)

308

■ You can delete a frame *and its contents* by selecting the frame and then pressing ⌐Del⌐. You can remove a frame without removing its contents by selecting the frame and then using the Frame command from the Format menu. You also can choose whether to print the border of a frame by selecting the frame and using the Border command from the Format menu.

■ You can insert a picture into a document without using a frame by choosing the Picture command from the Insert menu. You can add a frame to a picture by selecting the picture and then using the Frame button on the Toolbar or the Frame command on the Insert menu. You can insert a picture directly into a frame by selecting the frame and then choosing the Picture command from the Insert menu.

■ You can scale a picture by selecting the picture and then dragging its handles (when the mouse pointer is a two-headed arrow shape). You can crop a picture by selecting the picture, holding down ⌐⇧Shift⌐, and then dragging its handles (when the mouse pointer is a two-headed arrow shape). You can move a picture by inserting it into a frame and then moving the frame.

In the next chapter, you will learn how to use Word for Windows features to automate your work.

12

Automating Your Work

13

Word for Windows has several features you can use to automate your work. You already learned, in Chapter 10, about using bookmarks to mark places in a document to which you want to return quickly and about using cross-references to link a reference with its page number or with other text. In this chapter, you will learn how to define and use glossaries and how to record and use simple macros.

Using glossaries

Installing the macros provided with Word for Windows

Recording macros

Running macros

Deleting or renaming macros

Creating a macro to change directories

Creating a macro to insert a symbol

13

> ## Key Terms in This Chapter
>
> *Glossary*   Stores text or graphics. You can use glossary entries to save you the trouble of retyping or copying repetitive information.
>
> *Macro*   A user-defined series of instructions. You can use macros to automate repetitive tasks such as changing directories or inserting a frequently used symbol. In Word for Windows, you can assign a macro to a key combination, a menu, or a button on the Toolbar.

Using Glossaries

You can use glossaries to save words or phrases you use regularly. When you want to use a word or phrase you saved as a glossary entry, you don't have to retype it. Instead, you insert that glossary entry.

Suppose, for example, that you use the following standard complimentary closing for all your letters:

Sincerely yours,

WILLIAM G. WIDGET COMPANY, INC.

William G. Widget, Jr.

Vice President

WGW:cc

You can store this closing in a glossary entry named Close. Then, whenever you end a letter, you simply type **Close** and press F3. Word for Windows inserts all this information in the letter.

You also can apply formatting such as boldface or underlining to the glossary entries you create. When you insert the glossary entry, you can choose whether to include the formatting.

Creating a Glossary Entry

When you create a glossary entry, you use the Glossary dialog box to assign a name that indicates the contents of the entry. Then, whenever you want to use the glossary entry, you can simply type that name and press F3 . The name you assign, therefore, should be long enough to identify the entry, but short enough to type quickly.

To create a glossary entry, follow these steps:

1. Type the entry you want to store.
2. Select the entry you typed.
3. Open the Edit menu.
4. Choose the Glossary command.

   The Glossary dialog box appears.
5. In the Glossary Name text box, type the name you want to assign to the glossary entry.

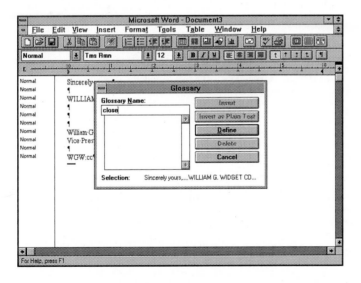

In the example, you would type Close.

6. Choose the Define button. (The Define button is not available unless you have selected text in the document *and* typed a name.)

Storing a Glossary Entry

You can store up to 150 glossary entries in a document template. If you create a glossary entry while working in any template other than NORMAL.DOT, Word for Windows prompts you to specify the storage location for the glossary entry.

You can store the glossary "as Global" or "in Template."

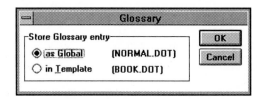

If you choose to store the glossary entry in the current template (the in Template option button), you can use that entry only when you are creating documents based on that template. If you choose to store the glossary entry "as Global," Word for Windows stores that entry in NORMAL.DOT, where it is available from any template.

If you don't want Word for Windows to display this prompt every time you create a glossary entry in a template other than NORMAL.DOT, you can tell the program where to store all future glossary entries. (If you later change your mind, just repeat these steps and choose a new location.)

To tell Word for Windows where to store glossary entries for a template other than NORMAL.DOT, follow these steps:

1. Open the File menu.
2. Choose the Template command.

   The Template dialog box appears. The name of the current template appears in the Attach Document To list box.

The Template dialog box provides three options for storing new glossary entries.

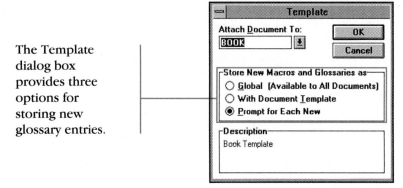

3. In the Store New Macros and Glossaries As box, choose Global (Available to all Documents), With Document Template, or Prompt for Each New.

   Global (Available to all Documents) and With Document Template are the same as the as Global or in Template options in the prompt dialog box. Prompt for Each New (the default option) makes Word for Windows display the Glossary dialog box each time you create a new glossary entry in a template other than NORMAL.DOT.

4. Choose OK.

13

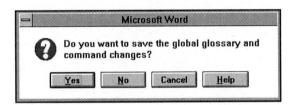

When you exit the program, Word for Windows prompts you to save glossaries and command changes.

Choose Yes to keep any glossaries you defined for future use.

Note: Word for Windows prompts you to save glossaries and command changes even if the document is based on NORMAL.DOT.

Inserting a Glossary Entry

You can insert a glossary entry by typing its name and pressing F3 or by choosing the Glossary command from the Edit menu. If you use the keyboard method, Word for Windows inserts the glossary entry exactly as you created it. If you use the Glossary command on the Edit menu, you can choose whether to include the formatting.

To use the keyboard method to insert a glossary entry, you must remember its name. Follow these steps:

1. Position the insertion point where you want the glossary entry to appear.

2. Type the glossary entry's name.

3. Press F3.

   Word for Windows inserts the glossary entry with any formatting you applied when you created the entry.

To use the Glossary command on the Edit menu to insert a glossary entry, follow these steps:

1. Position the insertion point where you want the glossary entry to appear.
2. Open the Edit menu.
3. Choose the Glossary command. (If you have not created any glossary entries, the Glossary command is not available.)

   The Glossary dialog box appears.
4. From the Glossary Name list box, choose the glossary entry you want to insert.
5. To insert the glossary entry with any formatting you applied when you created the entry, choose the Insert button. To insert the glossary entry without the formatting, choose the Insert as Plain Text button.

Editing or Deleting a Glossary Entry

To modify a glossary entry, follow these steps:

1. Insert the glossary entry you want to modify into a document.
2. Edit the glossary entry in the document.
3. Select the edited information you want to store as the glossary entry.
4. Open the Edit menu.
5. Choose the Glossary command.
6. From the Glossary Name list box, choose the name of the original glossary entry.
7. Choose the Define button.

   If Word for Windows prompts you to specify the storage location for the glossary entry, choose the as Global or in Template option button.

   A dialog box asks whether you want to redefine the glossary entry.
8. Choose Yes.

You also can delete a glossary entry. Please note, however, that you cannot "undo" such a deletion. (The only way you can recover the glossary entry is to exit Word for Windows and choose No at the prompt to save global glossaries and command changes.)

To delete a glossary entry, follow these steps:

1. Open the Edit menu.
2. Choose the Glossary command.
3. From the Glossary Name list box, choose the name of the glossary entry you want to delete.
4. Choose the Delete button.
5. Choose the Close button.

13

Renaming a Glossary Entry

You can rename a glossary entry by following these steps:

1. Insert the glossary entry you want to rename into a document. If you also want to modify the glossary entry, edit the entry in the document.
2. Select the information you want to store with a different name.
3. Open the Edit menu.
4. Choose the Glossary command.
5. From the Glossary Name list box, choose the name of the glossary entry you want to rename.
6. Choose the Delete button.
7. In the Glossary Name text box, type a new name for the glossary entry.
8. Choose the Define button.

Tip: If you want to create similar glossary entries, you can follow the preceding set of steps, but skip steps 5 and 6.

Printing Glossary Entries

You can print the contents of your glossary entries by using the Print dialog box. Follow these steps:

1. Open a document based on the template that contains the glossary entries you want to print.
2. Open the File menu.
3. Choose the Print command.

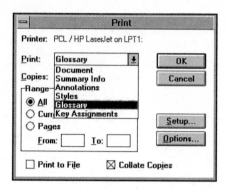

The Print dialog
box appears. The
Print list box
contains a Glos-
sary option.

4. From the **P**rint list box, choose Glossary.

5. Choose OK.

Installing Macros

Word for Windows comes with a collection of macros ready for you to use. Most of these macros not only are useful for performing repetitive tasks, but also provide examples you can study when you start writing your own macros.

The macros that come with Word for Windows are stored in the file NEWMACRO.DOC (in the Word for Windows program directory, WINWORD). Before you can use these macros, you must use this file to install the macros you want to use.

Follow these steps to install any or all of the macros provided with Word for Windows:

1. Open the **F**ile menu.

2. Choose the **O**pen command.

   The Open dialog box appears.

3. If you are working in a directory other than WINWORD, choose WINWORD from the **D**irectories list box.

4. From the File **N**ame list box, choose NEWMACRO.DOC.

5. Choose OK.

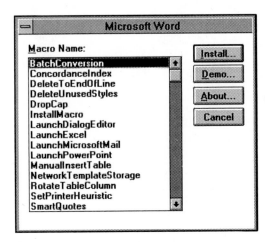

Word for Windows displays a dialog box from which you can learn about, demonstrate, or install any or all of the macros.

13

To learn about, demonstrate, or install a macro, follow these steps:

1. In the Macro Name list box, choose the macro you want to learn about, demonstrate, or install.

2. Choose the About, Demo, Install, or Cancel button on the right side of the dialog box.

   If you choose the About button, Word for Windows displays a dialog box that contains a brief description of the macro. If you choose the Demo button, Word for Windows demonstrates the macro. If you choose the Install button, Word for Windows displays another dialog box.

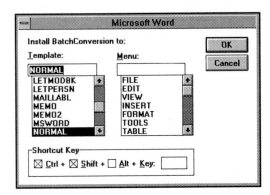

In this dialog box, you can choose the template in which you want to install the macro and the menu or key combination to which you want to assign the macro.

(For more information on assigning a macro to a key combination, a menu, or a Toolbar button, see the later sections of this chapter.)

If you choose the Cancel button, Word for Windows displays the document NEWMACRO.DOC

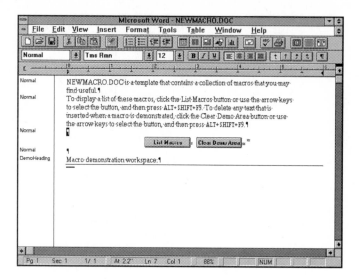

13

NEWMACRO.DOC explains how to list and demonstrate the macros.

The macro that deletes text from the insertion point to the end of the line is particularly useful, as are SmartBullets and ConcordanceIndex.

Follow these steps to install the DeleteToEndOfLine macro:

1. Open the File menu.
2. Choose the Open command.
3. If you are working in a directory other than WINWORD, choose WINWORD from the Directories list box.
4. From the File Name list box, choose NEWMACRO.DOC.
5. Choose OK.
6. In the Macro Name list box, choose DeleteToEndOfLine.
7. To demonstrate this macro, choose the Demo button.
8. To start the installation process, choose the Install button.
9. To make this macro available in all documents, choose NORMAL (the default) from the Template list box.

    For now, do not assign the macro to any menu or shortcut key combination. Later in this chapter, you will learn how to assign a macro to a key combination, a menu, or a Toolbar button. If you use this dialog box to assign the macro to a shortcut key, you risk assigning the macro to a key combination that is already assigned to some other feature.

10. Choose OK.
11. To install other macros now, repeat steps 6 through 10.

12. When you finish installing macros, choose Cancel to close the dialog box.

13. Close NEWMACRO.DOC (by opening the File menu and choosing the Close command).

Recording Macros

Although you can use WordBasic, a macro programming language, to write and edit macros, the easiest way to create a macro is to make Word for Windows record and store your actions. All you have to do is start the macro recorder, perform the action you want to record, and then stop the recorder.

Follow these steps to record a macro:

1. Open the Tools menu.

2. Choose the Record Macro command.

   Word for Windows opens a dialog box in which you can name the macro, assign it to a shortcut key, and provide a description. (Assigning a macro to a shortcut key combination is discussed later in this chapter.)

3. Accept the suggested macro name or type a name. You cannot include spaces in the name, but you can use uppercase letters to indicate the beginning of each word (for example, InsertDate).

4. Choose OK.

   Word for Windows closes the dialog box, and REC appears toward the right end of the status bar to indicate that the macro recorder is "on."

5. Perform the actions you want to record in the macro (such as changing to another directory).

6. When you complete the actions, open the Tools menu again.

7. Choose the Stop Recorder command.

   Word for Windows stores the macro in the template, and REC no longer appears on the status bar.

8. Save the template by using the Save All command on the File menu.
   Or
   Save the macro by responding to the dialog box that appears when you exit Word for Windows.

If you want to use WordBasic to write macros, previous experience with macro languages or some programming background is very useful. If you do not have this kind of experience, consider purchasing a book on this subject or taking a basic programming class. Describing how to use WordBasic is beyond the scope of this book.

13 Running Macros

Because macros are intended to help you work efficiently, running a macro should not be difficult, particularly if you need to use that macro often. You can run a macro from the Macro dialog box, or you can assign the macro to a shortcut key combination, a menu, or a Toolbar button.

Running Macros from the Macro Dialog Box

If you do not use a macro very often, you may want to run it from the Macro dialog box. Follow these basic steps:

1. Open the Tools menu.

2. Choose the Macro command.

The Macro dialog box appears.

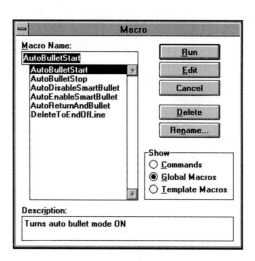

3. In the Show box, choose Commands, Global Macros, or Template Macros.

    If you choose Commands, all Word for Windows menu commands appear in the Macro Name list box. If you choose Global Macros, the macros stored in the NORMAL.DOT template appear in the Macro

Name list box. If you choose Template Macros, the macros stored in the current template appear in the Macro Name list box. (The Template Macros option button is available only when you are *not* working on a document based on the NORMAL.DOT template.)

4. From the Macro Name list box, choose the macro you want to run.

5. Choose the Run button.

The Macro dialog box also enables you to edit, delete, or rename macros.

Tip: You can execute a Word for Windows menu command by using the Macro dialog box. If you deleted a command from a menu (by using the Options command on the Tools menu), you can execute the command from the Macro dialog box.

Assigning Macros to Shortcut Keys

You should assign a macro you want to run more frequently to a shortcut key combination, a menu, or a Toolbar button. You can choose whichever method you find easiest to use.

You can assign a macro to a shortcut key combination in two ways:

- Assign a shortcut key combination when you create the macro.
- Assign a shortcut key combination by using the Options command on the Tools menu.

Earlier in this chapter, you learned how to record a macro. In the Record Macro dialog box, you can specify a macro name, a shortcut key combination, and a description of the macro. To assign a shortcut key combination, you choose a combination of the Ctrl key check box, the Shift key check box, and a key from the Key list box. When you select a key combination, its current assignment appears at the bottom of the Shortcut Key box. If the key combination is currently unassigned, Word for Windows displays [unassigned].

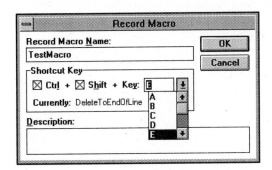

In this example, the shortcut key combination Ctrl + Shift + E is currently assigned to a macro called DeleteToEndOfLine.

13

You can also use the Options command on the Tools menu to specify shortcut key combinations for macros. Follow these steps:

1. Open the Tools menu.

2. Choose the Options command.

   The Options dialog box appears.

3. From the Category options, choose Keyboard.

   The Options dialog box displays keyboard options.

4. In the Show box, choose Macros.

5. If you are working in a document based on a template other than NORMAL.DOT, choose Template or Global in the Context box. (If you are working in a document based on NORMAL.DOT, only the Global option button is available.)

6. From the Macros list box, choose the macro to which you want to assign a shortcut key combination.

   If the macro is currently assigned to any key combination, that key combination appears next to the macro name and in the Current Keys For list box. (You *can* assign a macro to more than one key combination, but you probably will not want to do this.)

7. In the Shortcut Key box, choose a combination of the Ctrl and Shift check boxes and choose a key from the Key list box. Check the bottom of the Shortcut Key box to see whether that key combination is currently assigned.

In this example, the current template is BOOK.DOT, the key combination Ctrl + ⇧Shift + A is currently unassigned, and the AutoBulletStart macro is not currently assigned to any key combination.

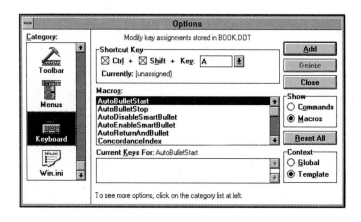

8. When you find an available key combination, choose the Add button.

9. Repeat steps 6 through 8 to assign other macros to key combinations.

10. Choose the Close button.

You can delete a shortcut key combination by highlighting the macro (in the Macros list box) and the key combination (in the Current Keys For list box). After you highlight both items, the Delete button becomes available. Note that you are deleting only the *shortcut key combination*, not the macro itself.

Assigning Macros to Menus

You also can use the Options command on the Tools menu to assign macros to Word for Windows menus. Follow these steps:

1. Open the Tools menu.

2. Choose the Options command.

   The Options dialog box appears.

3. From the Category options, choose Menus.

   The Options dialog box displays menu options.

4. In the Show box, choose Macros.

5. If you are working in a document based on a template other than NORMAL.DOT, choose Template or Global in the Context box. (If you are working in a document based on NORMAL.DOT, only the Global option button is available.)

6. From the Menu list box, choose the menu to which you want to assign a macro.

7. From the Macros list box, choose the macro you want to assign to the menu.

   The macro name appears in the Menu Text text box as it will appear in the menu you chose from the Menu list box. Notice that Word for Windows automatically inserts spaces into the name and adds an ampersand symbol (&) before the letter you can type to execute the menu command.

8. In the Menu Text text box, you can change the name that will appear on the menu or the letter you can type to execute the command.

13

In this example, the current template is BOOK.DOT, &Insert represents the Insert menu, and ⬚ will be the key you press to run the macro InsertFig from the Insert menu.

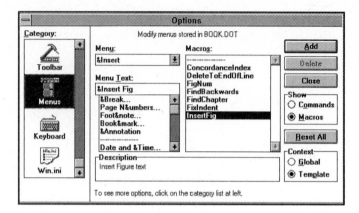

9. Choose the Add button.

10. Repeat steps 6 through 9 to assign other macros to menus.

11. Choose the Close button.

You can delete any menu item by highlighting the menu (in the Menu list box) and the menu item (in the Menu Text list box) you want to delete. After you highlight both items, the Delete button becomes available. Note that you are deleting the *appearance* of that item on the menu, not the menu item itself. To restore the menu item to the menu, choose the Reset All button.

Assigning Macros to the Toolbar

You also can use the Options command on the Tools menu to assign macros to the Toolbar. You can change an existing button or add a new button to the Toolbar. Follow these steps:

1. Open the Tools menu.

2. Choose the Options command.

   The Options dialog box appears.

3. From the Category options, choose Toolbar.

   The Options dialog box displays Toolbar options.

4. In the Show box, choose Macros.

5. If you are working in a document based on a template other than NORMAL.DOT, choose Template or Global in the Context box. (If you are working in a document based on NORMAL.DOT, only the Global option button is available.)

326

6. To change an existing button, choose that button from the Tool to Change list box. To add a button, choose one of the [space] options from the Tool to Change list box (the [space] option you choose determines the location of the button on the Toolbar).

7. From the Macros list box, choose the macro you want to assign to the Toolbar button.

8. From the Button list box, you can choose the button to which you want to assign the macro. (This step is optional.)

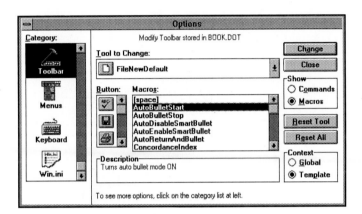

In this example, the current template is BOOK.DOT, the first tool on the Toolbar appears in the Tool to Change list box, and description of the macro AutoBulletStart appears in the Description box.

9. Choose the Change button.

10. Repeat steps 6 through 10 to assign other macros to the Toolbar.

11. Choose the Close button.

You can reset any or all the buttons on the Toolbar to their original meanings. To reset a specific button, highlight the button (in the Button list box) and then choose the Reset Tool button. To reset all the buttons on the Toolbar to the meanings they had when you installed Word for Windows, choose the Reset All button.

Deleting or Renaming Macros

You can delete or rename macros by using the Macro dialog box.

To delete a macro, follow these steps:

1. Open the Tools menu.

327

13

2. Choose the Macro command.

   The Macro dialog box appears.

3. In the Show box, choose Global Macros or Template Macros.

4. From the Macro Name list box, choose the macro you want to delete.

5. Choose the Delete button. Note, however, that you cannot "undo" this action.

6. Choose the Close button.

To rename a macro, follow these steps:

1. Open the Tools menu.

2. Choose the Macro command.

   The Macro dialog box appears.

3. In the Show box, choose Global Macros or Template Macros.

4. From the Macro Name list box, choose the macro you want to rename.

5. Choose the Rename button.

The Rename
dialog box
appears.

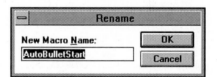

6. Type a name in the New Macro Name text box and then choose OK.

7. Choose the Close button.

Creating a Macro To Change Directories

Suppose that you store Word for Windows documents in four directories. You can create the following macro four times (one time for each directory) and assign each macro to a different shortcut key combination. Then, you can easily switch directories when you want to open a document in another directory.

Follow these steps to create a macro that changes directories:

1. Open the Tools menu.

2. Choose the Record Macro command.

3. In the Record Macro Name text box, type a name for the macro. You cannot include spaces in the name, but you can use uppercase letters to indicate the beginning of each word. In this example, name the macro **ChangeDirectory**.

4. Assign the macro to a shortcut key combination. In this example, choose the Ctrl and Shift check boxes and choose the letter C from the Key list box to assign the ChangeDirectory macro to the key combination $\boxed{\text{Ctrl}} + \boxed{\text{⇧Shift}} + \boxed{\text{C}}$.

5. In the Description text box, type a description of the macro (such as **Macro that lets me change directories**). Although this description is optional, it can be very helpful later.

6. Choose OK.

   Word for Windows closes the dialog box, and REC appears toward the right end of the status bar to indicate that the macro recorder is "on."

7. Open the File menu.

8. Choose the Open command.

9. From the Directories list box, double-click the directory to which you want to change.

10. Choose OK.

11. Choose the Cancel button.

12. Open the Tools menu again.

13. Choose the Stop Recorder command.

To use this macro, press its key combination ($\boxed{\text{Ctrl}} + \boxed{\text{⇧Shift}} + \boxed{\text{C}}$). Word for Windows changes to the directory you double-clicked when you created the macro.

Creating a Macro To Insert a Symbol

Perhaps, in your work, you use the symbols $\frac{1}{4}$, $\frac{1}{2}$, ✓, and § a great deal. You can create a macro to insert each symbol into a document (remember to consider whether your printer can print these symbols).

The following sets of steps create macros which insert two of these symbols: $\frac{1}{2}$ and ✓. These macros were created with a Hewlett-Packard LaserJet Series II

329

printer installed without any font cartridges or software fonts. If your printer cannot print these symbols, you cannot use the following macros (and the symbols do not appear in the Symbol dialog box).

To create a macro that inserts $\frac{1}{2}$ into a document, follow these steps:

1. Open the Tools menu.

2. Choose the Record Macro command.

3. In the Record Macro Name text box, type a name for the macro. You cannot include spaces in the name, but you can use uppercase letters to indicate the beginning of each word. In this example, name the macro **InsertHalf**.

4. Assign the macro to a shortcut key combination. In this example, choose the Ctrl and Shift check boxes and choose the number 2 from the Key list box to assign the InsertHalf macro to the key combination `Ctrl`+`⇧Shift`+`2`.

5. In the Description text box, type a description of the macro (such as **Macro to insert 1/2**). Although this description is optional, it can be very helpful later.

6. Choose OK.

   Word for Windows closes the dialog box, and REC appears toward the right end of the status bar to indicate that the macro recorder is "on."

7. Open the Insert menu.

8. Choose the Symbol command.

The Symbol dialog box appears.

9. From the Symbols From list box, choose (Normal Text).

10. Choose $\frac{1}{2}$.

11. Choose OK.

12. Open the Tools menu.

13. Choose the Stop Recorder command.

To use this macro, position the insertion point where you want $\frac{1}{2}$ to appear and press `Ctrl`+`⇧Shift`+`2`.

330

To create a macro that inserts ✓ into a document, follow these steps:

1. Open the Tools menu.

2. Choose the Record Macro command.

3. In the Record Macro Name text box, type a name for the macro. You cannot include spaces in the name, but you can use uppercase letters to indicate the beginning of each word. In this example, name the macro **InsertCheck**.

4. Assign the macro to a shortcut key combination. In this example, first choose the Ctrl and Shift check boxes and choose the letter C from the Key list box to assign the InsertCheck macro to the key combination Ctrl + ⇧Shift + C.

   If you previously used this key combination for the ChangeDirectory macro, Word for Windows indicates its current assignment. Reassign this key combination to the new macro or choose another key.

5. In the Description text box, type a description of the macro such as **Macro to insert check mark**. Although the description is optional, it can be very helpful later.

6. Choose OK.

   Word for Windows closes the dialog box, and REC appears toward the right end of the status bar to indicate that the macro recorder is "on."

7. Open the Insert menu.

8. Choose the Symbol command.

9. From the Symbols From list box, choose MT Symbol.

10. Choose ✓.

11. Choose OK.

12. Open the Tools menu.

13. Choose the Stop Recorder command.

You can repeat these steps (changing the macro name, the shortcut key combination, and the symbol you insert) to create a macro for each commonly used symbol.

Chapter Summary

In this chapter, you learned how to use glossaries and simple macros to automate your work and to help you work more efficiently. You learned that glossary entries store text (or pictures) and that macros store instructions for

13

executing Word for Windows commands. Specifically, you learned that you can do the following:

- You can create a glossary entry by using the Glossary command on the Edit menu.

- You can store a glossary entry by using the Template command on the File menu or by specifying a location when you exit Word for Windows.

- You can insert a glossary entry by typing the glossary name and then pressing F3 or by using the Glossary command on the Edit menu.

- You can edit or delete a glossary entry by using the Glossary Name dialog box, which you open by choosing the Glossary command from the Edit menu.

- You can print the contents of glossary entries by using the Print command on the File menu.

- You can install the macros provided with Word for Windows by opening NEWMACRO.DOC.

- You can use the Macro Recorder to record your own macros by using the Record Macro and Stop Recorder commands on the Tools menu.

- You can run macros by choosing the Macro command from the Tools menu. You also can assign frequently used macros to shortcut key combinations, menus, or the Toolbar by using the Options command on the Tools menu.

- You can delete and rename macros by using the Macro command on the Tools menu.

This chapter also included the steps to create a glossary entry for the complimentary close of a letter, a macro that changes directories, and macros that insert frequently used symbols.

In the next chapter, you will learn about merging.

Merging

14

Although you can use merging for other purposes, you most commonly use this feature to create form letters. To merge information, you create two types of documents: a main merge document and a data file. The main merge document contains the information that doesn't change from one copy of the document to the next—for example, the standardized information in a form letter. The data file contains the information that does change—for example, the names and addresses of the people to whom you want to send the form letter.

In this chapter, you will learn how to create a main merge document, how to create a data file, and how to attach the data file to the main merge document. You will learn how to plan a data file so that it contains all the information you need, how to edit a data file, and how to attach a different data file to a main merge document. You will learn how to sort a data file before you merge and how to merge to the printer or to a document on-screen. This chapter discusses all these procedures in the context of creating form letters, but you can use the same steps to create any kind of merged document.

Merging can be a complex process. Advanced merging procedures, such as using variable expressions to include only portions of information in the merged document or prompting the user to provide information at the time of the merge, are beyond the scope of this book.

Understanding records and fields

Planning a merge

Working with data files

Adding merge fields to the main merge document

Executing a merge

Using IF statements

Key Terms in This Chapter

Merge	The process of combining information from one document with information from another document. You usually use merging to create form letters.
Main merge document	Contains the information you want to repeat from one copy of the document to another (for example, from one letter to another) and the fields you want to use to merge information from the data file.
Data file	Contains the information that changes from one copy of the document to another (for example, the names and addresses of the people to whom you want to send a form letter). You organize a data file so that Word for Windows can identify what fields each record contains and where each record ends.
Field	One item of information in a record.
Record	A group of related, nonrepeating fields. One record contains all the information about one entry in the data file. If the data file were the contents of a Rolodex, for example, one record would contain all the information on one card in the Rolodex.
Header record	A record that contains the names of the fields in a data file.
Merge field	The name of a field in the data file. You insert merge fields into the main merge document at the locations where you want the information from the corresponding fields in the data file to appear in the merged documents.

Understanding Records and Fields

Data files consist of records, which consist of fields. A data file also can include a header record (later in this chapter, you will learn that you can store header records in separate files). The main merge document includes standardized text and merge fields. To successfully merge information, you must understand records and fields.

Understanding Records

A *record* is all the information about one entry in a data file. If the data file is an address file for form letters, a record is all the information about one person to whom you want to send the form letter—the name, street address, city, state, zip code, and any other information you choose to include.

For Word for Windows to merge the information successfully, you also must define a header record. The header record contains the titles or names of the fields. In a form letter data file, the header record might contain the words *Title*, *Name*, *Address1*, *Address2*, *City*, and so on.

Understanding Fields

You already have read about fields in other chapters of this book. In most cases, those fields were instruction fields, which contain codes that Word for Windows uses to insert information (such as the date) into a document. In a data file, the term *field* has a different meaning.

In a data file, a field is one item of information from a record, such as the name of one person to whom you want to send a form letter. The names of the fields (which appear in the header record) must be unique and must begin with a letter. A field name can have up to 32 characters and can include letters, numbers, and the underscore (_) character, but not spaces. You can enter field names in a data file in any order.

In the main merge document, you use merge fields to identify the locations where you want to insert information from the data file. Merge fields are the field names in the header record.

You can think of fields and records as a table. In fact, Word for Windows typically stores data files in a table.

14

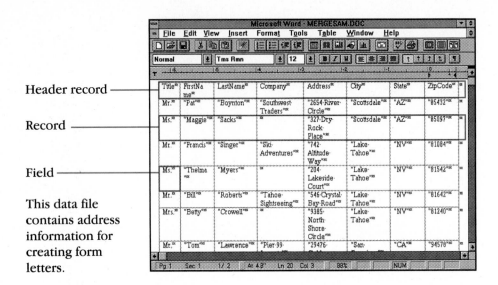

Header record ——

Record ——

14

Field ——

This data file
contains address
information for
creating form
letters.

Planning a Merge

To help you create a data file with the correct information, you probably
should create the main merge document first, leaving a blank (_____) or a
place holder (such as ZZ) wherever you want information from the data file to
appear. Add the merge fields to the main merge document after you create the
data file (when you know the merge field names). Adding merge fields to the
main merge document is discussed later in this chapter.

To create a main merge document that includes blanks or placeholders for
fields, follow these steps:

1. Open the File menu.
2. Choose the New command.
3. Type the main merge document, including blanks or placeholders for
   the fields you will use to merge data from the data file.
4. Save and close the document.

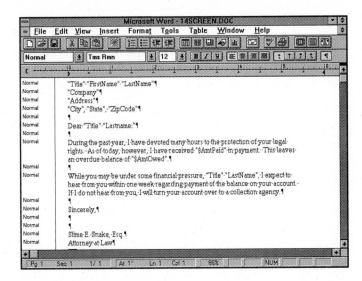

This main merge document indicates place-holders for the fields with quotation marks.

By default, Word for Windows organizes a data file in a table. You can include up to 31 fields in a data file with the default organization. You cannot include a Word for Windows table, an item in a frame, or an instruction field (a field that contains codes) in a field of a data file.

Note: If you need to include the result of an instruction field in a data file, position the insertion point in the instruction field, select the field (by pressing Ctrl + ⇧Shift + F9), and calculate the result of the field (by pressing ⇧Shift + F9).

To decide how many—and which—fields to include in a data file, look at the main merge document and consider the following questions:

- Do you want to sort the data?
- Do you want to include some records that have more information than others?
- Do you want to use the same information in different ways?
- Do you want to use the data file with more than one main merge document?

After evaluating these issues, add or delete placeholders in the main merge document to reflect the decisions you made.

Sorting Data

You can sort the records in a data file. If you are preparing a bulk mailing of form letters, for example, you can save time by sorting the data file and printing the letters and their mailing labels or envelopes by zip code. In this case, be sure to create a separate field for the zip code—do not include the zip code in the State field. In general, create a separate field for any information by which you may want to sort.

14

Handling Records of Different Sizes

All records in a data file must have the same size; however, creating a data file in which each record has the same amount of information (for example, in which each street address has exactly one line or exactly two lines) is very unusual. In general, create the record to accommodate the largest amount of information you think you will need. When a record does not have that much information, leave the extra fields blank. Blank fields do not necessarily create blank lines in the merge document.

Using the Same Information in Different Ways

You can use the information in a data file in different ways. In a form letter, for example, you can use the full name and title of the recipient (Ms. Mary Smith) in the inside address, but the last name and title (Ms. Smith) in the body of the letter. To use the same information in more than one way, divide the information into separate fields (for example, Title, First Name, and Last Name).

Using a Data File with More than One Main Merge Document

You can use a data file with more than one main merge document. If you create a name and address data file, for example, you can use the data file to produce form letters and to produce their mailing labels or envelopes. Because you can choose which fields you include in each main merge document, include in the data file all the information you will need for *all* the uses of the data file.

Working with Data Files

After you identify the information you need to include in a data file, you create the data file and attach it to the main merge document. If the data file already exists (for example, if you are using an existing mailing list), you simply attach the data file to the main merge document.

Creating and Attaching a New Data File

You can create a new data file in three ways:

- Use the Print Merge command on the File menu.
- Use Insert Table command on the Table menu.
- Use paragraphs.

Using the Print Merge Command To Create a Data File

Using the Print Merge command on the File menu is the easiest way to create a data file and attach it to a main merge document. If the data file will contain more than 31 fields, however, you cannot use this method—you must use paragraphs (described later in this section).

When you use the Print Merge command to create and attach a data file, you first attach an empty data file to a main merge document. Then, you create the header record for the data file. When you save the header record, Word for Windows opens a document that contains a table; the first row of the table contains the field names you defined as the header record. The second row is blank, ready for you to begin entering data.

Follow these steps to create and attach a new data file to a main merge document:

1. Open the main merge document you set up when planning the data file.
2. Use the blanks or place holders in the main merge document to identify the fields you must include in the data file.
3. Open the File menu.
4. Choose the Print Merge command.

14

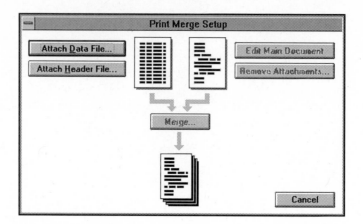

The Print Merge
Setup dialog box
appears.

14

5. Choose the Attach **D**ata File button.

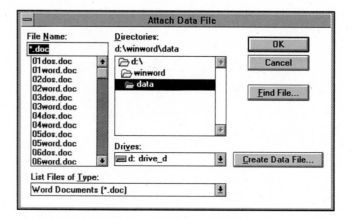

The Attach Data
File dialog box
appears.

6. Choose the **C**reate Data File button.

The Create Data
File dialog box
appears. You use
this dialog box to
create the header
record.

7. In the Field Name text box, type the name of the field you want to appear first in the data file.

8. Press ⏎Enter or choose the Add button.

    Word for Windows adds this field name to the header record. The field name appears in the Fields in Header Record list box.

9. Repeat steps 7 and 8 for each field in the data file.

    Word for Windows adds each field name to the header record in the order you enter it. The field names appear in the Fields in Header Record list box.

    If you make a mistake, you can delete a field by choosing the field name from the Fields in Header Record list box and then choosing the Delete button. After you delete a field, you can re-enter it correctly.

10. After you enter all the field names in the header record, choose OK.

    The Save As dialog box appears.

11. Type a file name for the data file.

12. Choose OK.

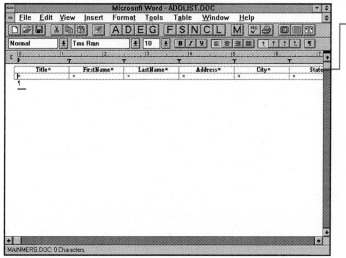

Header record

Word for Windows opens the data file. The first row is the header record. The insertion point appears in the first cell of the second row.

13. Type the data for the first field of the first record (in the first cell of the second row of the table).

    If the cell is not big enough to display all the data on one line, Word for Windows wraps the data. In the main merge document, the information will appear on one line.

341

You can press ⏎Enter to insert a paragraph mark or ⇧Shift + ⏎Enter to insert a line break in the data. When you merge the data, the information will appear on multiple lines. In general, you do not need to do this.

14. Press Tab⇄ to move to the next field.

15. Type the data for that field. If the record does not include information for that field, do not type anything in the field, even a space.

16. Repeat steps 13 and 14 to enter data for the rest of the record.

17. When you reach the end of a record (the end of a row), press Tab⇄ to add another row and continue entering data.

This data file contains names and addresses for a mailing list. Notice that Word for Windows wrapped the data in many of the fields.

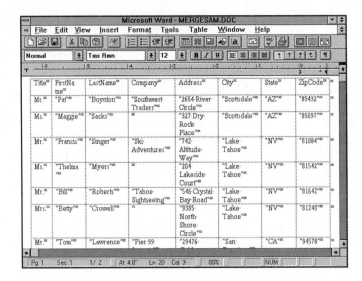

18. When you are done entering data, choose the Save command from the File menu or the Save button on the Toolbar.

    Word for Windows displays the Summary Information dialog box.

19. After entering the summary information, choose OK.

Using the Table Menu To Create a Data File

You can use the Insert Table command on the Table menu to create a data file manually. This method is more difficult; Word for Windows does not "walk you through" the steps for creating the header record and the data file. If you choose to create a data file manually, make sure that you enter the header record in the top row of the table. You then can use other Table menu commands to add rows for additional data. Note, however, that your table must remain rectangular—do not delete any individual cells.

Using Paragraphs To Create a Data File

To create a data file that has more than 31 fields per record, you cannot use the Print Merge command or the Insert Table command. (Both commands use tables to create data files, but Word for Windows tables cannot have more than 31 columns.) To create a data file that has more than 31 fields, you must organize the data in paragraphs, separating the fields with tabs or commas.

Create a paragraph for each record. Within each record (paragraph), use tabs or commas to separate fields. Because you often need commas within the data (for example, to separate a city from a state), you usually use tabs to separate the fields. The first record in the file must be the header record.

Attaching an Existing Data File

After you create a data file, you can use the same data with more than one main merge document. If, for example, you created a name and address file to use with a form letter to solicit new business, you can use the same names and addresses for a follow-up form letter that offers an introductory special.

To attach an existing data file to another main merge document, you follow the steps you used to create a new data file with the Print Merge command, but you choose the existing data file and then choose the OK button rather than the Create Data File button.

Follow these steps to attach an existing data file to another main merge document:

1. Open the main merge document to which you want to attach the existing data file.
2. Open the File menu.
3. Choose the Print Merge command.

   The Print Merge Setup dialog box appears.
4. Choose the Attach Data File button.

   The Attach Data File dialog box appears.
5. From the File Name list box, choose the data file that contains the information you want to merge with the main merge document.
6. Choose OK.

14

343

Print Merge bar —

Word for Windows opens the main merge document and displays the Print Merge bar.

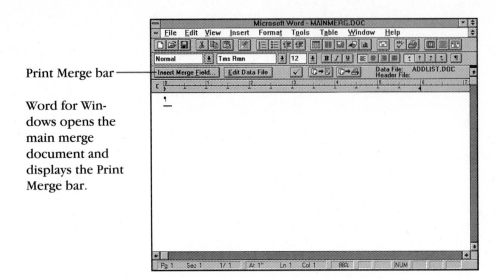

Type or edit the main merge document and then choose the Save command from the File menu or the Save button on the Toolbar.

The Print Merge bar appears in all main merge documents to which you have attached a data file. You will learn more about the Print Merge bar in the "Adding Merge Fields to the Main Merge Document" section later in this chapter.

Changing to Another Data File

You can attach only one data file to a main merge document at one time, but you can change the attached data file at any time.

To change the data file attached to a main merge document, follow these steps:

1. Open the main merge document to which you want to attach a different data file.
2. Open the File menu.
3. Choose the Print Merge command.

   The Print Merge Setup dialog box appears.
4. Choose the Attach Data File button. (You do not need to choose the Remove Attachments button to change the data file.)

   The Attach Data File dialog box appears.

5. From the File Name list box, choose the data file you want to attach to the main merge document.

6. Choose OK.

   On the Print Merge bar, the name of the attached data file changes.

Removing an Attached Data File

You can convert a main merge document to a regular document by removing the attached data file and changing the merge fields in the document to regular text.

Note: You cannot "undo" the removal of an attached data file.

To remove an attached data file, follow these steps:

1. Open the main merge document from which you want to remove the attached data file.

2. Open the File menu.

3. Choose the Print Merge command.

   The Print Merge Setup dialog box appears.

4. Choose the Remove Attachments button.

   A warning dialog box appears.

5. Choose Yes to remove the data file.

To change the merge fields to regular text, see "Adding Merge Fields to the Main Document" later in this chapter.

Editing a Data File

You can edit a data file (for example, to add or delete records) by opening both the main merge document and the data file and then using special editing commands in the data file.

Word for Windows bases merge data files on the DATAFILE.DOT template, which contains macros that help you to edit the data file. These macros appear on the Tools menu as the Record Management Tools and Database Management Tools commands.

345

14

When you choose the Record Management Tools command from the Tools menu, the Record Management Tools dialog box appears.

When you choose the Database Management Tools command from the Tools menu, the Database Management Tools dialog box appears.

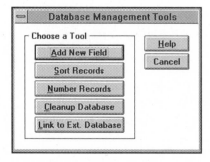

Both dialog boxes contain command buttons. which run macros that help you to modify the data file. The command buttons also appear on the Toolbar, temporarily replacing some of the usual Toolbar buttons.

On the Toolbar, the macro buttons replace existing buttons while you are working in the data file.

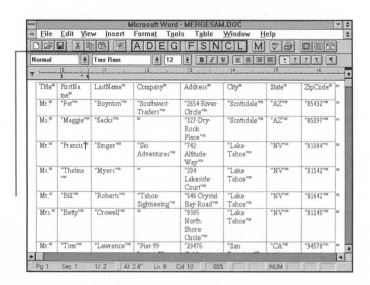

346

If you are using a mouse, you may find it faster to use these buttons than to open the Record Management Tools or Database Management Tools dialog box. Table 14.1 lists the record and database management tools.

Table 14.1
Macro Buttons for Editing a Data File

Macro Button	Effect
A	Adds a record to the end of the file.
D	Deletes a record.
E	Edits a record.
G	Goes to a specific record.
F	Adds a new field.
S	Sorts the file.
N	Numbers the records.
C	Converts an external database file.
L	Links to an external database file.
M	Switches to the main document.

14

To edit a data file, follow these steps:

1. Open a main merge document to which the the data file you want to edit is attached.
2. Open the data file you want to edit.
3. Use the the macro buttons on the Toolbar or the command buttons in the Record Management Tools and Database Management Tools dialog boxes to edit the data file.

To add a new record to the data file, for example, choose the A button on the Toolbar or choose the Record Management Tools command from the Tools menu and then choose the Add New Record button. Word for Windows asks where you want to insert the new record (at the end of the file is the safest location) and prompts you for the data for each field.

4. After you make all the changes, save the data file.

Using Data Created in Other Programs

You can use data you created in other programs as long as you installed the proper conversion filters when you installed Word for Windows. If you installed Word for Windows completely (see the Appendix), you have conversion filters available for WordPerfect (Versions 4 and 5), dBASE, Microsoft Excel, and Lotus 1-2-3. You can check your Word for Windows program directory for the following files to be sure you installed the conversion filters:

Program	Filter name
WordPerfect (Versions 4 and 5)	WPFT4.CNV and WPFT5.CNV
dBASE	DBASE.CNV
Microsoft Excel	XLBIFF.CNV
Lotus 1-2-3	LOTUS123.CNV

For details on converting data files from other programs, see the *Word for Windows User's Guide*. Carefully check data files you convert from other programs to ensure that each field contains the proper information (for example, that fields within a record are properly aligned). Also, you may need to create a header record for the imported data.

Creating Header Records

Until now, you have created the header record as part of the data file. You can, however, create a header record that is separate from the data file.

You may *need* to create a separate header record if you are using data that you converted from another application. You may *want* to create a separate header record so that you can use a data file with several different header records. (Remember, however, that a data file can have only one header record at a time.)

Creating a Header Record for an Existing Data File

If you find that you have a data file that has no header record, you can create a header record and store it in the data file.

If the data file is in paragraph form (with fields separated by tabs or commas), you insert a paragraph that contains the header record (with fields separated by tabs or commas) at the beginning of the data file.

If the data is in a table, you use commands on the Table menu to add a row at the beginning of the table and then type the header record field names in the new row. Follow these steps:

1. Position the insertion point in the first row of the data file table.

2. Open the Table menu.

3. Choose the Insert Cells command.

    The Insert Cells dialog box appears.

4. Choose the Insert Entire Row button.

    Word for Windows inserts a new row at the beginning of the table.

5. Type the header record field names in the cells of the new row (press `Tab` after each field name to move to the next cell).

Storing a Header Record in a Separate File

You may find that one header record will work well with several different data files or that one data file will need different header records when attached to different main merge documents. In either case, storing the header record in a separate file is convenient because you can attach the header record to any data file. (Remember, however, that a data file can have only one header record at a time.)

Creating and attaching a separate header record file is very similar to creating and attaching a data file by using the Print Merge command. Follow these steps:

1. Open the main merge document to which you want to attach the header record file.

2. Use the blanks or place holders in the main merge document to identify the fields you must include in the header record.

14

14

3. Open the File menu.

4. Choose the Print Merge command.

   The Print Merge Setup dialog box appears.

5. Choose the Attach Header File button.

   The Attach Header File dialog box appears.

6. Choose the Create Header File button.

   The Create Header File dialog box appears.

7. In the Field Name text box, type the name of the field you want to appear first in the header record.

8. Press ⏎Enter or choose the Add button.

   Word for Windows adds this field name to the header record. The field name appears in the Fields in Header Record list box.

9. Repeat steps 7 and 8 for each field in the data file.

   Word for Windows adds each field name to the header record in the order you enter it. The field names appear in the Fields in Header Record list box.

   If you make a mistake, you can delete a field by choosing the field name from the Fields in Header Record list box and then choosing the Delete button. After you delete a field, you can re-enter it correctly.

10. After you enter all the field names in the header record, choose OK.

    The Save As dialog box appears.

11. Type a file name for the header record.

12. Choose OK.

    A document containing just the header record (in table format) appears briefly on-screen. Then, Word for Windows displays the main merge document again.

If you open the Window menu, you can see that both the main merge document and the header record file remain open, and you can switch between these documents.

If you switch to the header record file, you can see that it looks like the data file you created by using the Print Merge command, except that the header record file does not contain the second row of the table.

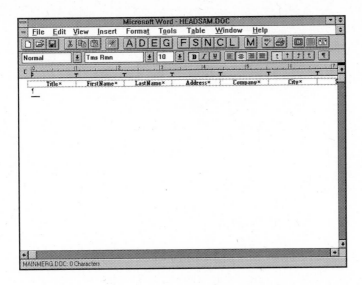

The header record file contains only the header record.

14

After you create a separate header record file and attach it to the main merge document, you also must attach a data file (without a header record) to both the main merge document and the header record file. With both the main merge document and the header record file open, follow these steps:

1. Open the File menu.

2. Choose the Print Merge command.

   The Print Merge Setup dialog box appears.

3. Choose the Attach Data File button.

   The Attach Data File dialog box appears.

4. From the File Name list box, choose the data file you want to attach to the main merge document and the header record file.

5. Choose OK.

Using an Existing Header Record File

To use an existing header record file, you must attach the header record file to a main merge document and attach a data file (without a header record) to both the main merge document and the header record file.

Follow these steps to attach a header record file and a data file to a main merge document:

1. Open the main merge document.

351

2. Open the **F**ile menu.

3. Choose the Print **M**erge command.

    The Print Merge Setup dialog box appears.

4. Choose the Attach **H**eader File button.

    The Attach Header File dialog box appears.

5. From the File **N**ame list box, choose the header record file you want to attach to the main merge document.

6. Choose OK.

    The header record file's name appears in the Print Merge bar.

7. Open the **F**ile menu again.

8. Choose the Print **M**erge command again.

    The Print Merge Setup dialog box appears.

9. Choose the Attach **D**ata File button.

    The Attach Data File dialog box appears.

10. From the File **N**ame list box, choose the data file you want to attach to the main merge document and the header record file.

11. Choose OK.

    The data file's name also appears in the Print Merge bar.

In this example, the header file HEADSAM.DOC and the data file MERGESAM.DOC are attached to the main merge document MAINMERG.DOC.

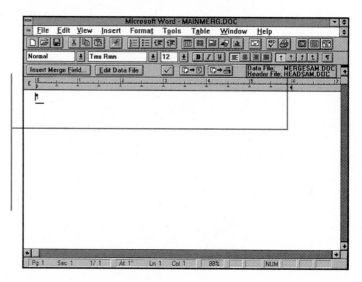

Note: Be sure to attach the header record file before you attach the data file. Word for Windows uses the first row of the first file you attach as the header record. If this row is not a valid header record, your merge will be unsuccessful.

Adding Merge Fields to the Main Merge Document

When you created a main merge document, you initially used blanks or place holders to identify the places in the document where you want to insert merge fields. Then, in a header record file or a data file, you named those fields. Now, you must replace the blanks or place holders in the main merge document with merge fields.

In the main merge document, merge fields can appear as codes or as "text," depending on whether you set your view options to display field codes (by choosing the Field Codes command from the View menu). If you do not choose the Field Codes command from the View menu, each merge field appears in the main merge document as the field name enclosed in double angle brackets: <<name>>. If you you do choose the Field Codes command from the View menu, each merge field appears in the main merge document enclosed in braces, with the keyword MERGEFIELD preceding the field name: {MERGEFIELD name}. The appearance of the merge fields (whether you display field results or field codes) has no effect on the merging process.

When you merge a data file with the main merge document, Word for Windows replaces merge fields in the main merge document with the information in the corresponding field of the data file. If you want to apply formatting (such as bold or italic) to the merged information, you can format the merge field in the main merge document. Select the merge field (position the insertion point anywhere in the merge field and press Ctrl + ⇧Shift + F9) and then apply the formatting.

The Print Merge bar provides the easiest way to insert merge fields into the main merge document. Follow these steps:

1. Open the main merge document.

   The Print Merge bar appears at the top of the text area.

2. Attach the header record file, if necessary. (Remember that you must attach the header record file before you attach the data file.) For more information, see the "Using an Existing Header Record File" section of this chapter.

3. Attach the data file. For more information, see the "Attaching an Existing Data File" section of this chapter.

14

353

4. Position the insertion point at the location where you want to insert a merge field into the main merge document.

Or

Select the blank or placeholder where you want to insert a merge field into the main merge document.

5. Choose the Insert Merge Field button from the Print Merge bar.

14

The Insert Merge Field dialog box appears.

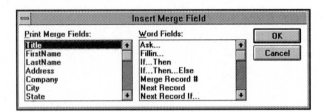

6. From the Print Merge Fields list box, choose the field you want to insert at that location in the main merge document.

7. Choose OK.

8. Repeat steps 4 through 7 to insert merge fields at all the locations you identified with blanks or place holders.

9. If you did not select the blanks or place holders in step 4, delete the blanks or place holders in the main merge document.

10. Save the main merge document.

If you make a mistake and want to replace a merge field you inserted, simply select the merge field you want to replace and repeat steps 5 through 7.

Executing a Merge

After you set up a data file (and header record file, if necessary), attach it to the main merge document, and insert merge fields into the main merge document, you can merge the variable information from the data file with the static information in the main merge document.

Before performing the merge, you can sort the data file so that Word for Windows produces the merged documents in a certain order (perhaps by zip code or alphabetically by last name). You also can have Word for Windows check the merge to identify potential problems. You can choose whether to merge information directly to the printer or to create a file that contains the merged documents. When you merge, you can control whether Word for

Windows prints blank lines for empty fields and which records Word for Windows includes in the merge.

Sorting Data Before Merging

Before you merge the data file and the main merge document, you can sort the data file. If you are producing a form letter for a bulk mailing, for example, you may want to sort the data file so that Word for Windows produces the merged letters in order by zip code.

To sort a data file, you first must select the records you want to sort. You can sort some or all of the records, but be sure to select the entire row for each record you want to sort. If you sort only some columns of the records, Word for Windows will mix up the related data (for example, scrambling names and addresses). Sometimes, sorting produces unexpected results; although you can "undo" the sort, you should save the data file before you sort.

After you select the records you want to sort, you must indicate a key field, the field by which you want to sort. If the information in the key field contains a combination of letters, numbers, and special characters, Word for Windows uses rules to evaluate and sort the key fields.

The following rules describe how Word for Windows sorts key fields in *ascending* order. The information appears in reverse order when Word for Windows sorts key fields in descending order:

- Key fields beginning with punctuation marks appear first, key fields beginning with numbers appear next, and key fields beginning with letters appear last.

- Key fields beginning with uppercase letters appear before key fields beginning with lowercase letters.

- Diacritical marks (such as accents and umlauts) are ignored.

- International characters are sorted as if they were their nearest English language equivalent.

If the key fields of several records have the same first character, Word for Windows sorts the key fields by evaluating subsequent characters according to the same rules.

To sort all the information in a data file table, follow these steps.

1. Open the data file by using the Open button on the Toolbar, the Open command on the File menu, or the Edit Data File button on the Print Merge bar. If the data file was already open, *save* the data file by using

14

355

the Save button on the Toolbar or the Save command on the File menu.

2. Select all cells in all rows in the table *except* the header record. (If you make no selection before sorting, Word for Windows automatically selects the entire file, *including* the header record.)

3. Open the Tools menu.

4. Choose the Sorting command.

   The Sorting dialog box appears.

5. In the Sorting Order box, choose Ascending or Descending.

   If you choose Ascending, Word for Windows sorts the information according to the rules described above (for example, from 0 to 9 and then from A to Z). If you choose Descending, Word for Windows sorts the information in reverse order (for example, from Z to A and then from 9 to 0).

6. From the Key Type list box, choose Alphanumeric, Numeric, or Date. If you plan to sort by zip code, for example, choose Numeric.

7. The Comma and Tab option buttons are not available when you are sorting a data file organized as a table. If these option buttons are available, you selected something other than rows of data. Choose Cancel and start over.

8. From the Field Number list box, choose the number of the key field— the field by which you want to sort. (Word for Windows numbers fields from left to right).

9. If you chose Alphanumeric from the Key Type list box, you can choose the Case Sensitive check box. (The Sort Column Only check box is available only when you do not select all columns in a row. If the Sort Column Only check box is available, you did not select the data properly. Choose Cancel and start over.)

10. Choose OK.

If you do not get the results you anticipated, you can undo the sort by using the Undo button on the Toolbar or the Undo command on the Edit menu.

To sort all the information in a data file organized in paragraphs, follow these steps:

1. Open the data file by using the Open button on the Toolbar, the Open command on the File menu, or the Edit Data File button on the Print Merge bar. If the data file was already open, *save* the data file by using the Save button on the Toolbar or the Save command on the File menu.

2. Select all the paragraphs except the header record. (If you make no selection, Word for Windows automatically selects the entire file, *including* the header record.)

3. Open the Tools menu.

4. Choose the Sorting command.

   The Sorting dialog box appears.

5. In the Sorting Order box, choose Ascending or Descending.

   If you choose Ascending, Word for Windows sorts the information according to the rules described above (for example, from 0 to 9 and then from A to Z). If you choose Descending, Word for Windows sorts the information in reverse order (for example, from Z to A and then from 9 to 0).

6. From the Key Type list box, choose Alphanumeric, Numeric, or Date. If you plan to sort by zip code, for example, choose Numeric.

7. Choose the appropriate separator—Comma or Tab.

8. From the Field Number list box, choose the number of the key field— the field by which you want to sort. (Word for Windows numbers fields separated by commas or tabs from left to right).

9. If you chose Alphanumeric from the Key Type list box, you can choose the Case Sensitive check box. (The Sort Column Only check box is not available when you are sorting a data file organized in paragraphs. If the Sort Column Only check box is available, you did not select the data properly. Choose Cancel and start over.)

10. Choose OK.

Again, you can undo the sort by using the Undo button on the Toolbar or the Undo command on the Edit menu.

Checking the Merge

Before merging the data file and main merge document, Word for Windows can check the merge for potential problems.

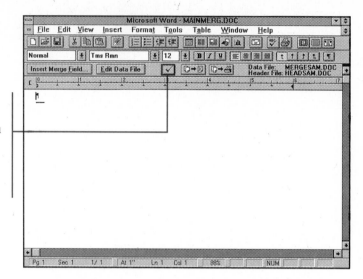

14

To check the merge for potential problems, you use the check mark button on the Print Merge bar.

If you choose the check mark button on the Print Merge bar, Word for Windows compares the header record, the data, and the merge fields in the main merge document. If Word for Windows finds potential errors, the program opens a document called Form Letter 1, where it displays each record and attempts to identify the problem. If Word for Windows finds no potential errors, the program displays a dialog box indicating that result.

One common merge error is to use a header record that does not match the data file. If you attached a separate header record file to the main merge document and data file, make sure that the header record and the data file match. Another common error is to insert merge fields into the main merge document that do not match the header record. If you insert merge fields into the main document by using the Print Merge bar, you should not encounter this problem.

Choosing Merge Options

You can perform a merge and send the result to a printer or to a document on-screen by using a button on the Print Merge bar or the Print Merge command on the File menu.

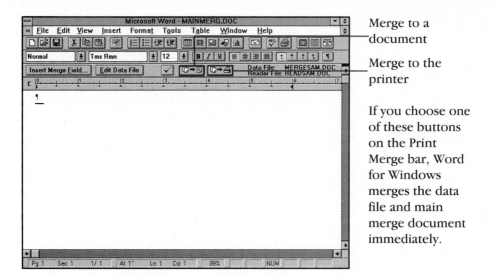

Merge to a document

Merge to the printer

If you choose one of these buttons on the Print Merge bar, Word for Windows merges the data file and main merge document immediately.

14

If you use the Print Merge command on the File menu, Word for Windows displays the Print Merge dialog box, which provides several merge options.

To perform a merge by using the Print Merge dialog box, follow these steps:

1. Activate the main merge document.

2. Open the File menu.

3. Choose the Print Merge command.

   The Print Merge Setup dialog box appears.

4. Choose the Merge button.

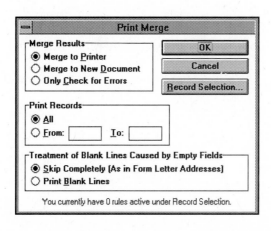

The Print Merge dialog box appears.

5. In the Merge Results box, choose Merge to Printer, Merge to a New Document, or Only Check for Errors.

   If you choose Merge to Printer, Word for Windows will merge the data file and main merge document and print the merged documents. If you choose Merge to a New Document, Word for Windows will merge the data file and main merge document to a new document. If you choose Only Check for Errors, Word for Windows will check for potential problems without actually performing the merge.

6. In the Print Records box, choose the All or From option button. If you choose From, type record numbers in the From and To text boxes. (Word for Windows numbers records consecutively without counting the header record.)

7. In the Treatment of Blank Lines Caused by Empty Fields box, choose Skip Completely or Print Blank Lines.

8. To control which records Word for Windows includes in the merge, choose the Record Selection button. After specifying merge rules, choose OK to return to the Print Merge dialog box. (Merge rules are explained at the end of this section.)

9. Choose OK.

To control which records Word for Windows includes in the merge by specifying merge rules, you choose the Record Selection button in the Print Merge dialog box.

When you choose the Record Selection button, the Record Selection dialog box appears.

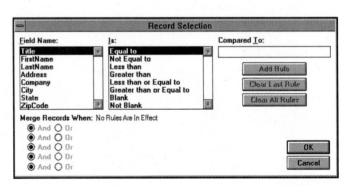

In the Record Selection dialog box, you use the Field Name list box to identify the field by which you want Word for Windows to restrict the merge. In the Is list box, you choose the way in which you want Word for Windows to compare the field you identified in the Field Name list box (for example, Equal to or Greater than). In the Compared To text box, type the information you want

Word for Windows to use when it makes the comparison. You use the And and Or option buttons to link rules together. If you want to send a form letter to only those customers whose zip codes are between 33549 and 33626, for example, you can set up the following two merge rules:

- From the Field Name list box, choose ZipCode. From the Is list box, choose Greater than. In the Compared To text box, type 33548. Then, choose the Add Rule button. The first set of And and Or option buttons becomes available. Choose the And option button.

- From the Field Name list box, choose ZipCode. From the Is list box, choose Less than. In the Compared To text box, type 33627. Then, choose the Add Rule button. The second set of And and Or option buttons becomes available. Because this rule is the last rule you want to create, however, the And and Or buttons are not relevant. Choose OK to accept the rules and return to the Print Merge dialog box.

When you perform the merge, Word for Windows produces form letters for only those customers whose zip codes are between 33549 and 33626.

Note: When no rules are in effect, the And and Or option buttons are not available. When rules *are* in effect, you use each set of option buttons to link a pair of rules. And takes precedence over Or, so Word for Windows evaluates all rules linked by And before any rules linked by Or. When you choose the And option button, Word for Windows selects only those records that meet all linked rules. When you choose the Or option button, Word for Windows selects any record that meets any linked rule. In general, choosing the And option button reduces the number of records Word for Windows selects, and choosing the Or option button increases the number of records Word for Windows selects.

Using IF Statements

Word for Windows provides several instruction fields you can use to customize a main merge document. In this section, you will learn about the IF field. For complete information about all the instruction fields, see the *Word for Windows User's Guide*.

To include certain text in the merged document if the specified conditions are true, you use the The If...Then option. To include certain text in the merged document if the specified conditions are true, but to include other text if those conditions are false, you use the If...Then...Else option.

Suppose, for example, that you own and operate a minor league baseball team, and you are using a mass mailing to try to build attendance. In the letters to women, you want to include the dates for Ladies Days. In the letters to men, you want to include the dates for Father/Son Days.

To create all the necessary form letters, you use the Insert Merge Field dialog box to include an If...Then...Else statement at the beginning of the main merge document. Follow these steps:

1. Position the insertion point at the beginning of the main merge document.
2. On the Print Merge bar, choose the Insert Merge Field button.

The Insert Merge Field dialog box appears.

3. From the Word Fields list box, choose If...Then...Else.
4. Choose OK.

Word for Windows inserts an IF statement at the beginning of the document.

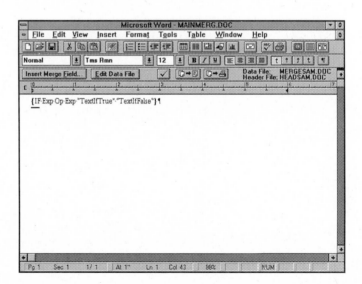

In this IF statement, you must provide substitutions for Exp, Op, Exp, TextIfTrue, and TextIfFalse and create an expression that Word for Windows can evaluate.

To provide these substitutions and create this expression for the baseball team example, follow these steps:

1. Select the first Exp.
2. From the Print Merge bar, choose the Insert Merge Field button.
3. From the Print Merge Fields list box, choose the Title field.
4. Select Op and type = (an equal sign).
5. Select the second Exp and type **Mr.**. Be sure that you include a period after *Mr.*, because a period appears in that field of the data file.
6. Select TextIfTrue (but not the quotation marks) and type **Father/Son Days are February 12, March 10, and April 3**. Be careful not to delete the quotation marks.
7. Select TextIfFalse (but not the quotation marks) and type **Ladies Days are February 14, March 17, and April 19**. Be careful not to delete the quotation marks.

The IF statement now tells Word for Windows to check the title field of each record in the data file. If a person's title is *Mr.*, Word for Windows will include the phrase about Father/Son Days. If the person's title is anything other than *Mr.*, Word for Windows will include the phrase about Ladies Days.

Chapter Summary

In this chapter, you learned how to set up a merge in Word for Windows. You learned about fields and records and about the factors to consider when planning a merge file. You learned that you can create separate header record files that you can use with more than one data file. You also learned that you can use data created in other programs for merges. Specifically, you learned the following information:

■ You can create a new data file by using the Print Merge command on the File menu, by using the commands on the Table menu, or by using paragraphs.

■ You can attach an existing data file to a main merge document by using the Print Merge command on the File menu. You also can change or remove the data file attached to a main merge document by using the Print Merge command on the File menu.

14

■ You can edit a data file by using special macro buttons on the Toolbar or by using the Record Management Tools command or the Database Management Tools command on the Tools menu.

■ You insert merge fields into a main merge document by using the Print Merge bar.

■ Before you merge a data file and a main merge document, you can sort the data file by using the Sorting command on the Tools menu, and you can check the merge for potential problems by using the check mark button on the Print Merge bar or the Only Check for Errors option in the Print Merge dialog box (which you open by choosing the Print Merge command from the File menu).

■ You can merge to the printer or to a document by using a button on the the Print Merge bar or the Merge to Printer or Merge to a New Document option in the Print Merge dialog box (which you open by choosing the Print Merge command from the File menu).

■ You can use the Print Merge bar to insert IF statements in a main merge document. IF statements direct Word for Windows to include information in the merge documents only *if* certain conditions are met.

In the next chapter, you will learn how to use Microsoft Graph to create charts and graphs that you can include in Word for Windows documents.

Using Microsoft Graph

15

Microsoft Graph is a software package that comes with Word for Windows. Microsoft Graph enables you to convert data from many Windows and non-Windows programs into a wide variety of charts and graphs. Microsoft Graph also works with many Windows programs other than Word for Windows.

In this chapter, you will learn how to use Microsoft Graph to create charts in Word for Windows documents. You don't need to exit Word for Windows because Microsoft Graph works inside Word for Windows.

An overview of Microsoft Graph

Using the datasheet

Creating a chart

15

Key Terms in This Chapter

Datasheet window   The window where you enter and edit the data from which Microsoft Graph creates a chart. The Datasheet window appears in the Microsoft Graph window when you open Microsoft Graph. The datasheet closely resembles a Word for Windows table.

Cell   The intersection of a row and a column in the datasheet.

Data point   The information stored in a cell.

Data series   A collection of related data points. A data series can be a row or a column of the datasheet.

Data series name   A label that identifies a data series. Microsoft Graph uses the information that appears in the first row or the first column of the datasheet as the data series names. These names appear in the legend of the chart.

Chart window   The window that contains the chart of the data in the Datasheet window. The Chart window appears in the Microsoft Graph window when you open Microsoft Graph.

Chart type   A category of charts (such as bar, line, area, or three-dimensional) that Microsoft Graph can produce.

Chart format   A variation of a chart type (such as the side-by-side bar, stacked bar, and 100-percent stacked bar formats available for bar charts) that Microsoft Graph can produce.

Axis   The vertical or horizontal line that provides the scale for plotting data. In two-dimensional charts, you usually plot categories of data along the horizontal axis (the X-axis) and data values along the vertical axis (the Y-axis).

Tick mark labels	The labels that appear along the X-axis and Y-axis. In a two-dimensional chart, the Y-axis labels usually are numbers, and the X-axis labels are labels taken from the datasheet that are *not* associated with the data series.
Data marker	A symbol that represents a data point. In line and XY charts, the data marker is a dot or a symbol. In bar and column charts, the data marker is a bar. In area and pie charts, the data marker is a shape (or slice of the pie).

15

An Overview of Microsoft Graph

Microsoft Graph enables you to create charts from data formatted in a table. You can create data inside Microsoft Graph, use a table in a Word for Windows document, or import data from other programs, such as Microsoft Excel or Lotus 1-2-3. If you use a table in a Word for Windows document or import data from another program, the new data appears in the datasheet. Microsoft Graph automatically creates a column chart based on all the data you provide and updates the chart as you make changes.

You also can change the chart style and apply formatting and shading. Microsoft Graph enables you to choose from 12 chart styles, each with its own set of formats. Remember that although you see the chart in color on a color monitor, the chart will print in shades of gray unless you have a color printer.

You don't need to exit Word for Windows to use Microsoft Graph. Rather, you can use the Word for Windows Toolbar or menus to open Microsoft Graph. Then, two additional windows appear in the Microsoft Graph window: the Datasheet window and the Chart window. When you work in these windows, Microsoft Graph provides menus from which you choose commands. Working in Microsoft Graph is easiest when you use a mouse, but you also can use the keyboard.

Opening Microsoft Graph

To open Microsoft Graph, follow these steps:

1. Open the Insert menu.
2. Choose the Object command.

The Object dialog box appears.

3. From the Object type list box, choose Microsoft Graph.

4. Choose OK.

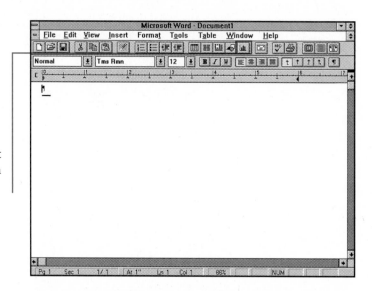

You also can open Microsoft Graph by choosing the Microsoft Graph button on the Toolbar.

15

When you open Microsoft Graph, the Datasheet window and Chart window appear in the Microsoft Graph window.

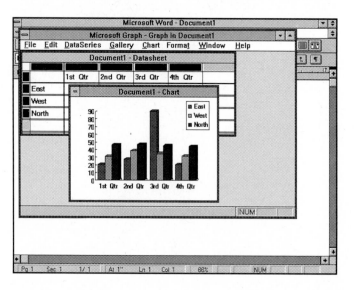

If you do not provide data, Microsoft Graph displays a default datasheet and chart. If you do provide data, this default graph and chart appear first, but then Microsoft Graph replaces them with the information you provided. The default chart format is a column chart.

You can switch between the Datasheet window and Chart window by using the mouse or the keyboard. To switch windows by using the mouse, click inside the other window. To switch windows by using the keyboard, press Ctrl + F6.

The menu bar at the top of the Microsoft Graph window provides menus that apply to both the Datasheet window and the Chart window. On each menu, the commands available for the active window are black and the commands for the inactive window are gray.

15

Closing Microsoft Graph

You can exit Microsoft Graph with or without including the chart in a Word for Windows document. To exit Microsoft Graph, follow these steps:

1. Open the File menu.
2. Choose the Exit and Return to *Document1* command (where *Document1* is the Word for Windows document's name).

   Microsoft Graph displays a dialog box that asks whether you want to update the document.
3. Choose Yes to include the chart in the active Word for Windows document. Choose No to exit Microsoft Graph without including the chart in the Word for Windows document.

Note: Including a chart in the Word for Windows document does not automatically save the chart. To save the chart, you must save the Word for Windows document after you include the chart.

Identifying New Mouse Pointer Shapes

When working in the datasheet, you may notice two new mouse pointer shapes:

appears when you position the mouse pointer over cells.

appears when you position the mouse pointer between the headings of the columns.

Getting Help

You can get Microsoft Graph Help the same way you get Word for Windows Help—by pressing F1. In fact, all the help information described in Chapter 1 of this book applies to Microsoft Graph as well as to Word for Windows.

15

Using the Datasheet

In the datasheet, you can enter and edit the information that Microsoft Graph will use in the chart. You also can use information from a Word for Windows document or information from other programs. In this section, you will learn how to work in the datasheet. Make sure that you switch to the datasheet before following the examples in this section.

The datasheet contains rows and columns of information.

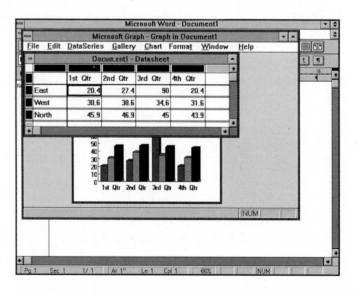

In the datasheet, the active cell is surrounded by a black box. The double lines indicate that data series are plotted in rows. For example, the numbers 45.9, 46.9, 45, and 43.9 make up the North data series. The data series names (East, West, and North) appear in the legend. 1st Qtr, 2nd Qtr, 3rd Qtr, and 4th Qtr are the tick mark labels that appear on the X-axis.

Note: When you move to a cell by using the mouse *or* the keyboard, Microsoft Graph selects that cell.

Using the Mouse in the Datasheet

You can move to any cell (and simultaneously select it) by clicking the cell. You can select a group of cells by dragging.

15

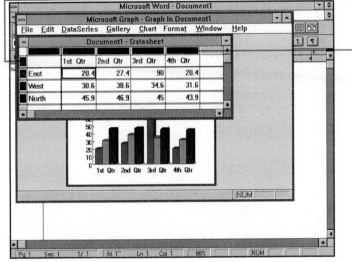

Row heading marker

Column heading marker

You can select an entire row or column by clicking the row or column heading marker.

You can select the entire datasheet by clicking the small box in the upper left corner of the datasheet.

To deselect a group of cells, click anywhere else in the datasheet. This action selects the cell you click, but deselects the group of cells.

Using the Keyboard in the Datasheet

Table 15.1 lists common key combinations for moving around the datasheet and selecting cells. For a complete list, see the *Microsoft Graph User's Guide*.

Table 15.1
Using the Keyboard in the Datasheet

Press	*To*
↑, ↓, ←, or →	Moves to and selects a cell.
⇧Shift + ↑, ↓, ←, or →	Selects more than one cell.
Home	Moves to and selects the first cell in the row containing the active cell.
⇧Shift + Home	Selects all cells between the active cell and the first cell in the row.
Ctrl + Home	Moves to and selects the first cell containing data.
End	Moves to and selects the last cell in the row containing the active cell.
⇧Shift + End	Selects all the cells between the active cell and the last cell in the row.
Ctrl + End	Moves to and selects the last cell containing data.
⇧Shift +space bar	Selects the entire row containing the active cell.
Ctrl +space bar	Selects the entire column containing the active cell.
Ctrl + ⇧Shift +space bar	Selects the entire datasheet.
⇧Shift + ⬅Backspace	Deselects the selection.

You also can select the entire datasheet by choosing the Select All command from the Edit menu.

15

Understanding and Defining the Data Series

A data series is a collection of related data points. Because the information in each row and each column of the datasheet is related, you can use each row of data points as a data series or each column of data points as a data series.

By default, Microsoft Graph defines data series in rows. When the data series are defined as rows, the row labels appear in the chart legend. The column labels usually appear along the X-axis. In the datasheet, double lines appear between the rows.

When the data series are defined as columns, the column labels appear in the legend and the row labels usually appear along the X-axis. In the datasheet, the double lines appear between the columns.

Note: Don't confuse the data series labels with tick mark labels. Data series labels appear in the chart legend. Tick mark labels appear on the X-axis and the Y-axis.

To define the data series for a chart, follow these steps:

1. Activate the datasheet.
2. Open the DataSeries menu.
3. Choose the Series in Rows or Series in Columns command.

Entering and Editing Data

You can enter data directly into the datasheet by moving to the active cell and typing. (Before you enter information, however, be sure to decide whether you want the data series to be in rows or columns.) Type the row headings in the first column, but type the first row heading in the *second* cell in the column. Type the column headings in the first row, but, again, start with the *second* cell in the row. Leave the cell in the upper left corner of the datasheet blank.

If you type in a cell that already contains data, you replace the original contents of the cell. To edit the contents of a cell, double-click the cell you want to edit or select the cell and press F2.

15

The Cell Data
dialog box
appears.

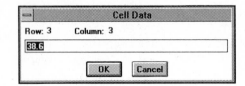

In the Cell Data dialog box, you can edit just as you do in Word for Windows. You can press ← or → to move left or right, Home or End to move to the beginning or end of the line, ◆Backspace and Del to delete characters, and so on. You also can use the mouse to select characters. You can paste selected data *to* the Clipboard by pressing Ctrl+X. You can copy data *from* the Clipboard by pressing Ctrl+V. If you select data and then press Ctrl+V, you replace the selected data with the contents of the Clipboard.

Undoing Your Actions

If you don't like a change that you made, you can "undo" the action by choosing the Undo command from the Edit menu.

Using a Word for Windows Table of Data

You do not have to enter data in the datasheet. Instead, you can use data you already typed into a Word for Windows table. Follow these steps to use data from an existing Word for Windows table:

1. Open the document that contains the table.

2. Position the insertion point anywhere in the table.

3. Open the Table menu.

4. Choose the Select Table command.

5. Open Microsoft Graph (choose the Microsoft Graph button on the Toolbar or open the Insert menu, choose the Object command, choose Microsoft Graph, and then choose OK).

Microsoft Graph first displays the default data and chart, but then replaces the default data with the data from the Word for Windows table and creates a corresponding chart. When you add the chart to the document, Microsoft Graph inserts the chart immediately after the table. The table and chart are completely independent; if you delete the table, the chart will remain.

Moving and Copying Cells

You can move and copy information in the datasheet. Microsoft Graph uses the Clipboard and Cut and Paste commands, just as Word for Windows does.

To move cell information, follow these steps:

1. Activate the datasheet.
2. Select the cells you want to move.
3. Open the Edit menu.
4. Choose the Cut command.
5. Select the cells where you want to move the information.
6. Open the Edit menu.
7. Choose the Paste command.

To copy cell information, follow these steps:

1. Activate the datasheet.
2. Select the cells you want to copy.
3. Open the Edit menu.
4. Choose the Copy command.
5. Select the cells where you want the copied information to appear.
6. Open the Edit menu.
7. Choose the Paste command.

Clearing Cells

You can delete the contents or formatting of cells by clearing the cells. (Later in this chapter, you will learn how to format the contents of cells.)

To clear cells, follow these steps:

1. Activate the datasheet.
2. Select the cells you want to clear.
3. Open the Edit menu.
4. Choose the Clear command.

   The Clear dialog box appears.
5. Choose Data, Format, or Both to clear the contents of the cells, the formatting of the cells, or both.

15

Inserting or Deleting Rows or Columns

You can insert or delete rows or columns in the datasheet. The datasheet can contain up to 4,000 rows and 256 columns.

Microsoft Graph inserts rows above the row containing the active cell and inserts columns to the left of the column containing the active cell. You can insert more than one row or column at a time.

To insert rows or columns, follow these steps.

1. Select any cell in the row below or the column to the right of the location where you want to insert a row or column. To insert more than one row or column, select the number of rows or columns you want to insert. To insert five rows, for example, select five rows.
2. Open the Edit menu.
3. Choose the Insert Row/Col command.

    The Insert Row/Col dialog box appears.
4. Choose Rows or Columns.
5. Choose OK.

When you delete rows or columns, Microsoft Graph deletes the row or column containing the active cell. You can delete more than one row or column at a time. When you delete a row or rows, all rows below move up. When you delete a column or columns, all columns to the right move left.

To delete rows or columns, follow these steps:

1. Select any cell in the row or column you want to delete. To delete more than one row or column, select the rows or columns you want to delete.
2. Open the Edit menu.
3. Choose the Delete Row/Col command.

    The Delete Row/Col dialog box appears.
4. Choose Rows or Columns.
5. Choose OK.

Sizing Columns

Sometimes, you may want to change the size of a column. Suppose, for example, that formatting increased the size of the information in the cells so that Microsoft Graph cannot display the information in the allotted space.

When this occurs, Microsoft Graph displays the number in exponential format (for example 1E+05) if the column is wide enough (at least 5 characters). If the column is not wide enough to display exponential format, Microsoft Graph displays number signs (#) in the cells rather than the information (the information is still in the cell, but you cannot see it). To display the formatted information, you must change the width of the cells.

To change a column's width by using the mouse, follow these steps:

1. In the column headings area, position the mouse pointer at the right edge of the column you want to size. (Watch for the mouse pointer to change shapes.)

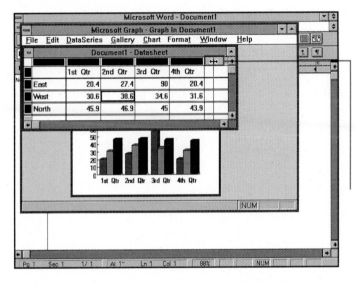

When you position the mouse pointer at the edge of a column heading, the mouse pointer changes shape.

2. Drag the right edge of the column to the right to make the column wider or to the left to make the column narrower.

   As you drag the edge of the column, a vertical bar appears as a guide.

To change a column's width by using the keyboard, follow these steps:

1. Select any cell in the column you want to size.

2. Open the Format menu.

3. Choose the Column Width command.

4. Type the number of characters (from 1 to 255) you want the column to display or choose Standard Width to make the column nine characters wide.

5. Choose OK.

Including or Excluding Data on the Chart

Initially, Microsoft Graph displays the chart using all data in the datasheet. If the datasheet contains data that you don't want to include in the chart, you can tell Microsoft Graph to exclude the data without deleting the data.

To exclude rows or columns of data, follow these steps:

1. Select the rows or columns you want to exclude from the chart.
2. Open the DataSeries menu.
3. Choose the Exclude Row/Col command.

    The Exclude Row/Col dialog box appears.
4. Choose Rows or Columns.
5. Choose OK.

    The data markers for the excluded rows or columns disappear from the chart. In the datasheet, the excluded information appears gray.

To include rows or columns of data that you previously excluded, follow these steps:

1. Select the rows or columns you now want to include in the chart.
2. Open the DataSeries menu.
3. Choose the Insert Row/Col command.

    The Insert Row/Col dialog box appears.
4. Choose Rows or Columns.
5. Choose OK.

    The data markers for the selected rows or columns reappear on the chart, and the selected rows or columns no longer appear gray in the datasheet.

Applying Numeric Formats

You can format the text and the numeric information in the datasheet. For the numeric data, you can apply different number formats.

To assign a number format to cells, follow these steps:

1. Select the cells you want to format.
2. Open the Format menu.
3. Choose the Number command.

4. Choose a format from the Number Format list.

5. Choose OK.

The *Microsoft Graph User's Guide* provides a very complete chart that demonstrates the effects of various formats.

If all the numbers in the data sheet have the same formatting, you can format the appearance of numeric tick mark labels by using a special technique. Follow these steps:

1. Select the cell in the second row and second column.

2. Open the Format menu.

3. Choose the Number command.

4. Choose a format from the Number Format list.

5. Choose OK.

15

Applying Character Formats

You also can change the font, size, and style of the information in the datasheet. To format the data in the datasheet, follow these steps:

1. Open the Format menu.

2. Choose the Font command.

   The Datasheet Font dialog box appears.

3. Choose a font name from the Font list box and a size from the Size list box.

4. From the Style box, choose from the Bold, Italic, Underline, and Strikeout check boxes.

5. Choose a color from the Color list box.

6. Choose OK.

These steps do *not* affect the tick mark labels. Formatting tick mark labels is discussed later in this chapter.

Note: You also can open the Number Format dialog box and the Col Width dialog box from the Datasheet Font dialog box.

Creating a Chart

When you create a chart, you are creating a picture of the data. In Microsoft Graph, you can produce 12 different types of charts: seven two-dimensional and five three-dimensional charts. Each chart type has several built-in formats. The default chart type is a column chart.

You can change the type of the chart at any time. You can add, modify, and delete legends, gridlines, text, and chart arrows. You can format the text on a chart as well as the X- and Y-axes of the chart. You also can adjust the layout and patterns of the data markers.

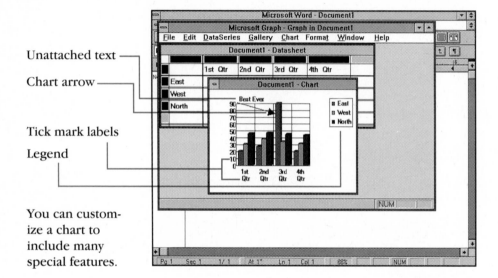

Unattached text

Chart arrow

Tick mark labels

Legend

You can customize a chart to include many special features.

Choosing a Chart Type and Chart Format

A chart type is a category of charts (such as bar, line, three-dimensional, or area) that Microsoft Graph can produce. The *Microsoft Graph User's Guide* includes an excellent presentation of samples of each graph type and their possible uses. When you first open Microsoft Graph and enter data, Microsoft Graph displays the data as a column chart.

Microsoft Graph provides 12 chart types. In addition, each chart type has several formats (variations of the chart type).

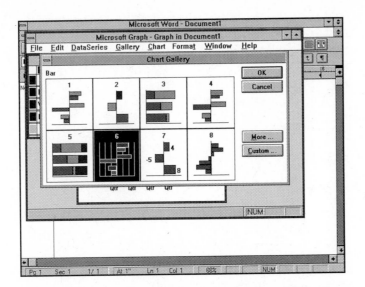

Side-by-side bar (1), stacked bar (3), and 100% stacked bar (5) are some of the formats available for bar charts.

15

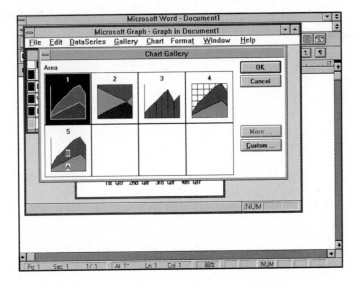

Microsoft Graph provides five formats for area charts.

15

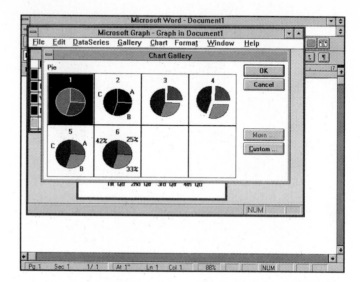

Six formats are available for pie charts.

You can easily change to another chart type or format by following these steps:

1. Open the Gallery menu.

2. Choose a chart type command: Area, Bar, Column, Line, Pie, Scatter (XY), Combination, 3-D Area, 3-D Bar, 3-D Column, 3-D Line, or 3-D Pie.

3. Choose a chart format by clicking the format or by pressing ⬆, ⬇, ⬅, or ➡. If more than eight formats are available for that chart type, the More button is also available.

4. Choose OK.

You also can create a custom chart format by choosing the chart type closest to the chart you want to create and then choosing the Custom button. Microsoft Graph displays a dialog box that enables you to define a custom chart format.

Copying a Chart

You can use the Clipboard to copy a chart from a Word for Windows document to another location in the same document, to another Word for Windows document, or to another program.

To copy a chart to another Word for Windows document, follow these steps:

1. In the document containing the chart you want to copy, open Microsoft Graph.
2. Activate the Chart window.
3. Open the Edit menu.
4. Choose the Copy Chart command.

    Microsoft Graph places a copy of the chart on the Clipboard.
5. Close Microsoft Graph.
6. Open the document where you want the copied chart to appear.
7. Position the insertion point where you want the chart to appear.
8. Choose the Paste button from the Toolbar or the Paste command from the Edit menu.

Selecting Chart Items

To edit, format, or clear an item from a chart, you first must select the item in the chart. When you select a chart item, one of two types of handles appears. You can move, size, or format items with black handles—such as the legend—by dragging or by using menu commands. You cannot move or size items with white handles, but you can format those items.

Table 15.2 provides guidelines for selecting items in a chart by using the mouse.

Table 15.2
Selecting Chart Items by Using the Mouse

To select	Action
A single item	Click the item.
A data series	Click any marker in the data series.
A single data marker	Hold down Ctrl and click the marker.
Gridlines	Click any gridline (Be sure to point to the gridline exactly.)
An axis	Click any tick mark label for that axis.
The plot area	Click any empty space in the plot area.
The entire chart	Click near the edge of the window, but outside any chart item.

15

To cancel the selection, click just inside the Chart window, but outside any item. If this action selects the entire chart, click closer to the edge of the window or press ⌊Esc⌋.

To select items by pressing ⌊↑⌋, ⌊↓⌋, ⌊←⌋, or ⌊→⌋, you need to understand how Microsoft Graph organizes chart items. Microsoft Graph divides chart items into the following classes:

- Entire chart
- Plot area
- Text
- Arrows
- Legend
- Axes
- Gridlines
- Data series
- 3-Dimensional walls
- 3-Dimensional floors
- Drop lines
- Hi-lo lines
- Series lines
- Up/down bars

You can press ⌊↑⌋ and ⌊↓⌋ to move between classes of items. You can press ⌊←⌋ and ⌊→⌋ to select items within a class. Press ⌊↑⌋ or ⌊↓⌋, for example, to move to the second data series. Press ⌊←⌋ or ⌊→⌋ to select one data bar in the second data series.

To cancel a selection, press ⌊Esc⌋.

Clearing a Chart

You can remove data or formatting from the chart by using the Clear command on the Edit menu. Follow these steps to clear a chart item:

1. Activate the Chart window.
2. Choose the item you want to clear.
3. Open the Edit menu.
4. Choose the Clear command.

If the item is a data series, Microsoft Graph displays a dialog box in which you can choose whether to clear the data or the formatting for the series. Choose Series or Formats and then choose OK.

You can undo most actions by choosing the Undo command from the Edit menu.

Working with Legends

A legend helps the reader to identify what each data marker on the chart represents. When you first create a chart, Microsoft Graph includes a legend.

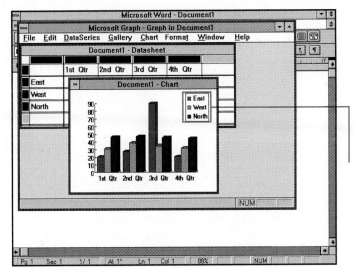

The legend appears at the right side of the chart.

15

You can delete the legend from the chart by following these steps:

1. Open the Chart menu.
2. Choose the Delete Legend command.

To restore the legend, open the Chart menu and choose the Add Legend command. (When the chart does not include a legend, the Delete Legend command changes to Add Legend.)

You can move a legend by using the mouse or the keyboard. To move a legend by using the mouse, simply select the legend and drag it to the new location. To move a legend by using the keyboard, follow these steps:

1. Select the legend.
2. Open the Format menu.

3. Choose the Legend command.

   The Legend dialog box appears.

4. From the Type box, choose Bottom, Corner, Top, Right, or Left to indicate on which side of the chart you want to position the legend.

5. To format the border and the area (foreground and background), choose the Patterns button.

6. To change the font used in the legend, choose the Font button.

7. Choose OK.

Working with Gridlines

Gridlines are lines that extend from each axis tick mark across the plot area to help the reader identify the values associated with the data markers. When you first create a chart, Microsoft Graph does not include gridlines. You can add gridlines to the chart by following these steps:

1. Open the Chart menu.

2. Choose the Gridlines command.

The Gridlines dialog box appears.

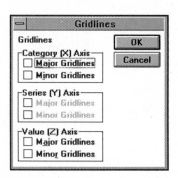

3. For each axis, choose the check boxes for the gridlines you want to add. Major gridlines indicate each data series and each main tick mark. Minor gridlines divide each data series in half and indicate each tick mark.

   (If the chart is three-dimensional, you can choose gridlines for the Z-axis. Z-axis gridlines appear along the back and side walls of the plot area. Depending on the three-dimensional chart type, you may be able to add gridlines for the X-axis and the Z-axis only.)

4. Choose OK.

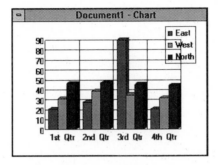

This chart has major gridlines for both axes.

15

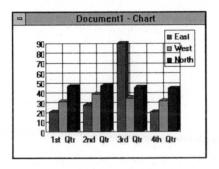

This chart has major gridlines for both axes and minor gridlines for the X-axis.

Tip: Be aware that adding major and minor gridlines on all axes does not necessarily make a chart more legible. In fact, too many gridlines can make the chart *harder* to read.

To delete gridlines, you follow the preceding steps, but deactivate the check boxes for the gridlines you want to remove.

You also can format gridlines by choosing style, color, and weight options. Follow these steps to format gridlines:

1. Select a major gridline to format all major gridlines. Select a minor gridline to format all minor gridlines.

2. Open the Format menu.

3. Choose the Patterns command.

   The Line Patterns dialog box appears.

4. Choose the Custom option button, then choose the style, color, and weight for the gridlines from the Style, Color, and Weight list boxes. If you change your mind, choose the Automatic option button to return the gridlines to their original format.

5. Choose OK.

Using Text on Charts

You can add, delete, and edit text on a chart. You can attach a title to the entire chart or to any of the axes. You also can create text that is not attached to any part of the chart. You can move, size, and format unattached text in a chart.

Using Attached or Unattached Text

Use attached text when you want to create a title for the entire chart or for any of the axes or when you want to create labels for the data markers. You cannot move attached text, so use unattached text when you want to add text that you can position.

Follow these steps to create attached title text:

1. Open the Chart menu.
2. Choose the Titles command.

   The Chart Titles dialog box appears.

3. Choose where you want to attach the title: Chart, Value (Z) Axis, Series (Y) Axis, or Category (X) Axis.
4. Choose OK.

   Microsoft Graph inserts sample text surrounded by white handles.

5. Type the text you want to appear in the chart.

   As you type the text, some of the text seems to disappear.

6. When you finish typing, press (Esc).

   You now can see all the text you typed.

To create attached data label text, follow these steps:

1. Open the Chart menu.
2. Choose the Data Labels command.

   Microsoft Graph opens the Data Labels dialog box.

3. Choose the type of information you want to use as the data series label: Value, Label, or (if applicable) Percent. You also can remove a data label by choosing None.
4. Choose OK.

To edit attached text, select the text you want to change and type the new text. To delete attached text, select the text and press (Del).

Follow these steps to create unattached text:

1. Make sure that no other text is selected.

2. Type the unattached text.

   The text you type appears in the middle of the chart.

3. When you finish typing, press (Esc).

   Black handles appear around the text.

To edit unattached text, select the text you want to change and type the new text. To change the size of unattached text, select the text and drag the black handles. To move unattached text, select the text, position the mouse pointer between any two black handles, hold down the left mouse button, and drag the border that appears to the new location. To delete unattached text, select the text and press (Del).

Formatting Text

You can format attached and unattached text in a chart by changing fonts, sizes, styles, colors, and the background area of the text. You also can format the text borders and area patterns.

To format text in a chart, follow these steps:

1. Select the text you want to format. To format the tick mark labels, select the appropriate axis. To format the text in the legend, select the legend. To format all text on the chart, select the entire chart.

2. Open the Format menu.

3. Choose the Font command.

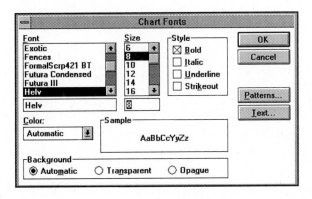

The Chart Fonts dialog box appears.

4. From the Font list box, choose a font name.

5. From the Size list box, choose a font size.

6. From the Style box, choose from the Bold, Italic, Underline, and Strikeout check boxes.

7. From the Color list box, choose a color.

8. In the Background box, choose Automatic, Transparent or Opaque.

9. To format the text borders and patterns, choose the Patterns button.

   The Area Patterns dialog box appears. Format the borders and patterns and then choose OK to return to the Chart Fonts dialog box.

10. To align text, choose the Text button. (The Text button is not available if you are formatting all text on the chart.)

    The Chart Text dialog box appears. Align the text and then choose OK to return to the Chart Fonts dialog box.

11. Choose OK.

You also can open the Area Patterns dialog box directly by choosing the Patterns command from the Format menu. You can open the Chart Text dialog box directly by choosing the Text command from the Format menu.

Working with Chart Arrows

You can add an arrow to a chart to direct the reader's attention to a specific item. Follow these steps:

1. Activate the Chart window.

2. Open the Chart menu.

3. Choose the Add Arrow command.

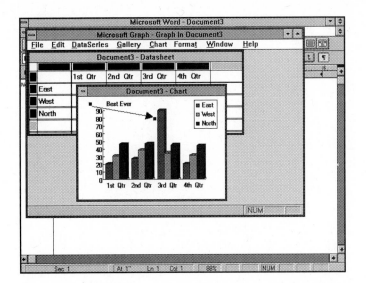

Microsoft Graph
inserts a chart
arrow with black
handles.

15

You can size the chart arrow by selecting it and dragging either end. You can move the chart arrow by selecting it and dragging its shaft to the new location. You can control a chart arrow's style, color, line weight, width, and length from the Patterns dialog box. (To open the Patterns dialog box, choose the Patterns command from the Format menu.)

You can delete a chart arrow in three ways:

- Select the arrow and then press Del.
- Select the arrow and then choose the Delete Arrow command from the Chart menu.
- Select the arrow and then choose the Clear command from the Edit menu.

Formatting Chart Axes

All two-dimensional charts, except pie charts, have two axes—the horizontal X-axis and the vertical Y-axis. (The pie chart has no axes.) For most two-dimensional charts, you plot the values along the Y-axis and the categories of data along the X-axis. The three-dimensional charts have three axes: a category X-axis, a series Y-axis, and a value Z-axis. (The Z-axis is vertical.) You can control which axes appear on the chart and the format of those axes.

To add or delete axes from the chart, follow these steps:

1. Open the Chart menu.

2. Choose the Axes command.

3. Choose the axes you want to appear on the chart. Deactivate the axes you don't want to appear on the chart.

4. Choose OK.

When you format axes, the available options depend on which axis you are formatting. In general, follow these steps to format an axis:

1. Select the axis you want to format.

2. Open the Format menu.

3. Choose the Scale command.

   The Format Axis Scale dialog box appears. The available options depend on the type of chart you selected.

4. For the Value axis, you generally can type values in the Minimum, Maximum, Major Unit, Minor Unit, and Floor (XY Plane) Crosses At text boxes or you can choose a check box for each option to set these values automatically. You also can choose the Logarithmic Scale, Reverse Order, or Floor (XY Plane) Crosses At Minimum check boxes.

   For the Category and Series axes, you generally can type values in the Number of Categories (or Series) between Tick Labels and Number of Categories (or Series) between Tick Marks text boxes. You also can choose the Reverse Order check box.

   To open the Axis Patterns, Chart Fonts, or Axis Text dialog boxes, choose the Patterns, Font, or Text button.

5. Choose OK.

Notice that you can open the Axis Patterns, Chart Fonts, or Axis Text dialog boxes from the Format Axis Scale dialog box. From the Axis Patterns dialog box, you can control the appearance of tick marks and axis lines, and the position of tick mark labels. From the Axis Text dialog box, you can control the tick mark label orientation.

Working with the Data Markers

You can control the placement and pattern of data markers. You also can control the appearance of the lines that border data markers.

To format data markers for a bar or column chart, follow these steps:

1. Open the Format menu.

2. Choose the Chart command.

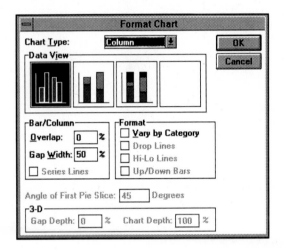

The Format Chart dialog box appears. The options available in this dialog box depend on the chart type.

3. If necessary, change the Chart Type.

4. Choose a Data View for the chart.

5. For bar or column charts, you can specify an Overlap that affects the spacing of data markers *within* a category.

6. For bar or column charts, you can specify a Gap Width that affects the spacing of data markers *between* categories.

7. If the chart contains more than one data series, you can choose the Vary by category check box to vary the color pattern.

8. Choose OK.

Working with the Plot Area

The plot area is different in two-dimensional and three-dimensional charts.

15

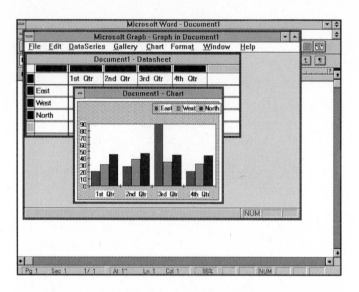

In a two-dimensional chart, the plot area includes the axes.

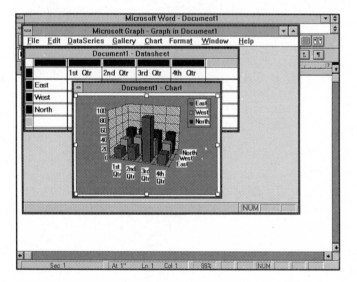

In a three-dimensional chart, the plot area includes the axes, labels, and titles.

You can control the color and pattern for the plot area and plot border. To format the plot area, you first must select it. To select the plot area (or the walls or floor of a three-dimensional chart), click anywhere inside the plot area (or wall or floor) that isn't occupied by another chart item (or press ↑ or ↓).

To format the patterns and colors for the plot area, follow these steps:

1. Open the Format menu.

2. Choose the Patterns command.

   The Area Patterns dialog box appears.

3. To change the border, choose the None option button, or choose a style, color, or weight from the Style, Color, or Weight list box. If you change your mind, choose the Automatic option button to return the border to its original format.

   To change the area, choose the None option button, or choose a pattern, foreground, or background from the Pattern, Foreground, or Background list box. If you change your mind, choose the Automatic option button to return the area to its original format.

4. Choose OK.

15

Chapter Summary

In this chapter, you learned the basics of using Microsoft Graph. You learned how to open and close Microsoft Graph and how to use the Datasheet window or a Word for Windows table to enter and edit data for a graph. You learned the following specific information:

■ You can move, copy, and clear cells by using the Copy, Cut, Paste, and Clear commands on the Edit menu.

■ You can insert or delete columns and rows by using the Insert Row/Col or Delete Row/Col command on the Edit menu. You can size columns by dragging or by using the Column Width command on the Format menu.

■ You can include or exclude data on the chart by using the Insert Row/Col or Exclude Row/Col command on the DataSeries menu.

■ You can apply numeric and character formatting by using the Font or Number command on the Format menu.

■ You can choose a chart type and format from the Gallery menu.

■ You can copy a chart to the Clipboard by choosing the Copy Chart command from the Edit menu.

■ You can select chart items by using the mouse or the keyboard.

■ You can remove data or formatting from a chart by using the Clear command on the Edit menu.

■ You can include legends, gridlines, and chart arrows on a chart by using commands on the Chart menu. You can format legends by using the Patterns, Fonts, and Legend commands on the the Format menu. You can format gridlines, chart arrows, and the plot area by using the Patterns command on the Format menu.

■ You can add titles to a chart by creating attached text with the Titles command on the Chart menu. You can add data labels to a chart by creating attached text with the DataLabels command on the Chart menu. You can add unattached text to any area of the chart by typing when no other text is selected and then dragging the text to the correct location.

■ You can format data markers by using the Chart command on the Format menu. You can format chart axes by choosing the Axes command from the Chart menu.

In the next chapter, you will learn the basics of using Microsoft Draw.

15

Using Microsoft Draw

Microsoft Draw is a software package that comes with Word for Windows. Microsoft Draw enables you to create drawings and import graphic files created in other programs. Microsoft Draw works with clip art, Windows bitmaps (files that have the extension BMP) and metafiles (files that have the extension WMF). You can use Microsoft Draw with a wide variety of graphic filters and with many Windows programs other than Word for Windows.

In this chapter, you will learn the basics of using Microsoft Draw to create drawings in Word for Windows documents. You also will learn how to import pictures created in other programs. You do not need to exit Word for Windows because Microsoft Draw works inside Word for Windows.

You can use the keyboard to work with some features of Microsoft Draw, but you need a mouse for other features. For a complete list of hardware and software requirements, see the *Microsoft Draw User's Guide*.

An overview of Microsoft Draw

Drawing objects

Changing objects

Working with text

16

Key Terms in This Chapter

Object   Any image you create or import when working in Microsoft Draw. When you select an object, handles appear.

Handles   Small black boxes that mark the edges of an object.

Tools   Implements you use to draw objects. Tools appear along the left side of the Microsoft Draw window.

Fill   A color or pattern you place inside an object.

Frame   The outside edge of an object.

Grid   An invisible set of intersecting lines you can use to position objects.

Guides   Two intersecting lines (one horizontal, one vertical) you can use to align objects. You can hide or display the guides.

Vertex   The point where two lines meet.

An Overview of Microsoft Draw

Microsoft Draw enables you to create drawings in Word for Windows documents. You can use drawing tools to insert lines and shapes into a drawing. You can apply color, fill patterns, and frames to a drawing. You can add text to a drawing and then format that text. Microsoft Draw also enables you to import drawings you have created in other programs. Microsoft Draw works with clip art, Windows bitmaps (files that have the extension BMP) and metafiles (files that have the extension WMF).

Microsoft Draw does not work independently, though. You must use Microsoft Draw from inside another program, such as Word for Windows. You cannot save or print drawings from Microsoft Draw; you must use the other program's save and print features.

Opening Microsoft Draw

To create a new drawing, you can open Microsoft Draw by using the Microsoft Draw button on the Toolbar or the Object command on the Insert menu.

Follow these steps to use the Toolbar to open Microsoft Draw:

1. Open the Word for Windows document into which you want to insert a drawing.
2. Position the insertion point where you want the drawing to appear.
3. Choose the Microsoft Draw button from the Toolbar.

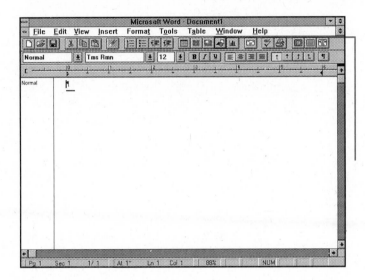

The Microsoft Draw button on the Toolbar.

16

The Microsoft Draw window appears.

If you prefer to use a menu command to open Microsoft Draw, follow these steps:

1. Open the Word for Windows document into which you want to insert a drawing.
2. Position the insertion point where you want the drawing to appear.
3. Choose the Insert menu.
4. Choose the Object command.

   The Object dialog box appears.
5. Choose Microsoft Drawing.
6. Choose OK.

   The Microsoft Draw window appears.

The Microsoft Draw window contains a drawing area, tools, menus, scroll bars, and Line and Fill color palettes.

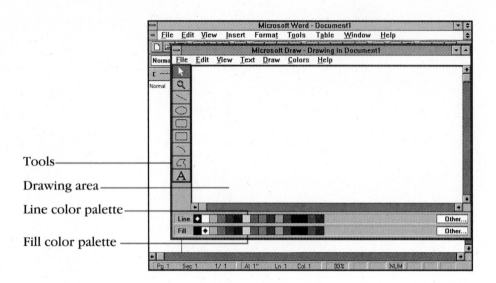

Tools

Drawing area

Line color palette

Fill color palette

16

To choose a tool, position the mouse pointer over the tool and click the left mouse button.

Table 16.1
Mouse Pointer Shapes for Drawing Tools

Tool	Name	Mouse pointer shape
	Arrow tool	
	Zoom tool	
	Line tool	
	Ellipse tool	
	Rounded Rectangle tool	
	Rectangle tool	
	Arc tool	

Tool	Name	Mouse pointer shape
	Freeform tool	+
	Text tool	↓

Getting Help

You can get Microsoft Draw Help the same way you get Word for Windows Help—by pressing [F1]. In fact, all the help information described in Chapter 1 of this book also applies to Microsoft Draw.

16

Saving and Printing Your Work

Because Microsoft Draw does not work independently, you must use the main program to save and print your drawings. You can transfer a drawing from Microsoft Draw to the document at any time, or you can wait until you finish a drawing and close Microsoft Draw. After you update the main document you can save or print the document and the drawing. When you save the main document, you are also saving the drawing. When you print the main document, you are also printing the drawing.

To update the document, but remain in Microsoft Draw, follow these steps:

1. Open the File menu on the Microsoft Draw menu bar.
2. Choose the Update command.

   Microsoft Draw copies the information in its window to the active Word for Windows document.

To exit Microsoft Draw, follow these steps:

1. Open the File menu on the Microsoft Draw menu bar.
2. Choose the Exit and Return to *Document1* command (where *Document1* is the name of the active Word for Windows document).

   A dialog box asks whether you want to update the Word for Windows document.

3. Choose Yes to transfer the drawing. Choose No to close Microsoft Draw without transferring the drawing. (If you choose No, you will lose the work you did in Microsoft Draw.) Choose Cancel to remain in Microsoft Draw.

401

Setting Menu Defaults

Some of the commands on Microsoft Draw's menus are actually settings that determine how Microsoft Draw operates. You can choose menu commands to change these settings. Microsoft Draw indicates the current settings with diamonds (◆) and check marks (✓).

When you first open Microsoft Draw, for example, and no objects are selected, diamonds appear on the Line and Fill color palettes. Diamonds also appear on the Text menu next to Plain and Left and on the Draw menu next to Framed and Filled.

16

Diamonds (◆) indicate the defaults Microsoft Draw will use when you create an object or text.

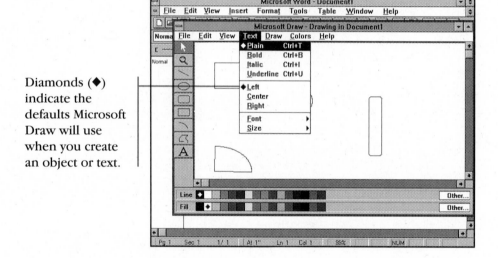

If any object is selected, check marks indicate options in effect for the selected object. If no object is selected, check marks indicate options in effect for the entire Microsoft Draw window.

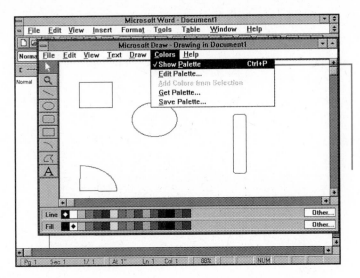

Check marks (✓) also appear on some menus in Microsoft Draw.

Selecting Objects

You must select an object before you can modify it.

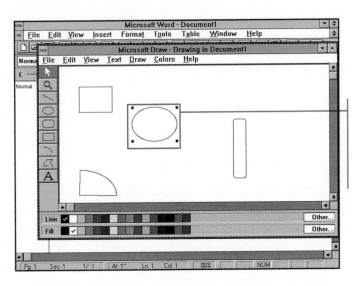

When you select an object, handles (small black boxes) appear around that object.

You can select an object in two ways:

- Choose the Arrow tool and then click the object.
- Use a Selection Rectangle.

403

If an object is filled, you can click anywhere over the object to select it. If an object is not filled, you must click its outline to select it.

Note: Filling an object with white (the background color of the screen) is not the same as leaving the object unfilled.

Selection Rectangles are particularly useful when you want to select more than one object. To use a Selection Rectangle, follow these steps:

1. Choose the Arrow tool.

2. Position the mouse pointer in an empty area above and to the left of the object(s) you want to select. Hold down the left mouse button.

3. Drag the mouse pointer down and to the right (diagonally).

    As you drag, a dotted rectangle appears. This rectangle is the Selection Rectangle.

4. Release the mouse button when the Selection Rectangle encloses the object(s) you want to select.

If you click an unselected object, Microsoft Draw selects that object, but deselects any previously selected objects. To add objects to a selection, hold down ⇧Shift and then click the objects you want to add. You can remove objects from a selection the same way.

You can select all objects in the drawing by choosing the Select All command from the Edit menu. You can cancel all selections by clicking any empty location in the drawing.

Drawing Objects

Microsoft Draw provides six tools you can use to create drawings:

*   The Line tool
*   The Ellipse tool
*   The Rounded Rectangle tool
*   The Rectangle tool
*   The Arc tool
*   The Freeform tool

If you make a mistake at any time, you can use "undo" the action by choosing the Undo command from the Edit menu.

16

You also can use the grid and the guides to help you align objects as you create them.

Working with the Grid and the Guides

The grid is an invisible set of lines you can use to align objects. To turn on or off the grid, choose the Snap to Grid command from the Draw menu. When the grid is turned on, the corners of a boundary box automatically align to the grid.

The guides are two intersecting lines (one horizontal, one vertical) you can use to align objects. To turn on or off the guides, choose the Show Guides command from the Draw menu.

To move the guides, follow these steps:

1. Choose the Arrow tool.
2. Position the mouse pointer on a guide.
3. Drag the guide to its new location.

   As you move the guide, Microsoft Draw displays the guide's distance from the edge of the drawing.

Tip: If you hold down Ctrl as you drag a guide, you can use the guide to measure the distance between objects. Position the guide at the point from which you want to start measuring, hold down Ctrl, and then drag the guide to the other position. Microsoft Draw displays the distance between the start and end points.

16

Drawing with the Line Tool

You use the Line tool to draw straight lines in any direction.

To draw a line, follow these steps:

1. Choose the Line tool.
2. Position the mouse pointer where you want the line to start. Hold down the left mouse button.
3. Drag the mouse pointer to the location where you want the line to end. To limit the line to a horizontal, vertical, or 45-degree diagonal line, hold down Shift as you drag.
4. When the line is the correct length, release the mouse button.

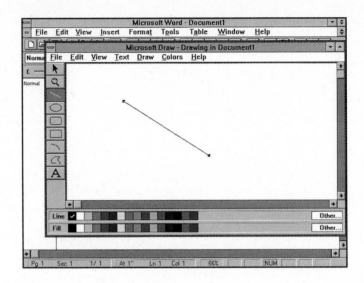

When you release the mouse button, the line is selected and handles appear at each end.

16

You also can draw a line that extends in both directions from the mouse pointer. Choose the Line tool and position the mouse pointer in the location you want to be the *center* of the line. Hold down Ctrl and then drag the mouse pointer to draw the line. To limit the line to a horizontal, vertical, or 45-degree diagonal line, hold down Ctrl + ⇧Shift as you drag.

Drawing with the Ellipse Tool

You use the Ellipse tool to draw ellipses or circles.

To draw an ellipse or circle, follow these steps:

1. Choose the Ellipse tool.

2. Position the mouse pointer where you want the ellipse or circle to start. Hold down the left mouse button.

3. Drag the mouse pointer down and to the right (diagonally). To create a circle, hold down ⇧Shift as you drag.

4. When the ellipse or circle is the correct size, release the mouse button.

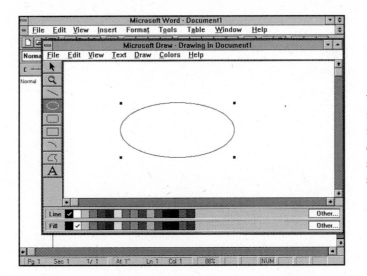

When you release the mouse button, the ellipse or circle is selected and four handles appear around it.

16

You also can draw an ellipse or circle that extends in both directions from the mouse pointer. Choose the Ellipse tool and position the mouse pointer in the location you want to be the *center* of the ellipse or circle. To draw an ellipse, hold down Ctrl as you drag the mouse pointer. To draw a circle, hold down Ctrl + ⇧Shift as you drag.

Drawing with the Rounded Rectangle Tool

You use the Rounded Rectangle tool to draw rectangles or squares with rounded corners.

To draw a rounded rectangle or square, follow these steps:

1. Choose the Rounded Rectangle tool.
2. Position the mouse pointer where you want the rounded rectangle or square to start. Hold down the left mouse button.
3. Drag the mouse pointer down and to the right (diagonally). To create a rounded square, hold down ⇧Shift as you drag.
4. When the rounded rectangle or square is the correct size, release the mouse button.

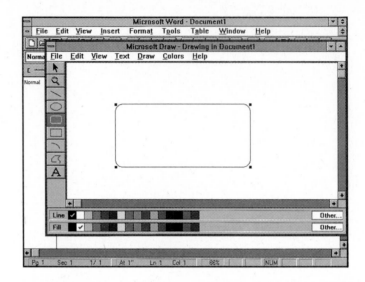

When you release the mouse button, the rounded rectangle or square is selected and four handles appear at its corners.

16

You also can draw a rounded rectangle or square that extends in both directions from the mouse pointer. Choose the Rounded Rectangle tool and position the mouse pointer in the location you want to be the *center* of the rounded rectangle or square. To draw a rounded rectangle, hold down Ctrl as you drag the mouse pointer. To draw a rounded square, hold down Ctrl + ⇧Shift as you drag.

Drawing with the Rectangle Tool

You use the Rectangle tool to draw rectangles or squares.

To draw a rectangle or square, follow these steps:

1. Choose the Rectangle tool.
2. Position the mouse pointer where you want the rectangle or square to start. Hold down the left mouse button.
3. Drag the mouse pointer down and to the right (diagonally). To create a square, hold down ⇧Shift as you drag.
4. When the rectangle or square is the correct size, release the mouse button.

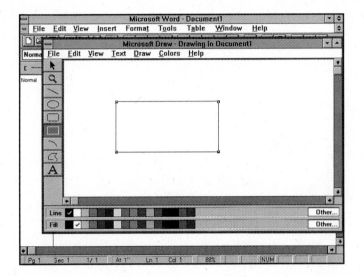

When you release the mouse button, the rectangle or square is selected and four handles appear at its corners.

16

You also can draw a rectangle or square that extends in both directions from the mouse pointer. Choose the Rectangle tool and position the mouse pointer in the location you want to be the *center* of the rectangle or square. To draw a rectangle, hold down Ctrl as you drag the mouse pointer. To draw a square, hold down Ctrl + ⇧Shift as you drag.

Drawing with the Arc Tool

You use the Arc tool to draw arcs (curves) and pie wedges (filled curves). Initially, arcs and pie wedges are 90 degrees (1/4 of an ellipse or circle). After you draw an arc or a pie wedge, you can change its size in area or in degrees.

To draw a pie wedge, make sure that a check mark appears to the left of the Filled command on the Draw menu. To draw an arc, make sure that a check mark does *not* appear to the left of the Filled command.

To draw an arc or a pie wedge, turn on or off the Filled command and then follow these steps:

1. Choose the Arc tool.

2. Position the mouse pointer where you want the arc or pie wedge to start. Hold down the left mouse button.

3. Drag the mouse pointer to where you want the arc to end. The direction you drag determines the section of an ellipse you draw. If you drag down and to the left, for example, you draw the upper left

409

section of an ellipse. If you drag up and to the right, you draw the lower right section of an ellipse.

To make the arc a section of a circle (that is, to make the height and width of the arc equal), hold down ⇧Shift as you drag.

4. When the arc or pie wedge is the correct length, release the mouse button.

16

When you release the mouse button, the arc or pie wedge is selected and handles appear at its ends and on each side of the arc.

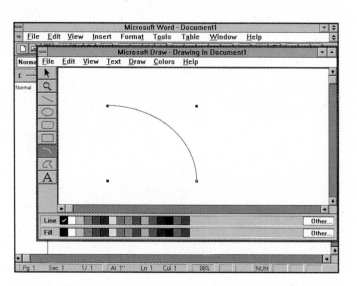

You also can draw an arc or pie wedge that extends in both directions from the mouse pointer. Choose the Arc tool and position the mouse pointer in the location you want to be the *center* of the ellipse or circle. To draw the arc or pie wedge, hold down Ctrl and then drag the mouse pointer. To draw an arc or pie wedge of equal height and width, hold down Ctrl+⇧Shift as you drag.

Drawing with the Freeform Tool

You use the Freeform tool to draw shapes that do not fall into any of the preceding categories. For example, you can draw polygons such as triangles or octagons with the Freeform tool. You also can draw freehand objects such as clouds. Or, you can create drawings that are combinations of polygons and freehand shapes, such as flowers.

Freeform objects actually consist of several connected lines. (Even freeform curves consist of several small connected lines.)

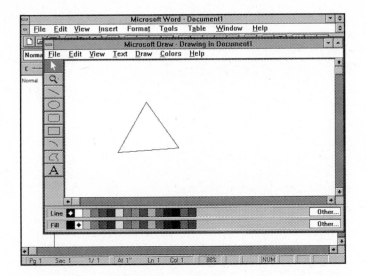

You can use the Freeform tool to draw closed objects.

16

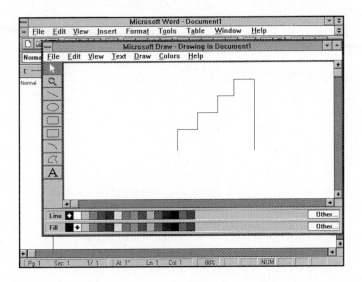

Or, you can draw open objects.

The procedures for drawing a polygon are different from those for drawing freehand. To draw a polygon by using the Freeform tool, follow these steps:

1. Choose the Freeform tool.
2. Position the mouse pointer where you want the polygon to start and click the left mouse button to anchor the drawing.

   You now can draw the first line of the polygon.

3. Move the mouse pointer (don't hold down the mouse button) to the end of the first line (and the beginning of the second line) in the object. Click the left mouse button again. (To limit the line to a horizontal, vertical, or 45-degree diagonal line, hold down ⇧Shift before you click the mouse button again.)

   Microsoft Draw creates a straight line between the positions you clicked.

4. Repeat step 3 to draw all the other lines in the polygon. If you are drawing an open object, double-click the end of the last line. If you are drawing a closed object, connect the starting point of the object to the ending point by double-clicking close to the starting point.

   When you double-click, Microsoft Draw selects the object.

If you make a mistake while drawing with the Freeform tool, you can delete the last vertex by pressing ←Backspace.

To draw a freehand object, follow these steps:

1. Choose the Freeform tool.

2. Position the mouse pointer where you want the object to start. Hold down the left mouse button.

   The mouse pointer changes to a pencil.

3. Drag the mouse pointer to draw the object.

4. If you are drawing an open object, double-click the end of the last line. If you are drawing a closed object, connect the last line to the starting point by double-clicking close to the starting point.

   When you double-click, Microsoft Draw selects the object.

To mix freehand drawing and polygons, you switch between the two forms. To switch from polygon lines to freehand drawing, hold down the left mouse button. When the mouse pointer changes to a pencil, you can draw freehand. To change from freehand to polygon lines, release the mouse button and move the mouse pointer (without dragging). Click the left mouse button at the position where you want to place the end of the line. Double-click to complete the drawing.

Adding Frames to Objects

You can add frames of different styles and colors to objects. If the Framed command on the Draw menu is turned on before you draw an object, Microsoft Draw automatically frames the object. You can choose frame colors

16

from the Line color palette at the bottom of the Microsoft Draw window. You can choose frame styles from the Draw menu.

To change the color of a line or frame, follow these steps:

1. Select the line or the framed object.
2. From the Line color palette at the bottom of the Microsoft Draw window, choose a color for the line or frame.

To change the style or width (thickness) of a line or frame, follow these steps:

1. Select the line or the framed object.
2. Open the Draw menu.
3. Choose the Line Style command.
4. Choose a style or width (thickness) for the line or frame. If you choose Other, you can define a specific width for the line or frame.

16

You also can remove frames. Before you remove a frame, however, fill the object with color (see the next section); otherwise, the object seems to disappear from the window.

To remove a frame from an object, follow these steps:

1. Select the object.
2. Open the Draw menu.
3. Choose the Framed command.

    Microsoft Draw removes the frame.

Filling Drawings

You can fill objects with colors and patterns. If the Filled command on the Draw menu is turned on before you draw an object, Microsoft Draw automatically fills the object. You can choose fill colors from the Fill color palette at the bottom of the Microsoft Draw window. You can choose fill patterns by using the Pattern command on the Draw menu.

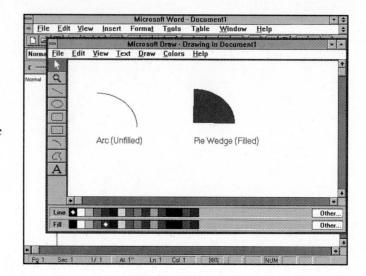

A filled arc is a pie wedge.

To change an object's fill color, follow these steps:

1. Select the object.
2. From the Fill color palette, choose the color with which you want to fill the object. If you already filled the object with a pattern, choose a foreground color from the Line color palette and a background color from the Fill color palette.

To change an object's fill pattern, follow these steps:

1. Select the object.
2. Open the Draw menu.
3. Choose the Pattern command.
4. Choose the pattern with which you want to fill the object.

You also can remove fill colors and patterns. If you have removed the frame of an object, replace the frame before you remove the fill color or pattern; otherwise, the object seems to disappear from the window.

To remove a fill color or pattern from an object, follow these steps:

1. Select the object.
2. Open the Draw menu.
3. Choose the Filled command.

    Microsoft Draw removes the fill color or pattern.

Importing Images

You can import images created in other programs as long as the images are clip art or formatted as bitmaps or Windows metafiles.

To import a picture, follow these steps:

1. Open the File menu.
2. Choose the Import Picture command.

   The Import Picture dialog box appears.
3. Choose the drive and directory where the files are stored.
4. Select the file from the Files list.
5. Choose OK.

Zooming

16

You can enlarge or reduce an object or drawing by using the Zoom tool or the commands on the View menu. You can enlarge an object or drawing to two, four, or eight times its regular size. You can reduce an object or drawing to 75 percent, 50 percent, or 25 percent of its regular size.

To use the View menu to enlarge or reduce an object or drawing, follow these steps:

1. Select the object you want to enlarge or reduce. If you don't select an object, Microsoft Draw zooms the upper left portion of the drawing.
2. Open the View menu.
3. Choose a size.

To use the Zoom tool to enlarge or reduce an object, follow these steps:

1. Choose the Zoom tool.

   The mouse pointer changes to a magnifying glass.
2. Position the magnifying glass on the object you want to enlarge or reduce.
3. To enlarge the object, click the object. If the object was originally full size, the first click enlarges the object to 200 percent, the second click enlarges the object to 400 percent, and the third click enlarges the object to 800 percent.

   To reduce the object, hold down ⇧Shift and click the object. If the object was originally full size, the first click reduces the object to 75 percent of its normal size, the second click reduces the object to 50 percent, and the third click reduce the object to 25 percent.

Changing Objects

When you want to edit an existing object, you can open Microsoft Draw by double-clicking the drawing in the Word for Windows document. Microsoft Draw opens, and the drawing appears in the Microsoft Draw window. You can move, copy, delete, size, rotate, and flip objects.

Moving, Copying, or Deleting Objects

To move an object, follow these steps:

1. Choose the Arrow tool.
2. Click the object to select it.
3. Drag the object to the new location.

   A dotted outline of the object indicates its changing position.

To copy an object, follow these steps:

1. Choose the Arrow tool.
2. Click the object to select it.
3. Open the Edit menu.
4. Choose the Copy command.
5. Choose the Paste command.

   A copy of the object appears in the Microsoft Draw window.

6. Drag the object to the location where you want the copy to appear.

To delete an object, select the object and then press Del or choose the Cut command from the Edit menu.

Sizing Objects

You can change the size of an object by dragging. Follow these steps:

1. Choose the Arrow tool.
2. Click the object to select it.
3. Drag one of the object's handles.

   An outline of the object indicates its changing size.

4. Release the mouse button when the object is the correct size.

16

416

When you resize an object by using this method, you do not maintain its proportions. To maintain the proportions of the object, hold down [⇧Shift] and drag the handle diagonally. To maintain the object's height, hold down [⇧Shift] and drag the handle horizontally. To maintain the object's width, hold down [⇧Shift] and drag the handle vertically. To resize the object using its center as a focal point, hold down [Ctrl] as you drag the handle.

If the object you are sizing is a bitmap, you can restore its proportions by double-clicking any of the object's handles. You also can restore a bitmap object to its original size by holding down [⇧Shift] and double-clicking any of its handles.

When you resize an arc or pie wedge by dragging, you change the *area* the arc or pie wedge covers, but not its size in degrees (90 degrees of a 360-degree ellipse or circle). To change an arc's or pie wedge's size in degrees, follow these steps:

1. Choose the Arrow tool.
2. Select the arc or pie wedge.
3. Double-click the arc or pie wedge.

   Or

   Open the Edit menu and choose the Edit Arc command.

   Two handles disappear, and two remain.
4. Drag one of the remaining handles until the arc is the correct size.

Rotating or Flipping Objects

You can rotate or flip objects that are not bitmaps. To rotate or flip an object, follow these steps:

1. Choose the Arrow tool.
2. Click the object to select it.
3. Open the Draw menu.
4. Choose the Rotate/Flip command.

   A submenu appears at the side of the Rotate/Flip command.
5. From the submenu, choose the Rotate Left, Rotate Right, Flip Horizontal, or Flip Vertical command.

   Rotating to the left turns the object counter-clockwise. Rotating to the right turns the object clockwise. Flipping horizontally reverses the object from left to right. Flipping vertically reverses the object from top to bottom.

16

417

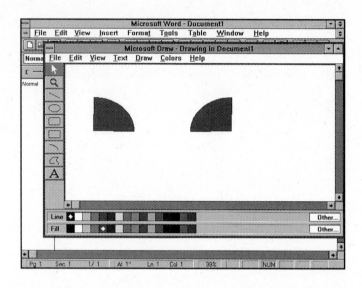

The object on the right is a copy of the object on the left, flipped horizontally.

16

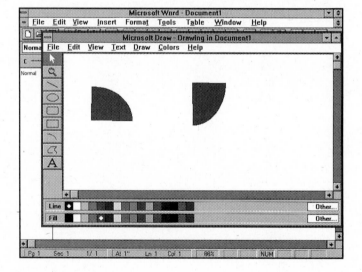

The object on the right is a copy of the object on the left, rotated to the right.

Changing a Freeform Object

A freeform object consists of many lines and vertices. You can change the shape of a freeform object by moving, adding, or deleting vertices. To make changes to a freeform object, you must switch to edit mode.

To switch to edit mode, follow these steps:

1. Select the freeform object.
2. Double-click the freeform object.

   Or

   Open the Edit menu and choose the Edit Freeform command.

   The mouse pointer changes to an arrowhead pointing up and slightly to the left, and handles appear at all vertices of the object.

To move a vertex, follow these steps:

1. Position the mouse pointer on the vertex you want to move.
2. Drag the vertex to the new location.

To add a vertex, follow these steps:

1. Position the mouse pointer on a line where you want to add a vertex. You can add a vertex anywhere on a line.
2. Hold down Ctrl.

   The mouse pointer changes to a plus sign inside a circle.
3. Click the left mouse button.

To delete a vertex, follow these steps:

1. Hold down ⇧Shift+Ctrl.

   The mouse pointer changes to a minus sign inside a square.
2. Click the vertex you want to delete.

   Microsoft Draw deletes the vertex and joins the segments on both sides of the vertex into one segment.

Working with Text

You can add text to your drawings by creating text objects. Each text object can be one line long and can contain up to 255 characters. Unlike Word for Windows, Microsoft Draw does not wrap text. If the text you type extends beyond the page, Microsoft Draw crops the text and stores the portion that does not fit on the page. If you move or size the text so that it all fits on the page, the cropped portion reappears. To create two lines of text, you must create two separate text objects.

16

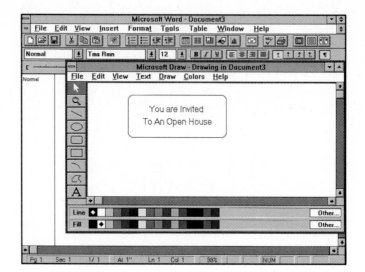

This text consists
of two text
objects.

You can set the font, style, size, color, and alignment for each text object, but you cannot rotate or flip text objects. (When you create a text object, you do not actually add text to an existing object; rather, you place text on top of the object. When you rotate or flip objects that "contain" text objects, the text objects are not affected.)

Adding a Text Object

You can set the color, size, font, style and alignment of text before you add the text object. You also can change any or all of these attributes after you add the text object.

To add a text object, follow these steps:

1. Choose the Text tool.
2. Position the mouse pointer where you want the text to appear and click the left mouse button.

   The mouse pointer changes to an I-beam shape, and an insertion point appears in the drawing area.

3. Type the text.
4. Press ↵Enter or Esc.

Editing a Text Object

You can add, change, or delete characters in a text object. Follow these steps:

1. Choose the Arrow tool.

2. Double-click the text object you want to modify.

   Or

   Select the text object you want to modify and then choose the Edit Text command from the Edit menu.

   The insertion point appears.

3. Add, change, or delete characters. In Microsoft Draw, ⟨◆Backspace⟩ and ⟨Del⟩ function just as they do in Word for Windows.

4. Press ⟨◄Enter⟩ or ⟨Esc⟩ or click anywhere else on-screen.

   The insertion point disappears, and the text object handles appear.

Moving or Copying Text

You can move or copy text in a drawing, but, because the text is a text *object*, you must use the mouse for the first part of the process.

To move text, follow these steps:

1. Choose the Arrow tool.

2. Double-click the text object you want to move.

   Or

   Select the text object you want to move and then choose the Edit Text command from the Edit menu.

   The insertion point appears.

3. Drag the mouse to highlight the text you want to move.

4. Press ⟨◆Shift⟩+⟨Del⟩.

   Microsoft Draw cuts the text object and stores it on the Clipboard.

5. Choose the Text tool. (You may have to click two times to choose the Text tool.)

6. Position the mouse pointer where you want the text to appear and click the left mouse button.

   The insertion point appears.

7. Press ⟨◆Shift⟩+⟨Ins⟩.

   Microsoft Draw inserts the text object in the new location.

16

To copy text, follow these steps:

1. Choose the Arrow tool.

2. Double-click the text object you want to copy.

   Or

   Select the text object you want to copy and then choose the Edit Text command from the Edit menu.

   The insertion point appears.

3. Drag the mouse to highlight the text you want to copy.

4. Press Ctrl + Ins.

   Microsoft Draw stores a copy of the text object on the Clipboard.

5. Choose the Text tool. (You may have to click two times to choose the Text tool.)

6. Position the mouse pointer where you want the copy to appear and click the left mouse button.

   The insertion point appears.

7. Press Shift + Ins.

   Microsoft Draw inserts a copy of the text object in the new location.

Enhancing Text

You can use the Text menu to select the font, size, style, alignment, and color of the text object.

Follow these steps to change font, size, style, or alignment of a text object:

1. Select the text object.

2. Open the Text menu.

3. Choose from the Bold, Italic, Underline, Left, Center, Right, Font, or Size commands.

   If you choose the Font or Size command, Microsoft Draw opens a submenu from which you can choose a font and a point size.

You can choose more than one style option (both Bold and Italic, for example). You can change the alignment of text, but if the text appears in relation to another object, you may have to move the text object or the other object to achieve the alignment you want. If you already enhanced a text object, you can remove the enhancement(s) by choosing the Plain command from the Text menu.

To change the color of a text object, select the text object and then choose a color from the Line color palette.

Chapter Summary

In this chapter, you learned the basics of using Microsoft Draw with Word for Windows. You learned how to use the drawing tools to draw lines, ellipses, circles, rounded rectangles, rectangles, squares, and arcs. You also learned how to use the Freeform tool to draw unspecified shapes and the Text tool to add text to drawings. Specifically, you learned the following information:

- You can open Microsoft Draw by using the Microsoft Draw button on the Toolbar or the Object command on the Insert menu.

- You save and print drawings by transferring them to a Word for Windows document and then using Word for Windows commands to save or print the document.

- You can select an object by choosing the Arrow tool and then clicking the object or by using a Selection Rectangle.

- You can select menu defaults by choosing commands from the View, Text, Draw, and Colors menus.

- You can turn on or off the grid by choosing the Snap to Grid command from the Draw menu. You can turn on or off the guides by choosing the Show Guides command from the Draw menu. You can move the guides by using the Arrow tool.

- You can add frames to or remove frames from an object by choosing the Framed command from the Draw menu. You can change the color of a line or frame by using the Line color palette. You can change the style of a line or frame by using the Line Style command on the Draw menu.

- You can add fills to or remove fills from an object by choosing the Filled command from the Draw menu. You can change an object's fill color by using the Fill color palette. You can change an object's fill pattern by choosing the Pattern command from the Draw menu.

- You can import pictures created in other software by using the Import Picture command on the File menu.

- You can zoom objects by using Zoom tool or the View menu.

- You can move, copy, and delete objects by using the Copy, Cut, and Paste commands from the Edit menu. You can size an object by dragging one of its handles. You can change the angle (in degrees) of

16

an arc or pie wedge by using the Edit Arc command on the Edit menu. You can rotate and flip an object by using the Rotate/Flip command on the Draw menu.

■ You can modify a freeform drawing by moving, adding, or deleting vertices. You move a vertex by dragging. You add a vertex by holding down Ctrl and clicking the location for the new vertex. You delete a vertex by holding down Ctrl+⇧Shift and clicking the vertex you want to delete.

■ You can edit a text object by selecting it and typing changes. You can move or copy a text object by using the Clipboard. You press ⇧Shift+Del to cut a text object to the Clipboard. You press Ctrl+Ins to copy a text object to or retrieve a text object from the Clipboard. You also can enhance a text object by using the commands on the Text menu.

In the next chapter, you will learn how to use Microsoft Equation Editor with Word for Windows.

16

Using Microsoft Equation Editor

17

Microsoft Equation Editor is a software package that comes with Word for Windows. Microsoft Equation Editor enables you to create and edit simple or complex equations easily. This capability is particularly valuable to users who regularly type technical information.

Microsoft Equation Editor is a version of the MathType equation editor developed by Design Science, Inc. Microsoft Equation Editor has been customized for use with Word for Windows, but also works with many other Windows programs.

In this chapter, you will learn how to use Microsoft Equation Editor to create equations in Word for Windows documents. You don't need to exit from Word for Windows because Microsoft Equation Editor works inside Word for Windows.

An overview of Microsoft Equation Editor

Understanding the basics

Creating and editing equations

Key Terms in This Chapter

Slot	A dotted box in the Microsoft Equation Editor window. You type information or insert symbols or templates in slots. Slots control the size and spacing of the text, symbols, and templates they contain.
Symbol palette	A group of related mathematical symbols, such as operators (+, −, ÷, and so on). To display a symbol palette, you click its icon (one of the ten icons in the first row at the top of the Microsoft Equation Editor window).
Template palette	A group of standard mathematical relationships. To display a template palette, you click its icon (one of the nine icons in the second row at the top of the Microsoft Equation Editor window). Each template palette contains related combinations of slots and symbols, such as fences.
Primary slot	The slot you are most likely to use after inserting a template. When you insert a slot, Microsoft Equation Editor positions the insertion point in the primary slot.
Pile	A series of lines of equation information. You create a pile by pressing ⏎Enter between lines. You can align piles by using commands on Microsoft Equation Editor's Format menu.

17

An Overview of Microsoft Equation Editor

Microsoft Equation Editor enables you to create simple or complex equations in Word for Windows documents by using basic "point and click" techniques. You use palettes to insert symbols and templates into an equation. You can accept Microsoft Equation Editor's default formatting, or you can customize the formatting and styles of the symbols and templates you insert. You can easily combine text and mathematical symbols.

You typically use Microsoft Equation Editor from inside another program, such as Word for Windows. You cannot save or print equations from inside Microsoft Equation Editor; you must use the other program's save and print features.

If you work with equations extensively, you may want to use MathType, the extended version of Microsoft Equation Editor. MathType supports macros, advanced formatting based on tabs, and customized symbol and template palettes. To contact Design Science or one of its local distributors, see Appendix C of the *Microsoft Equation Editor User's Guide*.

Opening Microsoft Equation Editor

To open Microsoft Equation Editor from Word for Windows, follow these steps:

1. Open the Word for Windows document into which you want to insert an equation.
2. Position the insertion point where you want the equation to appear.
3. Open the Insert menu.
4. Choose the Object command.

   The Object dialog box appears.
5. Choose Equation.

   The Microsoft Equation Editor window appears.

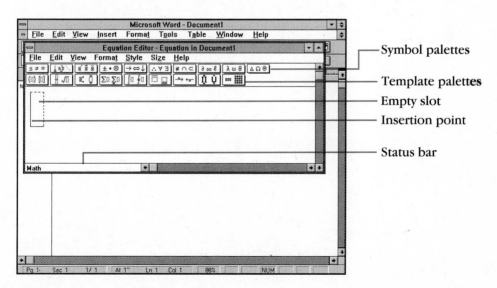

— Symbol palettes

— Template palettes

— Empty slot

— Insertion point

— Status bar

The Microsoft Equation Editor window contains a menu bar, ten symbol palettes, nine template palettes, an equation area, scroll bars, and a status bar.

The first time you use Microsoft Equation Editor, a warning dialog box tells you that Microsoft Equation Editor selects default fonts.

To check (and change) these defaults, follow these steps:

1. Open the Style menu.
2. Choose the Define command.

17

The Styles dialog box appears.

Styles				
Style	Font		Bold	Italic
Text	Tms Rmn	⬦	☐	☐
Function	Tms Math A	⬦	☐	☐
Variable	Tms Rmn	⬦	☐	☒
L.C. Greek	MT Symbol	⬦	☐	☒
U.C. Greek	MT Symbol	⬦	☐	☐
Symbol	MT Symbol	⬦	☐	☐
Matrix-Vector . . .	Tms Math A	⬦	☒	☐
Number	Tms Math A	⬦	☐	☐

Character Format

OK   Cancel   Help...

3. Choose default fonts and formatting for the parts of an equation. If your text font is a math font, for example, you may want to change the font; otherwise, unexpected characters may appear when you type in the text style.

   In your printer does not support the fonts Microsoft Equation Editor uses to produce equations, a dialog box warns you that symbols and characters will not print properly.

4. Choose OK.

Changing the Size of the View

You can enlarge or reduce the display size of an equation by using commands on the View menu. You can enlarge an equation to two or four times its regular size. Note that when you use the View menu to change the size of the equation, you are *not* changing the size at which the equation will print—you are changing only the display size. (To change the size at which the equation will print, you use commands on the Size menu.)

To use the View menu to zoom an item or an equation, follow these steps:

1. Select the item or equation you want to zoom.
2. Open the View menu on Microsoft Equation Editor's menu bar.
3. Choose a size command.

Saving and Printing

Because Microsoft Equation Editor does not work independently, you must use the main program to save and print your equations. You can transfer an equation from Microsoft Equation Editor to the document at any time, or you can wait until you finish an equation and close Microsoft Equation Editor. After you update the main document you can save or print the document and the equation. When you save the main document, you are also saving the equation. When you print the main document, you are also printing the equation.

To update the document, but remain in Microsoft Equation Editor, follow these steps:

1. Open the File menu on Microsoft Equation Editor's menu bar.
2. Choose the Update command.

   Microsoft Equation Editor copies the information in its window to the Word for Windows document.

To exit Microsoft Equation Editor, follow these steps:

1. Open the File menu on Microsoft Equation Editor's menu bar.
2. Choose the Exit and Return to *Document1* command (where *Document1* is the active Word for Windows document).

   A dialog box asks whether you want to update the Word for Windows document.

3. Choose Yes to transfer the equation. Choose No to close Microsoft Equation Editor without transferring the equation. (If you choose No, you will lose the work you did in Microsoft Equation Editor.) Choose Cancel to remain in Microsoft Equation Editor.

Getting Help

You can get Microsoft Equation Editor Help the same way you get Word for Windows Help—by pressing [F1]. In fact, all the help information described in Chapter 1 of this book also applies to Microsoft Equation Editor.

17

Understanding the Basics

Before you start typing equations, you need to understand how the insertion point works in Microsoft Equation Editor. You also need to know how to type, select, move, copy, and delete information in Microsoft Equation Editor. Finally, you need to learn about the palettes.

Understanding the Insertion Point

In Microsoft Equation Editor, the insertion point has several shapes. When you open Microsoft Equation Editor, the insertion point looks like the letter L and appears in the empty slot. The insertion point is really a vertical line and a horizontal line that intersect. As you work, the relationship of the vertical line to the horizontal line changes. The insertion point can, for example, look like a backward L, or the vertical bar may appear somewhere in the middle of the horizontal bar. The horizontal bar also may become longer. The position and size of the vertical bar determine the size and formatting of text.

The following examples show the changing location and appearance of the insertion point as you are creating and modifying a basic equation: $x + a\text{y} = z$.

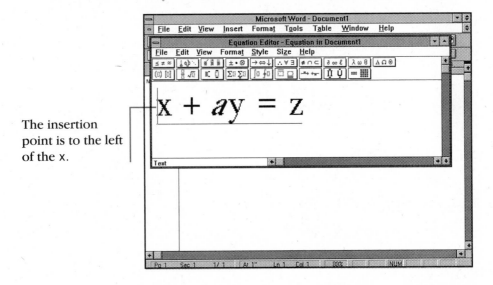

The insertion point is to the left of the x.

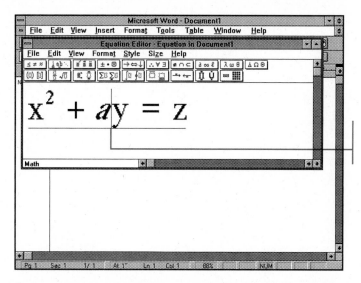

The insertion point is between *a* and y.

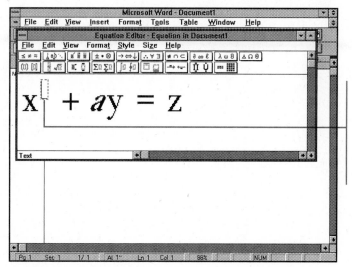

When you insert a template to enter an exponent for x, the insertion point flashes in the slot of the template.

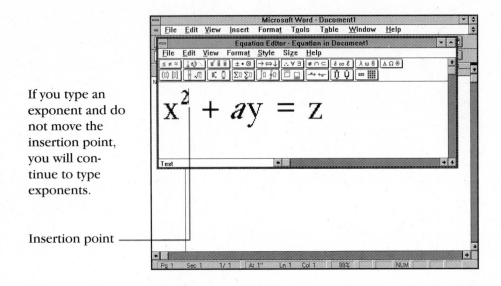

If you type an exponent and do not move the insertion point, you will continue to type exponents.

Insertion point ———

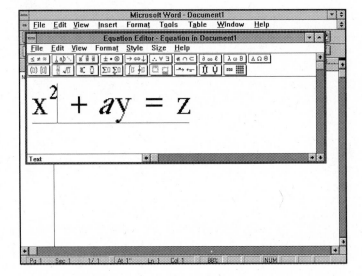

If you move the insertion point, you will no longer be typing in the exponent's slot.

Typing Rules

Most of the typing rules you follow in Word for Windows also apply in Microsoft Equation Editor, but a few important exceptions exist:

- In most cases, Microsoft Equation Editor automatically inserts spaces for numbers, symbols, and variables. For this reason, the **space bar** doesn't work unless you have selected the **T**ext command from the **S**tyle menu. If you press the **space bar** with any other style selected, Microsoft Equation Editor beeps.

- Microsoft Equation Editor automatically replaces certain characters with symbols unless you have selected the **T**ext command from the **S**tyle menu. Because Microsoft Equation Editor's symbols have been sized and positioned for equations, you should use the symbols from the symbol palettes rather than the symbol keys on the keyboard (for example, the bracket symbols on the keyboard do not have the correct size in Microsoft Equation Editor).

- Press ⏎Enter to begin a new line of an equation or to insert a new slot directly below the slot containing the insertion point.

Using the Palettes

You use Microsoft Equation Editor's symbol and template palettes to insert symbols or templates into an equation.

A symbol palette is a group of related mathematical symbols. Microsoft Equation Editor provides symbol palettes of relational symbols, spaces and ellipses, embellishments, operators, arrows, logical symbols, set theory symbols, miscellaneous symbols, and lower- and uppercase Greek letters.

The symbol palette icons appear in first row at the top of Microsoft Equation Editor window. To display a symbol palette, click its icon and hold down the left mouse button.

Table 17.1 lists the symbol palettes.

Table 17.1
The Symbol Palettes

Icon	Name	Use
≤ ≠ ≈	Relational	Inserts symbols that express the relationship (such as equality or inequality) between two math-ematical expressions.
⫶ ɑb ∴	Spaces and Ellipses	Aligns the expressions in a pile.

continues

433

Table 17.1 (continued)

Icon	Name	Use
⃓ ⃗ ⃛	Embellishments	Adds symbols such as primes, hats, and bars to variables.
± • ⊗	Operators	Inserts mathematical operators.
→ ⇔ ↓	Arrows	Inserts one of fourteen arrow styles.
∴ ∀ ∃	Logical	Inserts one of eight logical operators.
∉ ∩ ⊆	Set Theory	Designates set theory relationships (such as membership, union, and intersection).
∂ ∞ ℓ	Miscellaneous	Inserts symbols not found in any other symbol palette.
λ ω θ	Lowercase Greek	Inserts lowercase Greek characters.
Λ Ω Θ	Uppercase Greek	Inserts uppercase Greek characters.

A template palette is a group of standard mathematical relationships. Each template palette contains related combinations of slots and symbols. Microsoft Equation Editor provides template palettes of fences, fractions and radicals, subscripts and superscripts, summations, integrals, labeled arrows, product and set theory expressions, and matrices.

The template palette icons appear in second row at the top of Microsoft Equation Editor window. To display a template palette, click its icon and hold down the left mouse button.

Table 17.2 lists the template palettes.

Table 17.2
The Template Palettes

Icon	Name	Use
(⬚) [⬚]	Fences	Encloses mathematical expressions in symbols such as ( ) or { }.

17

Icon	Name	Use
	Fractions and Radicals	Creates fractions, square roots, and long division expressions.
	Superscript and Subscript	Creates exponents and subscript characters.
	Summations	Inserts expressions involving sums.
	Integrals	Creates expressions involving integrals.
	Overbars and Underbars	Adds bars over or under expressions.
	Labeled Arrows	Adds labels above or below arrows.
	Products and Set Theory	Inserts expressions related to products and set theory.
	Matrices	Builds expressions that require a table layout.

17

To insert a symbol or template, follow these steps:

1. Position the insertion point where you want to insert a symbol or template.

2. Click the icon of the symbol or template palette that contains the symbol or template you want to insert and hold down the left mouse button.

   Microsoft Equation Editor displays the palette of related symbols or templates.

3. Drag the mouse pointer across the palette to highlight the symbol or template you want to insert.

4. Release the mouse button.

Editing

Before you can change, move, or copy an item in Microsoft Equation Editor, you first must select that item. You select items in Microsoft Equation Editor similarly to the way you select items in Word for Windows, but you use some additional techniques to select the contents of a slot, a symbol inserted as part of a template, or a matrix:

- To select the contents of a slot, double-click the slot. If the equation has nested templates within slots, double-clicking selects the smallest, innermost slot.

- To select an embedded item (such as an embellishment, a summation sign, or expanding fences), hold down Ctrl. The mouse pointer changes to an outlined arrow pointing up. Click the symbol.

- To select any continuous area of an equation, including a matrix, highlight the area by dragging from the beginning of the area to the end or by holding down Shift and pressing ← or →. If the expression extends beyond the window, select to the edge of the window.

- To select the entire window, choose the Select All command from the Edit menu.

You can move or copy a selected item by using the Cut, Copy, and Paste commands on the Edit menu. You also can use key combinations to cut, copy, and paste a selected item: press Ctrl+X to cut the item to the Clipboard, Ctrl+C to copy the item to the Clipboard, and Ctrl+V to paste the item from the Clipboard.

You can delete the item to the left of the insertion point by pressing Backspace. You can delete the item to the right of the insertion point by pressing Del. You can delete a selected item by pressing Backspace or Del.

Creating and Editing Equations

This section provides steps for entering sample equations. The illustrations are screen images and do not demonstrate how the equation will appear when printed, but rather how the equation appears as you create it. For example, some lines appear broken and jagged when you are working in the Microsoft Equation Editor window. When you print the equation, however, the lines appear far less jagged.

This book uses the Fourier series, three equations used in mathematical physics and engineering, to demonstrate how to build equations.

The first equation is:

$$f(\theta) = \frac{A_o}{2} + \sum_{n=1}^{\infty} \left(A_n \cos n\theta + B_n \sin n\theta \right)$$

If you make a mistake as you follow these examples, press ⌫Backspace to delete the mistake.

To begin entering this equation, follow these steps:

1. Open a Word for Windows document and position the insertion point where you want the equation to appear.

2. Open the **Insert** menu and choose the **Object** command.

   The Object dialog box appears.

3. Choose Equation and then choose OK.

   Microsoft Equation Editor opens.

4. Open the **Style** menu and choose the **Variable** command.

5. Type **f**.

   Microsoft Equation Editor uses the font you defined for variables (in the Styles dialog box) to add the letter *f* to the equation.

6. From the Fences template palette, choose the first template (parentheses surrounding a slot).

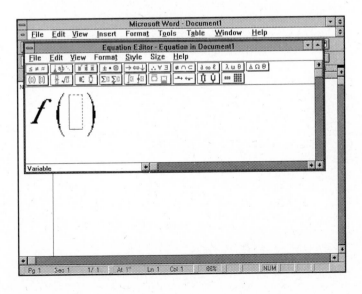

The equation should now look like this. The insertion point flashes in the slot.

17

To continue, follow these steps:

1. From the Lowercase Greek symbol palette, choose the Greek letter *theta*.

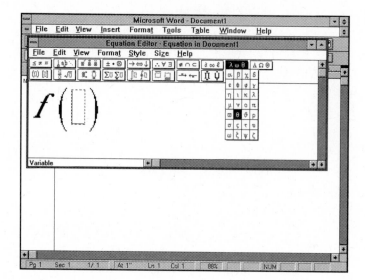

Theta is the fifth letter in the second column.

2. Press ⟶ to move the insertion point outside the slot.
3. Type =.

   Microsoft Equation Editor inserts an extra space automatically.

4. From the Fractions and Radicals template palette (the second template palette), choose the first box, a fraction.

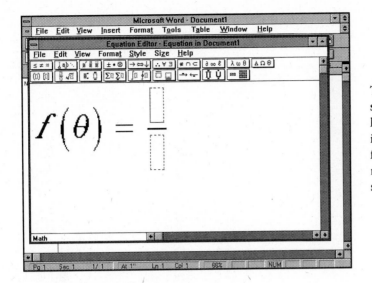

The equation should now look like this. The insertion point flashes in the numerator (top) slot.

17

Now follow these steps:

1. Open the **Style** menu and choose the **Variable** command.

2. Type **A**.

3. From the Superscript and Subscript template palette (the third template palette), choose the second box.

4. Type **o**.

5. Press ⬇ to move the insertion point to the denominator (bottom) slot of the fraction.

6. Type **2**.

7. Press ➡ to move out of the fraction.

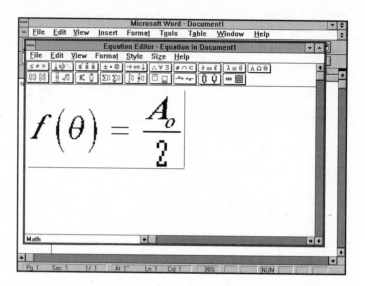

The equation
should now look
like this.

17

Continue with the following steps:

1. Type +.

   Microsoft Equation Editor automatically inserts extra space.

2. From the Summation template palette (the fourth template palette),
   choose the third box.

3. Press ⬆ to move the insertion point to the top slot.

4. From the Miscellaneous symbol palette (the eighth symbol palette),
   choose the infinity symbol (the third symbol).

5. Press ⬇ two times to move the insertion point to the slot below the
   summation symbol.

6. Open the **S**tyle menu and choose the **V**ariable command.

7. Type **n=1**.

   The slot expands to hold the information.

8. Press ➡ to move the insertion point out of the bottom slot.

9. Press ⬅ to move the insertion point to the empty slot next to the
   summation symbol.

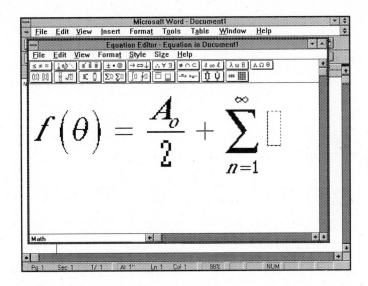

The equation should now look like this.

Now follow these steps:

1. From the Fences template palette, choose the left parenthesis with an empty slot.

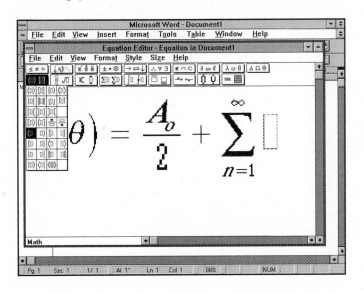

The left parenthesis is the fifth box in the first column of the Fences template palette.

2. Open the **S**tyle menu and choose the **V**ariable command.

3. Type **A**.

4. From the Superscript and Subscript template palette, choose the second box.

5. Type **n**.

6. Press → to move the insertion point out of the subscript slot.

7. Open the **S**tyle menu and choose the **T**ext command.

8. Press the **space bar** and type **cos**. Press the **space bar** again.

17

The equation should now look like this.

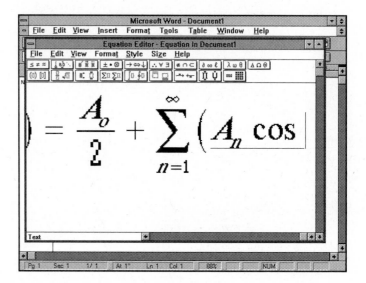

To continue creating the equation, follow these steps:

1. Open the **S**tyle menu and choose the **V**ariable command.

2. Type **n**.

3. From the Lowercase Greek symbol palette, choose *theta*.

4. Type **+B**.

5. From the Superscript and Subscript template palette, choose the second box.

6. Type **n**.

7. Press →.

8. Open the **S**tyle menu and choose the **T**ext command.

9. Press the **space bar** and type **sin**. Press the **space bar** again.

10. Open the Style menu and choose the Variable command.

11. Type **n**.

12. From the Fences template palette, choose the right parenthesis with an empty slot (the fifth box in the second column).

13. From the Lowercase Greek symbol palette, choose *theta*.

14. Open the File menu on Microsoft Equation Editor's menu bar.

15. Choose the Exit and Return to *Document1* command (where *Document1* is active Word for Windows document).

16. Choose Yes to save the changes.

In the Word for Windows document, the finished equation should look like this:

$$f(\theta) = \frac{A_0}{2} + \sum_{n=1}^{\infty} \left(A_n \cos n\theta + B_n \sin n\theta \right)$$

If, after you print the equation, you decide that some of the characters are too close together, you can use a technique called "nudging" to move a character one pixel (one dot on-screen). To "nudge" a character or symbol, follow these steps:

1. Double-click the equation to open Microsoft Equation Editor.

2. Select the character you want to "nudge."

3. Hold down $\boxed{\text{Ctrl}}$ and press $\boxed{\uparrow}$, $\boxed{\downarrow}$, $\boxed{\leftarrow}$, or $\boxed{\rightarrow}$ to move the character in that direction.

The second and third equations in the Fourier series are very similar, so you will learn how to copy and edit the second equation to create the third. In the third equation, you also will learn a new way to insert spaces—by using the Spaces and Ellipses symbol palette.

The second and third equations in the Fourier series are:

$$A_n = \frac{1}{\pi} \int_0^{2\pi} f(\theta) \cos n\theta \, d\theta$$

$$B_n = \frac{1}{\pi} \int_0^{2\pi} f(\theta) \sin n\theta \, d\theta$$

17

443

To create the second equation, follow these steps:

1. Open a Word for Windows document and position the insertion point where you want the equation to appear.
2. Open the Insert menu and choose the Object command.

   The Object dialog box appears.
3. Choose Equation and then choose OK.

   Microsoft Equation Editor opens.
4. Open the Style menu and choose the Variable command.
5. Type A.
6. From the Superscript and Subscript template palette, choose the second box.
7. Type n.
8. Press → to move the insertion point out of the subscript slot.
9. Type =.

The equation should now look like this.

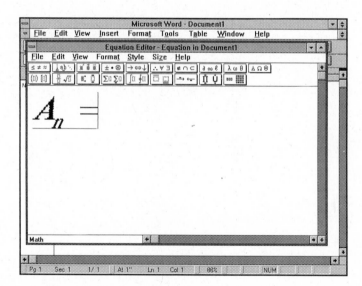

To continue creating this equation, follow these steps:

1. From the Fractions and Radicals template palette, choose the first box.
2. In the numerator slot, type 1.
3. Press ↓ to move the insertion point to the denominator slot.
4. From the Lowercase Greek symbol palette, choose *pi* (the fourth box in the fourth column).

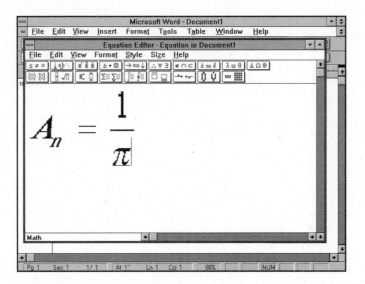

The equation should now look like this.

5. Press ⇥ to move the insertion point out of the denominator slot.

6. From the Integral template palette (the fifth template palette), choose the second box.

7. Press ⇧ to move the insertion point out of the primary slot, the integrand, into the slot above the integral symbol.

8. Type 2.

9. From the Lowercase Greek symbol palette, choose *pi*.

10. Press ⬇ two times to move the insertion point to the slot below the integral symbol.

11. Type 0.

12. Press ⇧ to move the insertion point to the integrand slot (the empty slot next to the integral symbol).

17

The equation
should now look
like this.

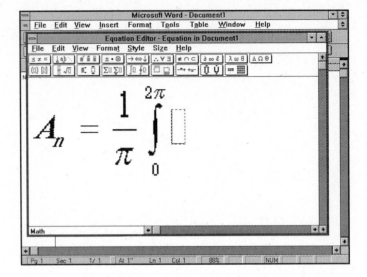

17

Now follow these steps:

1. Open the **S**tyle menu and choose the **V**ariable command.

2. Type **f**.

3. From the Fences template palette, choose the parentheses surrounding a slot (the first box).

4. From the Lowercase Greek symbol palette, choose *theta*.

5. Press → to move the insertion point out of the slot.

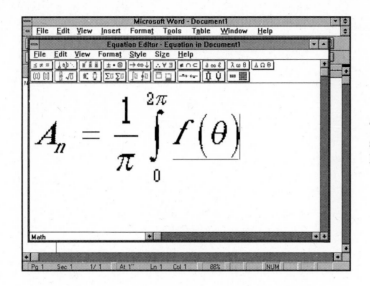

The equation
should now look
like this.

6. Open the Style menu and choose the Text command.

7. Press the **space bar** and type **cos**. Press the **space bar** again.

8. Open the Style menu and choose the Variable command.

9. Type **n**.

10. From the Lowercase Greek symbol palette, choose *theta*.

11. From the Spaces and Ellipses symbol palette, choose the second box in the second row to insert a wide space.

12. Type **d**.

13. From the Lowercase Greek symbol palette, choose *theta*.

14. Open the File menu on Microsoft Equation Editor's menu bar.

15. Choose the Exit and Return to *Document1* command (where *Document1* is active Word for Windows document).

16. Choose Yes to save the changes.

In the Word for Windows document, the finished equation should look like this:

$$A_n = \frac{1}{\pi} \int_0^{2\pi} f(\theta) \, \cos n\theta \, d\theta$$

To create the third equation, you can copy and modify the second equation. Follow these steps:

1. In the Word for Windows document, click the equation to select it.

    Gray handles appear around the equation.

2. Copy the equation to the Clipboard by using the Copy button on the Toolbar or the **Copy** command on the **Edit** menu.

    The gray handles are replaced by black handles.

3. Position the insertion point in the document where you want the copied equation to appear.

4. Insert the copy of the equation by using the Paste button on the Toolbar or the **Paste** command on the **Edit** menu.

5. Open Microsoft Equation Editor by double-clicking the copied equation.

    The copied equation appear in the Microsoft Equation Editor window and is selected.

6. Press ← to cancel the selection and move the insertion point to the beginning of the equation.

7. Change the *A* to a *B* by pressing Del and typing **B**.

8. Click the beginning of the word *cos*, or press → to move the insertion point to the beginning of *cos*.

9. Delete *cos* by pressing Del three times or by highlighting *cos* and then pressing Del or ←Backspace.

10. Type **sin**.

11. Open the **File** menu on Microsoft Equation Editor's menu bar.

12. Choose the E**x**it and Return to *Document1* command (where *Document1* is active Word for Windows document).

13. Choose **Y**es to save the changes.

In the Word for Windows document, the finished equation should look like this:

$$B_n = \frac{1}{\pi} \int_0^{2\pi} f(\theta) \, \sin n\theta \, d\theta$$

17

Chapter Summary

In this chapter, you learned the basics of using Microsoft Equation Editor. You learned about the position and size of the insertion point and how to type in Microsoft Equation Editor. Specifically, you learned the following information:

■ You can open Microsoft Equation Editor from Word for Windows by using the Object command on the Insert menu or by double-clicking an existing equation.

■ You can use the View menu to change the display size of an item or equation.

■ You save and print equations by transferring them to a Word for Windows document and then using Word for Windows commands to save or print the document.

■ You use the symbol and template palettes to insert symbols or combinations of symbols and empty slots into an equation.

■ You can select items in Microsoft Equation Editor by using new techniques in addition to the selection techniques you already learned in Word for Windows.

■ You can move and copy text, symbols, and templates by using the Cut, Copy, and Paste commands on Microsoft Equation Editor's Edit menu. You can delete text, symbols, and templates by using the Cut and Paste commands on Microsoft Equation Editor's Edit menu or by pressing ◆Backspace or Del.

This chapter completes your introduction to Word for Windows 2.0. Appendix A provides instructions for installing a single-user version of Word for Windows.

17

Installing Word for Windows 2.0

This appendix provides instructions for installing a single-user version of Word for Windows. The *Word for Windows User's Guide* contains complete instructions for installing Word for Windows in a network environment.

When you install Word for Windows 2.0, you can choose from three installation options. You can install just the basic program, which requires 1 megabyte of RAM and approximately 5.5 megabytes of free space on your hard disk. You can install the complete program, which requires 2 megabytes of RAM and approximately 15 megabytes of free space on your hard disk (with 4 megabytes available on the drive where you installed Windows). Or, you can perform a custom installation, during which you control what parts of Word for Windows you install.

Windows and Word for Windows

To install Word for Windows, you first must have installed Windows. In addition, before you can print in Word for Windows, you must define your printer(s) to Windows. (You do not install printers through Word for Windows, but rather use whatever printers you installed in Windows.)

See your Windows manual for details on installing Windows and setting up your printer. If you change printers or add a printer, you must make the changes or additions in Windows before you indicate the changes or additions to Word for Windows.

After Windows is installed and working, you use the Word Setup program to install Word for Windows.

Using the Setup Program

When you start the Setup program, it asks you to choose an installation option. The installation option you choose determines the amount of free space you need on your hard disk. If you do not choose the Complete installation option, you can add files later by running the Setup program again.

The Minimum installation installs only the basic files you need to run Word for Windows. For this installation option, you need about 5.5 megabytes of free space on your hard disk.

The Complete installation installs all the files that come with Word for Windows, including help, on-line tutorial lessons, the Spelling Checker, the Grammar Checker, the Thesaurus, and the three extra programs that come with Word for Windows (Microsoft Draw, Microsoft Graph, and Microsoft Equation Editor). For this installation option, the documentation specifies that you need about 14 megabytes of free space on your hard disk, but the Setup program specifies that you need about 15 megabytes of free space on your hard disk, with 4 megabytes (of that 15) on the drive where you installed Windows.

The Custom installation enables you to choose what files you install. As you choose files, the Setup program estimates the necessary disk space.

After Word for Windows is installed, the Word Setup icon appears in the Word for Windows group along with the icon for Word for Windows.

Performing a Complete Installation

To perform a Complete installation of Word for Windows, follow these steps:

1. Start Windows. If Windows is already running, close all applications except the Program Manager.
2. Insert Disk 1 of the Word for Windows disks into drive A. (If your floppy disk drive is not drive A, substitute the appropriate letter.)

3. Open the File menu.

4. Choose the Run command.

5. Type a:setup.

6. Choose OK.

   The Setup program starts.

7. On the first setup screen, personalize your copy of Word for Windows by typing your name and your company's name. (Use the ⟨Tab⟩ key to move between the boxes and the ⟨◆Backspace⟩ key to correct mistakes.) Then, choose Continue.

   Note: If you previously ran the Setup program, you will not see this screen again.

8. On the next setup screen, specify the drive and directory where you want to install Word for Windows. The Setup program suggests C:\WINWORD. You can change the drive or the directory, but this book assumes that you install Word for Windows in the WINWORD directory. After you make any necessary changes, choose Continue.

9. If the directory you specified does not exist, the Setup program asks whether you want to create it. Choose Yes. The Setup program checks for available disk space.

   If the directory you specified exists, but the Setup program detects another version of Word for Windows, you can choose to overwrite that version or to change the installation directory for Word for Windows 2.0.

10. On the next screen, the Setup program displays the installation options: Minimum, Custom, or Complete. Choose Complete.

11. On the next screen, the Setup program displays a dialog box directed to WordPerfect users. The dialog box asks whether you want more information on a feature that helps WordPerfect users learn Word for Windows.

   To see a screen that explains how to make WordPerfect Help available inside Word for Windows, choose Yes. The Setup program displays a screen where you can choose whether to use WordPerfect Help or Word Help. (If you do not enable WordPerfect Help now, you can enable this feature from inside Word for Windows later.)

   To continue the installation without displaying this screen, choose No.

12. On the next screen, the Setup program displays a dialog box that asks whether you want to let the Setup program automatically update your AUTOEXEC.BAT file, adding the Word for Windows directory to the path statement and inserting a statement that runs the SHARE utility whenever you start your system.

A

453

If you are unfamiliar with modifying your AUTOEXEC.BAT file, choose Update.

If you are an experienced computer user and prefer to make the modifications yourself, choose Do Not Update.

13. On the next screen, the Setup program displays a dialog box that indicates the percentage of the installation that the Setup program has completed and message boxes from Microsoft Corporation concerning support, new features, and so on.

    If you need to cancel the setup at any time, choose Cancel.

14. When setup is complete, the Setup program returns to the Windows Program Manager and displays two new icons in the Word for Windows group: one for Word for Windows and one for Word Setup. You now can use Word for Windows.

Performing a Minimum Installation

To perform a Minimum installation of Word for Windows, follow these steps:

1. Start Windows. If Windows is already running, close all applications except the Program Manager.

2. Insert Disk 1 of the Word for Windows disks into drive A. (If your floppy disk drive is not drive A, substitute the appropriate letter.)

3. Open the File menu.

4. Choose the Run command.

5. Type a:setup.

6. Choose OK.

    The Setup program starts.

7. On the first setup screen, personalize your copy of Word for Windows by typing your name and your company's name. (Use the `Tab⇄` key to move between the boxes and the `⬅Backspace` key to correct mistakes.) Then, choose Continue.

    Note: If you previously ran the Setup program, you will not see this screen again.

8. On the next setup screen, specify the drive and directory where you want to install Word for Windows. The Setup program suggests C:\WINWORD. You can change the drive or the directory, but this book assumes that you install Word for Windows in the WINWORD directory. After you make any necessary changes, choose Continue.

9. If the directory you specified does not exist, the Setup program asks whether you want to create it. Choose Yes. The Setup program checks for available disk space.

    If the directory you specified exists, but the Setup program detects another version of Word for Windows, you can choose to overwrite that version or change the installation directory for Word for Windows 2.0.

10. On the next screen, the Setup program displays the installation options: Minimum, Custom, or Complete. Choose Minimum.

11. On the next screen, the Setup program displays a dialog box that asks whether you want to let the Setup program automatically update your AUTOEXEC.BAT file, adding the Word for Windows directory to the path statement and inserting a statement that runs the SHARE utility whenever you start your system.

    If you are unfamiliar with modifying your AUTOEXEC.BAT file, choose Update.

    If you are an experienced computer user and prefer to make the modifications yourself, choose Do Not Update.

12. On the next screen, the Setup program displays a dialog box that indicates the percentage of the installation that the Setup program has completed and message boxes from Microsoft Corporation concerning support, new features, and so on.

    If you need to cancel the setup at any time, choose Cancel.

13. When setup is complete, the Setup program returns to the Windows Program Manager and displays two new icons in the Word for Windows group: one for Word for Windows and one for Word Setup. You now can use Word for Windows.

Performing a Custom Installation

To perform a Custom installation of Word for Windows, follow these steps:

1. Start Windows. If Windows is already running, close all applications except the Program Manager.

2. Insert Disk 1 of the Word for Windows disks into drive A. (If your floppy disk drive is not drive A, substitute the appropriate letter.)

3. Open the File menu.

4. Choose the Run command.

5. Type **a:setup**.

A

6. Choose OK.

   The Setup program starts.

7. On the first setup screen, personalize your copy of Word for Windows by typing your name and your company's name. (Use the `Tab⇥` key to move between the boxes and the `⬅Backspace` key to correct mistakes.) Then, choose Continue.

   Note: If you previously ran the Setup program, you will not see this screen again.

8. On the next setup screen, specify the drive and directory where you want to install Word for Windows. The Setup program suggests C:\WINWORD. You can change the drive or the directory, but this book assumes that you install Word for Windows in the WINWORD directory. After you make any necessary changes, choose Continue.

9. If the directory you specified does not exist, the Setup program asks whether you want to create it. Choose Yes. The Setup program checks for available disk space.

   If the directory you specified exists, but the Setup program detects another version of Word for Windows, you can choose to overwrite that version or to change the installation directory for Word for Windows 2.0.

A

10. On the next screen, the Setup program displays the installation options: Minimum, Custom, or Complete. Choose Custom.

11. On the next screen, the Setup program displays the Word Setup Options dialog box with all options activated. In the lower left corner of the dialog box, you see the disk space available and the disk space required to install the activated options.

    To cancel an option, choose its check box. The Setup program removes the X from the box.

    To see details about a file, choose its command button. If you choose the Conversions button, for example, the Setup program displays a dialog box with all conversions activated. If you know you will not convert from certain file formats to Word for Windows, you can cancel those file conversion options. By installing only the conversion filters you need, you save hard disk space. After you choose your file conversion options, choose Setup to return to the Word Setup Options dialog box.

12. On the next screen, the Setup program displays a dialog box directed to WordPerfect users. The dialog box asks whether you want more information on a feature that helps WordPerfect users learn Word for Windows.

To see a screen that explains how to make WordPerfect Help available inside Word for Windows, choose Yes. The Setup program displays a screen where you can choose whether to use WordPerfect Help or Word Help. (If you do not enable WordPerfect Help now, you can enable this feature from inside Word for Windows later.)

To continue the installation without displaying this screen, choose No.

13. On the next screen, the Setup program displays a dialog box that asks whether you want to let the Setup program automatically update your AUTOEXEC.BAT file, adding the Word for Windows directory to the path statement and inserting a statement that runs the SHARE utility whenever you start your system.

    If you are unfamiliar with modifying your AUTOEXEC.BAT file, choose Update.

    If you are an experienced computer user and prefer to make the modifications yourself, choose Do Not Update.

14. On the next screen, the Setup program displays a dialog box that indicates the percentage of the installation that the Setup program has completed and message boxes from Microsoft Corporation concerning support, new features, and so on.

    If you need to cancel the setup at any time, choose Cancel.

15. When setup is complete, the Setup program returns to the Windows Program Manager and displays two new icons in the Word for Windows group: one for Word for Windows and one for Word Setup. You now can use Word for Windows.

Installing Word for Windows Over an Earlier Version

If you install Word for Windows over an earlier version of the program, the Setup program overwrites all program files, but retains existing user directories. If the Setup program detects any documents or templates with the same names as the ones it is about to install, the program asks whether you want to overwrite existing files.

A

Index

Free Catalog!

Mail us this registration form today, and we'll send you a free catalog featuring Que's complete line of best-selling books.

Name of Book _____

Name _____

Title _____

Phone ( ) _____

Company _____

Address _____

City _____

State _____ ZIP _____

Please check the appropriate answers:

1. Where did you buy your Que book?
   - ☐ Bookstore (name: _____)
   - ☐ Computer store (name: _____)
   - ☐ Catalog (name: _____)
   - ☐ Direct from Que
   - ☐ Other: _____

2. How many computer books do you buy a year?
   - ☐ 1 or less
   - ☐ 2-5
   - ☐ 6-10
   - ☐ More than 10

3. How many Que books do you own?
   - ☐ 1
   - ☐ 2-5
   - ☐ 6-10
   - ☐ More than 10

4. How long have you been using this software?
   - ☐ Less than 6 months
   - ☐ 6 months to 1 year
   - ☐ 1-3 years
   - ☐ More than 3 years

5. What influenced your purchase of this Que book?
   - ☐ Personal recommendation
   - ☐ Advertisement
   - ☐ In-store display
   - ☐ Price
   - ☐ Que catalog
   - ☐ Que mailing
   - ☐ Que's reputation
   - ☐ Other: _____

6. How would you rate the overall content of the book?
   - ☐ Very good
   - ☐ Good
   - ☐ Satisfactory
   - ☐ Poor

7. What do you like *best* about this Que book?

   _____

   _____

8. What do you like *least* about this Que book?

   _____

   _____

9. Did you buy this book with your personal funds?
   - ☐ Yes   ☐ No

10. Please feel free to list any other comments you may have about this Que book.

   _____

   _____

   _____

QUE

Order Your Que Books Today!

Name _____

Title _____

Company _____

City _____

State _____ ZIP _____

Phone No. ( ) _____

Method of Payment:

Check ☐ (Please enclose in envelope.)

Charge My: VISA ☐   MasterCard ☐

American Express ☐

Charge # _____

Expiration Date _____

Order No.	Title	Qty.	Price	Total

You can **FAX** your order to **1-317-573-2583**. Or call **1-800-428-5331, ext. ORDR** to order direct.
Please add $2.50 per title for shipping and handling.

Subtotal _____

Shipping & Handling _____

Total _____

BUSINESS REPLY MAIL
First Class Permit No. 9918   Indianapolis, IN

Postage will be paid by addressee

11711 N. College
Carmel, IN 46032

NO POSTAGE
NECESSARY
IF MAILED
IN THE
UNITED STATES

BUSINESS REPLY MAIL
First Class Permit No. 9918   Indianapolis, IN

Postage will be paid by addressee

11711 N. College
Carmel, IN 46032